CRUCIAL AGE SERIES

HURRICANE FROM CHINA

THE MACMILLAN COMPANY
NEW YORK · CHICAGO
DALLAS · ATLANTA · SAN FRANCISCO
LONDON · MANILA

IN CANADA
BRETT-MACMILLAN LTD.
GALT, ONTARIO

HURRICANE FROM CHINA

罒罒罒罒罒罒 by Denis Warner 罒罒罒罒罒罒罒罒罒罒

NEW YORK - THE MACMILLAN COMPANY - 1961

The hurricane against U.S. imperialism sweeps across heaven and
    earth;
The storm breaks at the appropriate hour,
And with the heroic spirit.
O clouds, rush on bravely!
O lightning split the heavens sharply!
O thunder, roll ever more loudly!
O waves, smash every rock in your path!
O great hurricane, blow with all your might!
Blow in a brand new age
Where the earth is strewn with red flowers
And the sky is illumined with joy.

           From a poem "The Hurricane" by Kuo Hsiao-chuan,
written to celebrate Hate America Week in Peking, June, 1960

INTRODUCTION

Across the People's Square in Peking on October 1, 1960, students shouldered a model of the world surmounting a burning torch. Following them with an immense dummy of Mao Tse-tung's fourth volume of *Selected Works* embedded in a trough of roses came the staff of the New China Printing Press. Two thousand foreign guests from seventy different countries rose in the reviewing stands to cheer. Tall sallow Arabs stood beside their darker brothers from Central Africa. Southeast Asians mixed with Japanese and Latin Americans. Though they came from the different corners of the earth, spoke different tongues and had different customs, this was something that all could understand. The flames that licked around the globe were Mao's flames: the book told how they should be lit.

Above the square five big balloons held five golden characters. "Long Live Chairman Mao," they proclaimed. One portrait of Mao hung from the rostrum: another came high over the heads of the honor guard as it went past in ranks of a hundred and fifty. Mao Tse-tung himself stood in the center of the rostrum, his moon face beaming over the scene. For this was Communist China's eleventh birthday celebration and the celebration also of the publication of Mao's latest book. China's two major Communist Party journals, the *People's Daily* and *Red Flag*, greeted the day with long editorials and special articles interpreting the book's revolutionary message for the masses. And now to its greater glory half a million men, women and children marched and danced their way across the square. Militia girls with long pigtails carried light machine guns: advanced workers wore red flowers on their breasts and held emulation banners in their hands. Housewives "liberated" to the fields and factories from the "four tyrannies"—the millstone, the grindstone, the stove and the oven—went past with spades and spanners, symbols of their new-found freedom. Their babies in the care of commune nurses rode in prams.

Thirty-four years before Mao had been a hunted, nondescript guerrilla. Now he led a nation of 650 million people in the vanguard of world revolution. Ferhat Abbas, the Algerian rebel leader, who had come to gather guns for his struggle against the French, stood on his right. Prime Minister U Nu, there to sign the Sino-Burmese Boundary Treaty, was on his left. The Algerian leader signified by his presence what Marshal Chen Yi, the Foreign Minister, described as Mao's determination to regard all struggles against colonialism and "imperialism" as "component parts of the common struggle for world peace and human progress." U Nu represented Mao's devotion to the cause of "peaceful coexistence."

It was a day of symbols. The ranks of militia, workers, peasants, intellectuals, students, women, children, babies, the emblems they wore, the banners they carried and the speeches they listened to represented the component parts of the new China. Here were the words of Marx and Lenin and Stalin and the rich interpretations of Mao transplanted into the peasant environment of China, given life and presented to the people of the world as the example they should follow. Those who sought "peace" could find it in the doves that soared from the marchers' baskets into the crisp fall air. The peasants were agrarian reform, the women emancipation, the children education, the workers industrialization, the militia security, and the militant declarations of Prime Minister Chou En-lai and Marshal Chen Yi the echo of Mao's strident call to the men and women of every land to rise and unite and struggle with the Chinese people against "imperialism" and its agents.

To Mao the world is a great guerrilla battlefield in which the principles he applied with such genius and success against Chiang Kai-shek on the plains of China may be used with equal success in the underdeveloped countries of Asia, Africa and Latin America for the isolation, and ultimate destruction, of the United States and its allies. The tinder of world revolution is dry. All it needs is the spark and the strong fresh breeze that blows from Communist China to create an anticolonial and "anti-imperialist" inferno among the forces that have been unleashed by the collapse of the Western empires and to inflame the passions in still dependent countries, or in countries where there are glaring injustices or inequalities of wealth.

It is with this battle, its nature and its prospects that this brief book is concerned. It is not directed to the specialist but to the general reader, to those who may know little of China and to whom events there may seem remote and perhaps not even of great significance. Comments and statements attributed to Chinese leaders and others are taken from official sources. Mr. Nehru's views on Communism and other matters were expressed in the course or interviews with the author. Opinions on the future of the Far East and Southeast Asia are based on many years of travel and work in all countries on China's western, southern and eastern borders from Afghanistan to Korea.

In parts of the text I have made use of articles of mine which have appeared in the *Reporter*, the *New Republic* and in the Atlantic Reports section of the *Atlantic Monthly*. The usual acknowledgments are made to the publishers concerned.

Denis Warner

July 1961

CONTENTS

Chapter I

A NOISE IN THE EAST

MAO TSE-TUNG likes to think of the Chinese revolution as a guiding star in the eastern sky. The brighter it shines the more clearly will it illumine the path and the more readily will the people of the underdeveloped world follow it to victory. To put it into more mundane terms, it is a combination of three distinct forces: the chauvinistic desire for expansion which has always marked the beginning of periods of unity and strength in China; the adaptation into Chinese peasant society of Marxism-Leninism; and the perception and flexibility of Mao Tse-tung, who, when it suits him, can argue that Marxism is not a dogma but only a criterion for action while insisting that Lenin laid down absolute rules.

Such contradictions are the rule rather than the exception in China today. It denounces nationalism and is ultranationalistic. It is anti-imperialist and imperialist. It is in a tearing hurry, but it is also patient. It is devious, as Mao puts it, only in order to be direct.

1

Mao himself holds no official government position other than that of honorary chairman of the National Committee of the Chinese People's Political Consultative Conference. He is no longer Head of State, or commander-in-chief of the armed forces. He is simply Chairman Mao, as he is habitually called, chairman, in particular, of the Central Committee of the Chinese Communist Party and of the standing committee of its Politburo. Yet it is also characteristic that on occasions when Mao has seemingly or in fact been pushed into the background, he has always emerged as a more important and powerful figure than before. His idea that he could stand Marx on his head and turn away from the proletariat and toward the peasantry in search of the material of revolution had him thrown out of the Central Committee, the Hunan Provincial Committee and perhaps even the Party in 1927. His further heresy in wanting to keep the revolution in the countryside led to another partial eclipse in the early thirties. On each occasion his reverses were only temporary. Now, nearly three years after he stood down as official leader of the People's Republic of China, discredited, it was erroneously thought by many, by the "failure" of the communes, Mao's influence is stronger and more assured than ever before.

His position is unique. He is the subject of a cult of the personality that dwarfs the campaign to project Stalin's father-image into the minds of the Soviet people. Though he continues to admire much of Stalin's work, he is not, and never has been, a Stalin. Stalin drove: Mao endeavors to persuade. Stalin was a ruthless dictator: Mao can be ruthless enough, but he is not, and never has been, a dictator in the accepted sense of the word.

For those who go further and seek analogies between Hitler and Mao there are *Mein Kampf* and the four volumes of Mao's selected writings to bear witness that megalomania is a common link, that Mao, like Hitler before him, wants to conquer the earth. The evidence is there: we deserve a rude shock, however, if we think of Mao in terms of Hitler, or Chinese Communism in terms of Naziism. In the top leadership of China today there is fanaticism but no gangsterism. Mao, Marx and Chinese nationalism have combined to produce a militant evangelism of a type the world has not seen since the Crusades.

Though Mao has not dictated, he has most certainly dominated this movement. The revolution has been his life and his life is also an essential part of the revolution. It owes something to the time of his birth, his peasant background, his early family life, his social and military experience, the books he read, the habits and friendships and prejudices he formed. Some aspects of Maoism which have most shocked the Western world have early roots in his youth in a South China village, and, though perhaps shocking, are not nearly so pointless as they may seem. As a schoolboy, for instance, Mao learned, like millions of other Chinese, to identify China's corruption and collapse with Western exploitation and the inadequacy of the Confucian system, which for two thousand years had shaped the country's social and economic systems and directed its political life. Since America, leader of what the Communists continue to refer to as the "imperialist" Powers, is the principal barrier to Mao's plans to change the nature of society everywhere, this early hatred of the West and its predatory activities in China is now channeled expediently against the United States.

Similarly, Mao's land reform campaign in 1951 was ideological and economic, but it was also his way of breaking down the family system, the cornerstone of the Confucian ethic, which, as a child, he had found personally hateful. It called for absolute filial loyalty: Mao loathed his father. It decreed absolute control of parents over children: Mao found he got fair treatment only by open revolt. Instead of honoring his father, he sneered at him for his ignorance. Required to be loyal to the family, he conspired with the underpaid coolies against his father's estate. Wed at the age of fourteen to a girl of twenty, with whom he never lived, he cursed arranged marriages. Lonely and shy in his early student days, an outsider among sons of well-to-do peasants, snubbed and humiliated, he became bitter against a society which provided scholarship and power only for the rich gentry. Only by breaking the hold of Confucianism, he later reasoned, could Chinese society be rebuilt. Only by destroying the power of the United States could the world be made safe for that society.

Mao has always read widely—"greedily, like an ox that has rushed into a vegetable garden, and, having tasted the vegetables, ate desperately," was the description he once applied. His reading turned him into a social scientist at the age of nineteen. Such books as Adam Smith's *Wealth of Nations*, Spencer's *Principles of Psychology*, John

Mills's *Ethics*, Darwin's *The Origin of Species*, and, in particular, Huxley's *Theory of Evolution*, which he read and reread, had a profound effect on his early thinking and writing.

For years he has written prodigiously, in a style that deliberately seeks to combine his knowledge of the Classics with the language of the people. It has an earthiness which appeals to the earthy Chinese people. He once described the Party's approach to economic work as "like the footbandages of a slut, long as well as smelly." At a time when the Kuomintang was calling for coalition government he said it "sold the dog meat of one-party dictatorship by displaying the sheep's head of unification." If you want to know the taste of pears, he says, you must eat them yourselves. If you want to know war, you must experience war. He is a phrasemaker, and such expressions as "imperialists are all paper tigers," and "the east wind is prevailing over the west wind," have stoked the ideological furnaces and warmed the Chinese people for the task that Mao has set them.

Until his late twenties Mao was not a revolutionary: he was a bookish reformer whose only real ambition was to become a teacher, specifically a teacher among the peasants. In the spring of 1918, for instance, and only a year before his discovery of the works of Marx and Lenin added the Communist arrowhead to his reformist staff, he founded a society to promote learning and morals. It forbade its members to visit brothels, to gamble, to have concubines and to misappropriate public or other people's funds.

Though he has been married three times by his own choice—his first wife died in 1935 and his eldest son, An-ying, was killed in Korea in November, 1950—Mao as a youth had no time for sex and none for frivolous living. For relaxation he used to go out into the hills, even in winter, and strip to do knee bends and deep-breathing exercises, or to plunge into icy rivers. Now a portly sixty-seven, he still lives a Spartan life. He dresses in a plain gray uniform. He takes a cold bath in the morning, even in winter, and though he seems to have become more sedentary in recent years, he actually swam across the Yangtze no less than four times in 1958.

His home is a simple villa near the Jade Temple in Peking's Western Hills, and his closest friends are comrades-in-arms for upwards of forty years, men like Liu Shao-chi, who succeeded him as Head of State in 1959, after an association that dates back to 1922, when Liu worked under Mao in a small Party branch in Hunan; Tung Pi-wu, who with Mao and ten others punted around a small lake in Chekiang Province in 1921 while they drafted the Constitution of the Party; Li Fu-chun, the State Planner, who played football with Mao in Changsha during World War I; Marshal Chu Teh, whose partnership with Mao saved the Communist cause from destruction in 1927 and again in 1934–1935; Teng Hsiao-ping, able secretary-general of the Party and Mao's most likely successor; and Chen Po-ta, Party theorist, editor-in-chief of the Central Committee's fortnightly, *Red Flag*, and, in recent years, Mao's ghost writer.

Like Ho Chi-minh, his contemporary in North Vietnam, Mao is a poet, and much of his verse is interesting and important for the insights it gives of his character and ambitions. Ho writes of a "spray of spring," and Mao observes that the "sighing" of the "sad autumn wind" is of the past. The winter winds may be cold, but he, too, looks for a spray of spring.

A typical example of his early interest in social reform appeared in the Changsha edition of the newspaper *Ta Kung-pao* when a young girl, who was about to be given in marriage to the proprietor of an old curiosity shop, took her life by cutting her throat with a razor while on the way to the home of her intended husband by sedan chair.

Mao at this time was still studying at a teachers' training college outside the city of Changsha in Hunan. In a first article on the incident he blamed Chinese society and the family system for the girl's death. "The incident was an important one," he wrote. "It occurred because of the foul system of arranged marriages, the darkness of the social system, the denial of the will of an individual, and the absence of freedom to choose one's mate." Mao wrote ten articles in all on the girl's death. "Since there are factors in our society which caused the death of Miss Chao, this society is an extremely dangerous thing," he said in one. In another he condemned superstition in marriage, using it to demand the emancipation of women.

This was a period of continuing turbulence and frustration in China. The Manchus had gone. Yuan Shi-kai, who succeeded them, had died of apoplexy. The war lords stripped the countryside like locusts. Strikes gripped the industries in the coastal ports. The end of imperial rule meant that Chinese nationalism could be directed now to foreign exploiters. There was a violent reaction to the Versailles Treaty and the substitution of Japanese rights in China for German. Meanwhile, crops failed and irrigation systems fell into disrepair.

About this time the appearance in Moscow of young Asian nationalists and their accounts of native uprisings and popular discontent led to Soviet appreciation that common opposition to imperialism provided the opportunity for mutual Communist-national endeavor. Watching the great imperialist Powers of Europe in the battle for world supremacy, Lenin had already concluded that the colonies and semicolonies were the imperialists' main supply bases on whose raw materials, manpower and markets their economies depended.

At the Conference of the Peoples of the Orient in 1920, Grigori Zinoviev again postulated Lenin's theory when he said that the real revolution would blaze up only when the hundreds of millions of people in Asia united with the Soviet Union. Partly in pursuit of this objective, the Comintern was established in 1919, the year that Mao, having graduated from the Hunan Provincial First Normal School at Changsha, read Marx and Lenin in the library of the Peking University.

Mao was now twenty-six and frustrated. Communism, it seemed, offered a way to effect the changes he envisaged for China. Two years later he attended the inaugural meeting of the Chinese Communist Party, and for a time became an orthodox Party worker, organizing trade unions among miners and the handful of industrial workers. His activities during the period of the Kuomintang-Communist honeymoon included service as alternate member of the Kuomintang Central Committee and propaganda chief at the Whampoa Military Academy in Canton. Subsequent experience among the peasants in Hunan Province confirmed his impression, however, that China could not hope to wage a successful revolution by using only the proletariat. To ignore the peasantry, the vast, potentially powerful, poverty-stricken and restless mass of the Chinese people, was folly.

In a Party report on his work in Hunan in 1927, he abandoned Marxist orthodoxy and launched an impassioned appeal for a peasant revolution. "All kinds of arguments against the peasant movement must speedily be set right," he said. "The erroneous measures taken by the revolutionary authorities concerning the peasant movement must be speedily changed. Only thus can any good be done for the future of the revolution. For the rise of the present peasant movement is a colossal event. In a very short time in China's central, southern and northern provinces, several hundred million peasants will rise like a tornado or tempest, a force so extraordinarily swift and violent that no power, however great, will be able to suppress it. They will break all trammels that now bind them and rush forward along the road to liberation. They will send all imperialists, war lords, corrupt officials, local bullies and bad gentry to their graves. All revolutionary parties and all revolutionary comrades will stand before them to be tested, and to be accepted or rejected as they decide. To march at their head and lead them? Or to follow at their rear, gesticulating at them and criticizing them? Or to face them as opponents?"

For Mao there was no doubt. His report, the most fundamental and important he has ever made, laid the foundations for both the civil war and the social and economic revolution that followed the victory twenty-two years later. It is basic to all his thoughts and plans for world revolution. Mao believed that four kinds of authority— political authority, clan authority, theocratic authority and the authority of the husband—represented the whole ideology and institution of feudalism and patriarchy and were the four great cords that bound the Chinese people and particularly the peasants. He saw the political authority of the landlords as the backbone of all other systems of authority. Once this was broken down the revolts against the other authorities would follow as a natural consequence. The family system could be destroyed, the influence of Confucianism broken and women emancipated. With the old system removed the opportunity would then exist to build the new. "Now, you want to have your rent reduced," he used to say to the peasants. "How will you go about it? Believe in the gods, or believe in the peasant associations?" The peasants, he reported smugly, rocked with laughter.

Puritan Mao was against many traditional Chinese pleasures. He was against vice and against gambling and opium smoking, against the wasteful use of rice to make wine, against religious ceremonies associated with festivals, against feasts—and even against pigs (the most succulent of all Chinese food) because they ate grain. He was for culture for the people, for a cooperative movement, for shock teams of peasant workers to repair roads and embankments, for a militia even though its weapons were only spears, and for violent revolution. "A revolution is not the same as inviting people to dinner, or writing an essay, or painting a picture, or doing fancy needlework: it cannot be anything so refined, so calm and gentle, or so mild, kind, courteous, restrained and magnanimous. A revolution is an uprising, an act of violence by which the peasantry overthrows the authority of the feudal landlord class." It was necessary, he said, to "bring about a reign of terror in every rural area," otherwise it would be impossible to suppress the activities of the counterrevolutionaries or to overthrow the authority of the gentry.

In the more than three decades that have passed since Mao proclaimed these fundamentals of his revolution he has never deviated. He knows exactly what he wants and how it should be achieved. But no one of significance in the Chinese Communist Party, not even the Hunan Provincial Committee, which was outraged by some of his heretical views, believed that he was right when, in the fall of 1927, he led a thousand survivors of a summer uprising against the Kuomintang to a pine-covered mountain called Chingkanshan, on the border of Hunan and Kiangsi provinces. Among them Mao's men had two hundred rifles. The rest were armed with double-edged spears mounted on long shafts. Yet from this beginning Mao won China—and believes he can win the world.

Mao's band was desperately poor. Many of the troops had no shoes. Those with guns had little or no ammunition. When money was available it was distributed in kind: in oil, salt, firewood and vegetables, and occasionally as pocket money. It was obtained from the plains in a way that did not at first seem to the suspicious peasants to differ very greatly from traditional Chinese banditry. Only slowly did they learn the difference: that Mao and his men neither molested nor robbed the poor peasants but only the rich peasants and landlords, whom they murdered. Of the spoils they took only enough for their needs: the rest they distributed.

It was not long before this form of "agitprop" began to have effect, and gradually Mao pushed deeper into the plains, winning more recruits among the poor peasants and establishing new base areas, harassing the Kuomintang with his guerrillas and conserving his small regular forces for overwhelming assaults against targets of opportunity. He resisted all temptation to seize real estate—to hold towns or cities. Cities had to be isolated and surrounded and captured only in the final annihilation phase.

This in the simplest terms is the essence of Mao's theory of expanding a guerrilla war into a "war of national liberation." This was the technique he employed during the war against the Japanese and against Chiang Kai-shek all through the civil war. He exported it to Indo-China, where it won victory for Ho Chi-minh in his war with the French. He has given it to the Algerians and to the Pathet Lao in Laos; to the Angolans in their struggle with the Portuguese and to many others. It is, he believes, a readily applicable formula for any underdeveloped country where there is rural poverty and discontent. If there is poverty there is also discontent, and if there is discontent there exists also a target against which discontent may be channeled and turned into revolutionary force. Long before the Second World War Mao had seen the global possibilities in his struggle. "This war is not only the banner of China's liberation," he said, "but is pregnant with significance for the world revolution. The eyes of the revolutionary masses of the world are upon us." The Communist Party, he believed, provided the essential theoretical framework. Though allies might be expediently and temporarily picked up, the successful outcome of a war of national liberation— and the world revolution—depended on the existence of a disciplined, dedicated and fully indoctrinated Communist Party.

To achieve this on Chingkanshan, Mao hammered Marxist principles into his troops over the campfires at night and in training programs by day. Beginning in every section there was a Communist group. At company level there were committees. At first the ratio of Party members to non-Party men in the Red Army was one to three, a proportion that Mao felt did not adequately guard against every loophole of independent thought. He therefore trained more political secretaries, devoted more time to political study and raised the ratio of Party members to one for two. The army, he directed, fought not merely for the sake of fighting but to "agitate the masses, to organize them, to arm them and to help them establish revolutionary military power."

He became more than ever convinced of the necessity for violent revolution. "War is the highest form of struggle, existing ever since the emergence of private property and social classes, for settling contradictions between classes, between nations, between states, or between political groups at given stages of their development," he said. There was only one way of eliminating it—"to oppose war by means of war, to oppose counterrevolutionary war by means of revolutionary war. . . . All counterrevolutionary wars are unjust, all revolutionary wars are just. We will put an end to man's warring era with our hands, and the war we are waging is undoubtedly part of the final war. . . . When human society advances to the point where classes and States are eliminated, there will no longer be any wars, whether revolutionary or counterrevolutionary, just or unjust, and that will be an era of lasting peace for mankind."

Political power grew out of the barrel of the gun, he said. His principle was that the Party should command the gun and that the gun should never command the Party. The army was the chief component of the political power of a State. Whoever wanted to seize the political power of the State and to maintain it had to have a strong army. "Some people have ridiculed us as advocates of the omnipotence of war," he added. "Yes, we are. We are the advocates of the omnipotence of revolutionary war, which is not bad at all, but is good and Marxist. With the help of guns the Russian Communists brought about Socialism. We are to bring about a democratic republic. Experience in the class struggle of the era of imperialism teaches us that the working class and the toiling masses cannot defeat the armed bourgeois and landlords except by the power of the gun: in this sense we can even say that the whole world can be remolded only with the gun. As we are the advocates of the abolition of war, we do not desire war: but war can be abolished only through war—in order to get rid of the gun, we must first grasp it in our hand."

This emphasis on the importance of military struggle flowed naturally from Mao's brilliance as a guerrilla strategist. His accounts of the battles against Chiang Kai-shek's encirclement campaigns in the early thirties are thrilling. Heavily outnumbered and with only the most elementary weapons, he tied down huge Nationalist forces with guerrilla groups while his mobile, élite Red Army raced through the mountains to hit and run and hit again in demoralizing raids that sought and fought and often destroyed the weakest links in Chiang's chain. He used his guerrillas to spread over Nationalist controlled areas, converting Chiang's rear into a front and tying down opposing forces out of all proportion to his own numbers. Defend in order to attack, he told his men. Retreat in order to advance. Take a flanking action in order to take a frontal action. Be devious in order to go direct.

He fought defensive battles to lull the Nationalists and their followers while he mobilized the poor peasants to join in the war. He fought only when he was sure of winning: he ran when defeat threatened. Counteroffensives should be launched, he directed, only when the people gave active support to the Red Army, the terrain was favorable for operations, the main forces of the Red Army were completely concentrated, the Nationalists were worn out physically and morally and their weak spots were discovered.

"Make a noise in the east but strike in the west," he said. "Our strategy is to pit one against ten, while our tactic is to pit ten against one. We defeat the many with the few but we also defeat the few with the many."

He rejected chance and lucky gambles. "The plucky determination to wipe out the enemy before breakfast is good, but any concrete plan to do this is inadvisable." Quick decisions required many specific conditions, including thorough preparation, correct timing, concentration of a preponderant force, the tactic of encirclement and outflanking, favorable positions and attacks on an enemy force on the move or on a stationary enemy in an unconsolidated position.

He eschewed a war of attrition. "To wound all the ten fingers of a man is not so effective as to chop one of them off," he said. "To rout ten of the enemy's divisions is not so effective as to annihilate one of them."

He was adamant on the necessity for establishing base areas and for the political indoctrination of all people in these areas. Without this preparation, he said, it was impossible to sustain guerrilla war in the enemy's rear. It was the duty of all guerrilla leaders operating behind the enemy's lines to build up separate guerrilla units and to develop them gradually into a guerrilla corps and eventually into regular units and regular corps. At all times these activities were to be coordinated with the masses of the people living in the base area, since without consolidation no vigorous expansion was possible.

By such tactics Mao in the early thirties routed four of Chiang Kai-shek's encirclement campaigns, and was ready to pass from strategic defensive into full-scale mobile offensive. He planned to break through Chiang's lines and to carry the campaign out of the Communist areas and to set all of east China aflame with revolutionary war, striking now at Hangchow, then at Soochow, at Nanking, Wuhu, Nanchang and Foochow. It was a bold and brilliant scheme, often and skillfully copied years later in Indo-China, where the bewildered French forces in the campaigns of 1953–1954 never knew where next the Vietminh regular forces might appear.

Obsessed with its own achievement in having created a Soviet State inside China, the Party was unwilling to go along with Mao's theories either of luring the enemy into Communist territory, there to destroy it, or of branching out, away from its well established base areas, on such a breath-taking mobile war as Mao proposed. Against Mao's opposition, the Red Army split into six columns and attempted unsuccessfully to beat Chiang at positional warfare. The campaign began in October, 1933. Three months later in the face of heavy defeats Mao appealed once again for a return to mobile war—and once again was refused. "All hope of smashing the fifth campaign of encirclement and annihilation was finally dashed and there was no alternative but the Long March," he noted subsequently.

The Long March, that fantastic 8,000-mile trek by the remnants of the Communist forces from Kiangsi to Yenan in northwest Shensi, which began in October, 1934, and ended a year later, was a feat of endurance, courage and determination without parallel in modern military history. The distance covered was greater than that from Anchorage to Panama and the terrain and hazards no less fearful. Attacked all the time and enduring fearful privations, the Communists died in tens of thousands. Ninety thousand men and 35,000 women began the march. Fewer than 30,000 survived. But among those who got through there was no questioning Mao's leadership. The intra-Party struggle that marked the early years in Kiangsi, when Mao's opponents rejected his "countryside" concept and wanted to storm the cities, and the disputes of the Long March, belonged to the bitter past. Mao lost his wife and abandoned a child on the march, but the future was now his to shape.

While the Red Army was still battling the Japanese, Mao predicted that there would be no interval between the Second World War and the great world war it would develop into. Owing to the existence of the Soviet Union and the heightened awakening of the peoples of the world, great revolutionary wars would emerge to oppose all counterrevolutionary wars, thus giving the war the character of a war for permanent peace.

He called for the continuous development of revolution, of the continuous development of a democratic revolution into a Socialist revolution. Stalin's works made a notable addition to his library and to his "thoughts" during the Yenan days. Stalin's article on the Bolshevization of the Party, which appeared in *Pravda* on February 3, 1925, became a basic document of the 1942–1944 Chinese Communist Party reform movement which, in many ways, set a pattern for Communist leadership in China after 1949.

Stalin laid down rigid rules. The Communist Party could not be an appendage of the elective machinery of parliament, or a voluntary annex to the trade unions. It had to be the highest form of the class alliance. The Party and its leaders had to be completely versed in Marxist revolutionary theory. Every step and every action of the Party should be designed to bring about the revolutionary development of the masses, so that they were cultivated and educated in the spirit of the revolution. The Party had to mold a leading nucleus from the outstanding elements of its vanguard. It had regularly to improve the social composition of its own organization and clean out opportunists and those who would corrupt the Party. It had to set up iron proletarian discipline based on unanimity in thought, a clear understanding of the movement's objectives, unity in practical activity and consciousness of the Party's mission.

Into these rules Mao breathed his own puritanical fervor. "A Communist Party member should be straightforward, loyal and positive," he insisted. "He should consider the interests of the revolution as the primary concern in his life, sacrifice individual interests, and, no matter where, or when, uphold correct principles of struggle untiringly against all incorrect thoughts and actions. He should want to consolidate the Party's collective livelihood, consolidate the relations between the Party and the masses, should be devoted to the Party and the masses rather than to the individual and should be devoted to others rather than to himself. Then only can he be considered a Communist Party member."

As the Communists extended their control over larger areas of China and more and more people came under their control, the need for qualified and indoctrinated officials increased rapidly. This had been anticipated. In 1937, in his concluding speech to the national Communist Party congress, Mao said that to guide a great revolution there had to be a great Party and many excellent officials. "It would be impossible to carry out an unprecedented great revolution in a country like China with a population of 450,000,000 if the leadership were but a small group founded on a narrow basis. It would also be impossible if the leaders and cadres in the Party were all narrowminded and lacking in a sense of proportion, without insight or ability. The organization of our Party must be expanded throughout the country: it must purposefully train tens of thousands of cadres and several hundreds of excellent mass leaders."

More than ten years before victory was in Mao's grasp thousands of Chinese had been politically indoctrinated and trained as teachers in the fields of military work, culture, education, propaganda, organization, popular movements, the liquidation of counterrevolutionaries, finance, economics, medicine, women's and children's activities, education and labor. Every function and aspect of society came within the Party orbit. Officials were taught, as Liu Shao-chi put it, to use the "most cold-blooded methods" in dealing with the people's common enemies, but under no circumstances to use such methods in dealing with their own brothers or comrades. The masses were not to be alienated but won over. The first step in reasoning, Mao prescribed, was to give the patient a powerful stimulus. "Yell at him 'you're sick,' so that the patient will have a fright and break out in an all-over sweat," he told the Reform Movement School in Yenan. "Then he can actually be started on the way to recovery."

Although the Party membership had increased sharply from 1,348,320 in 1946, it totaled only 4,488,080 in 1949. It had trained thousands of cadres, but even so it was still largely out of touch with the masses. Its principal asset was its army, which by its unique and exemplary behavior in the civil war had won many friends. It could have been used to implement Mao's controls by force. It was not Mao's intention, however, to destroy its prestige, and its morale, by the reckless use of the jackboot in enforcing Party control. Yet by the end of the first year of Communist rule, Prime Minister Chou En-lai, speaking at the National Committee of the People's Political Consultative Conference, could say with a fair measure of truth that "China's history has undergone more important changes during the past year than during the previous several hundred or even thousand years. The old China is fast disappearing and the new China— a people's China—has assuredly grown up."

During this first year, another 2,180,000 Kuomintang remnants fell to the Communists in massive mopping-up operations, bringing the total eliminated by the Red Army during the final phase of the civil war to more than 8 million. But it was one thing to mop up a defeated army and another to consolidate power in this vast land. Mao succeeded partly because of the lack of organized opposition and partly through his foresight in the training of cadres, who, if inadequate for the huge task that confronted them, did succeed in casting an intricate set of interlocking controls, a spider web of power, over much of China. At the center was the Party, firmly directed and led by the Politburo and the Central Committee. Interwoven with the Party was the Central People's Government. Beyond this came military and administrative committees, all under Communist leadership, or supervision, provincial governments and administrative district governments. Municipalities were directly subordinate either to the central government or to the six greater administrative areas established at that time. Sixty-seven municipal governments and 2,087 county governments came under the control of the provinces. In itself, this combination of military and bureaucratic control, even though linked directly with the Party, was only partly effective. Subordinate to it was the network of organizations, both vertical and horizontal, which brought hundreds of millions of people under direct Party surveillance. On the vertical level there were the Residents' Committees, Public Security Substations and Security Defense Committees. At the lowest level, the Residents' Committees were responsible for basic indoctrination, for getting everyone out to do their physical jerks in the morning, for organizing health and cleanliness procedures, such as the subsequent campaigns against spitting and against grain-eating sparrows, rats, mosquitoes and flies.

There were many loopholes in the system. In some areas and for some years it existed only on paper. But in the larger centers of population it was reinforced by the horizontal organizations, such as the All-China Federation of Trade Unions, which, during 1950, signed up more than 4 million workers. Thirty million women registered for the All-China Democratic Women's Federation during the same year. Seven million youths enrolled in the Young Pioneers and the New Democratic Youth League. These and other similar organizations were all intended to further the processes of indoctrination and control. The All-China Federation of Trade Unions, for instance, has as its principal function "to develop industrial and agricultural production and to increase labor productivity continuously." Members are required, under the leadership of the Party, to "intensify Communist education among the workers . . . to organize Socialist emulation and to develop the enthusiasm and initiative of all the workers so that they may consolidate labor discipline of their own conscious will and ensure the fulfillment and overfulfillment of the construction plans of the State."

Through these interlocking organizations large sections of the population came under the control of the Party. Since many people were members of two and sometimes three or more of the cell, or front, organizations, it became increasingly difficult even to hold incorrect thoughts. Self-criticism, family criticism, criticism of parents by children, children by parents, husband by wife and wife by husband brought espionage to the marriage bed. There was safety, perhaps, in the horizontal group when father, wife, son and daughter all were members of the same organizations. But when the nine-year-old went off to the Pioneers, the fifteen-year-old to the New Democratic Youth League, and the parents to their own separate organizations, there was no safety. The dossier dictated daily life. Failure to conform invited suspicion. Suspicion invited police inquiries.

A network of fifty-five broadcasting stations served to broaden the system of indoctrination. At work, in the streets, at rest, or at play, there was no escape. Books and films from Western countries were banned: foreign broadcasts were jammed. If this was not new, the intensity and orientation of it was. Political courses were universally introduced into the universities and middle schools. Teachers were required to participate in study groups under the direction of Party cadres. Special political colleges were set up in various parts of the country.

To many Chinese, however, the new regime, despite all its controls, seemed less onerous and fearful than they had expected. Most of even the conservative upper stratum of intellectuals, afraid of a last-minute blood bath by Chiang, found that there was a place for them in the Communist regime. Mao's New Democracy also had a place, though a temporary one, for small capitalists. Moreover, it had called a halt to inflation. By March, 1950, the drastic price rises in grain, yarn and cloth that characterized the closing years of Kuomintang rule had been ended. The police and the army, disciplined and efficient in a manner that the Chinese had never known before, had restored law and order. Streetwalkers had become street cleaners. And on the statute books were a number of new laws including the Agrarian Reform Law, the Regulations Governing the Organization of Peasants' Associations, the Regulations Governing the Organization of People's Tribunals, Decisions Concerning the Differentiation of Class Status in the Countryside, all of which seemed to promise spoils to the peasant victors. They promised other things, also.

Prime Minister Chou En-lai gave the first hint. In a speech commending the achievements of the Chinese people's judiciary he added that there had also been defects, the chief one being that "many local judicial workers have misinterpreted the policy of clemency with regard to the suppression of counterrevolutionary elements. They have only shown clemency to the counterrevolutionary elements without suppressing them, so that the masses of people blame them for their 'boundless clemency.' The masses of the people are right in blaming them, for the principles set out by Chairman Mao Tse-tung for the treatment of counterrevolutionary elements were to 'punish the ringleaders, leave their misguided followers alone and reward those who render assistance and service in the struggle.'"

On February 21, 1951, Peking promulgated Regulations for the Punishment of Counterrevolutionaries. For such crimes as "spreading rumors," or "splitting the solidarity between the government and the national minorities," Mao now prescribed the death penalty. To ensure the widest scope for the security net, the regulations were made retroactive.

Within two weeks the Chinese press began its reports of the terror. Huge mass trials presided over by Communist mayors brought summary justice to tens and hundreds of thousands of "counter-revolutionaries." The effect was liturgical. Enormous crowds rose to their feet to hurl their challenges and their sentences at the accused. "Kill, kill," they shouted, in a delirium of excitement that reached its crescendo at the moment of execution.

In describing this campaign, Mao's long-trusted Szechwanese political commissar, General Lo Jui-ching, then Minister of Public Security and now Chief of Staff in the People's Liberation Army, said: "The outstanding features [of the campaign] were the accusation, denunciation and spontaneous arrest of counterrevolutionaries by the broad mass of the people. In consequence, this campaign was an unprecedented one, whether in terms of the effect of elimination of counterrevolutionaries, in terms of the scope and extent of mobilization of the masses, or in terms of the soundness of the development of the campaign. . . . Through the campaign for the suppression of counterrevolutionaries, accompanied by much publicity, we succeeded basically in clearing up the remnant influence of counterrevolution on mainland China."

This campaign should have occasioned little surprise. Mao had foreshadowed it as early as 1927 in his report on the peasant movement in Hunan and in even more explicit terms in July, 1949, in *On People's Democratic Dictatorship.* "The army, the police and the courts of the State are instruments by which class oppresses classes," he said. "To the hostile class the State apparatus is the instrument of oppression. It is violent and not benevolent. 'You are not benevolent?' Just so. We decidedly will not exercise benevolence toward the reactionary acts of the reactionaries and reactionary class."

The cadres coaxed, urged, directed and the people of China, intoxicated by the blood-letting and the chance to vent old resentments, did the rest. In city streets, in public squares, in the villages, towns and cities, counterrevolutionaries and suspects were accused, stoned, spat upon and shot. Along with the campaign against the counterrevolutionaries, and sometimes confused with it, went the land reform campaign. Mao had laid down that peaceful redistribution of land was a contradiction of the Marxist theory of social revolution, that the landlord class would not disintegrate by itself but had to be knocked out and that the more violent the land reform the more successful it would be.

"Land reform is a systematic and fierce struggle," said an article in the *Yangtse Daily* in December, 1950. "Land reform is to shake the foundations of a feudal system that has a history of over two thousand years, to shatter the old order and establish a new one, to pass the countryside from the hands of the landlords to the hands of the peasants, to turn feudal rule into a People's Democratic Dictatorship. In other words, land reform rewrites history, as it were, by turning heaven and earth upside down."

Land reform, like the campaign against the counterrevolutionaries, was at once a systematically applied terror, a form of thought changing (or brain washing) and a social revolution. By eliminating the landlord class, by class war, it aimed to make a major break with the past, not merely a physical, or proprietorial, break, and to establish in the minds of those who participated in denouncing and destroying the landlords a revolutionary sense of identity with the regime and its ideology. The peasants who shouted for blood sipped from the same cup as those who brought the landlords to trial. Party and people were participants in the same revolutionary act.

Teams of land reformers traveled through the countryside. Their job was to work among the poorer peasants, looking for, and even inventing, grievances, and, by agitation, to stir up the people against the landlords. Barricades around each village during the reformation process served to produce an appropriate atmosphere of tension. All work stopped and all peasants were required to attend and to participate directly. In each region land reform began in a central village, worked outward to cover the next two and multiplied again by three to cover nine villages in each sector. Sometimes inadequate preparation by Communist officials failed to produce the desired violence. But the systematic repetition of the performance over a series of closely related villages usually provided a sufficient check against undue moderation. What began slowly in the first village could usually be counted a bloody success by the ninth. Passion, terror, hate, revenge and the emotional inspiration of bloodshed combined to root out the past.

The press and radio spared no detail. Assigned to the difficult task of handling the Western-contaminated city of Shanghai, Politburo member Marshal Chen Yi, who had proved himself a brilliant guerrilla leader when he covered the rear guard of the Long March, led the campaign against the counterrevolutionaries' there.

The *Liberation Daily* in Shanghai reported the following dialogue between Chen and a conference of Communist deputies:

Chen: "How shall we cope with this herd of beastly despots, traitors and special agents?"

Answer: "Kill them."

Chen: "Another thing. We have already disposed of a number of cases, but there are still some in jail. What shall we do with them?"

Answer: "Kill them all."

Chen: "Another thing. There are despots in the markets, among the fishmongers, real-estate brokers, water carriers and night soil scavengers. How shall we cope with these feudal elements?"

Answer: "Execute them by firing squad."

It is impossible to say how many men and women actually lost their lives before the two campaigns, under pressure from the top, began to taper off in October, 1951. A U.S. Congressional report put the total number killed during the first decade (1949–1959) of Communist rule at about 30 million. An official Communist report published on December 21, 1951, referred to the liquidation of 1,150,000 "native bandits" in the central-south region (one of the six administrative regions then in existence). It is said that 28 per cent, or 322,000 had been executed. The rest were undergoing "reform through labor," including 2 per cent under suspended death sentences. On the other hand, Mao Tse-tung in a speech on February 27, 1957, gave the total figure killed up to 1954 as 800,000. Mao's figure may not be a gross underestimation. The Communists did not kill for the sake of killing but for interrelated psychological, social and political purposes. They were intent on administering a shock, not on exterminating the population. People were much too valuable to be squandered, and increasing numbers were therefore sent to "reform through labor," the system by which millions worked out their suspended sentences of death. A United Nations estimate is that Peking put 25 million men and women into this form of slave labor. Nationalist China, which has its own obvious reasons for exaggeration, estimates the figure at 40 million. In any event, extensive "reform through labor" camps had been established in most parts of China by 1952.

Although the Regulations Governing Reforms Through Compulsory Labor were not introduced by General Lo Jui-ching until August 26, 1954, he made clear that they were based on the experiences of the preceding four years in "combining punishment and surveillance with ideological reform and labor and production with political education." For those under sentence of death who failed after two years to exhibit the required political reorientation, the firing squad was always ready. For those under lesser sentences who did not respond there were further years of labor and detention, since Article 72 of the regulations provided for the continued detention of those whose sentences had expired, in particular all major "counterrevolutionaries" along with those whose release might be regarded as "endangering public security," or who had failed to reform or to work with enthusiasm.

Among those who learned from their experience in the "reform through labor" camps were such people as Henry Pu Yi, last emperor of the Ching dynasty and Japanese puppet ruler of Manchukuo, who tended pigs while he studied Mao and Marx. "The crimes committed by me during the first half of my life were very grievous," he told Hsieh Chueh-tsai, President of the Supreme People's Court, and a crony of Mao's in his Changsha days. "I could die a hundred times without being able to repay the debt of blood."

Hsieh, in a speech to the National People's Congress on "reform through labor," said that Pu Yi once held the view that he could not be reformed and that he had no intention of being reformed. "However, after staying for a long period in custody, undergoing reform through education and participating in study and visiting various places, Pu Yi saw the great changes which had taken place in the fatherland, recognized the correct leadership of the Communist Party and Chairman Mao, and gradually began to understand his own crimes. He finally made up his mind to change from evil to good and decided to lead a new life. . . . After his release from prison, he requested to participate in labor and has become an employee at a botanical plantation, engaging in labor and study simultaneously."

In a vigorous defense of this thought reform, Hsieh said that "imperialist" elements had slandered it as "brain washing." "In point of fact, what is wrong with washing out all the vicious and dirty things—in transforming reactionary thinking into an acceptance of progressive thinking?" he asked.

Included among a group of former Nationalist soldiers released with Pu Yi was General Tu Yu-ming, formerly commander of the Manchurian Security Preservation Headquarters. Tu, the Communists said, was the kind of man who had never participated in labor, and he was also sick when captured. "Simultaneously with reforming his ideology," Peking claimed, "the People's Government also cured his neuralgia and rheumatism." He is now working in a rural commune. With five others released with him the general wrote to Mao Tse-tung to offer his thanks. "We were criminals guilty of heinous crimes against the people in the past," the letter began. "Death, even if it were repeated ten thousand times, could not atone for our crimes. In accordance with what is right we should have been condemned to death and would have rotted and turned into dust long ago. Yet the great leader of the people, Chairman Mao Tse-tung, let bygones be bygones. A long-term, thoroughgoing education was conducted to reform us according to the noble aim of transforming the human society and the policy of tempering punishment with leniency and linking corrective labor to education. We were enabled to submit to truth and gradually to restore our human nature. On the occasion of celebrating the tenth anniversary of our great national day we are pardoned and set free. We are enabled to turn from death to a new life and from darkness to light."

In the cities the "five-anti" campaign and the State acquisition of factories and businesses were the counterpart of the land reform program. Just as land reform was theoretically designed to improve the lot of the peasantry by giving land to the tillers, the five-anti campaign ostensibly sought to put morality into business by eliminating bribery, tax evasion, fraud, theft of State assets and leakage of State economic secrets. Like the land reform campaign, also, it was sometimes indistinguishable from the suppression of counterrevolutionaries. Its primary functions were to extend the process of wrecking the old social system and the consolidation of the Communist writ by shock treatment. It also had some attractive fringe benefits. A vast sum of additional revenue flowed into the government purse: and the "reform through labor" camps bulged with the surplus manpower that Peking was to find so useful in the execution of agricultural, irrigation and industrial projects then on its drawing boards.

The Communist Party did not escape in this nation-wide spring cleaning. Together with the five-anti movement went a similar campaign within the Party and the bureaucracy to eliminate corruption, waste and bureaucratism. Some indication of its extent is indicated by the fact that Party membership, even in this period of growth, dropped by more than a hundred thousand in 1951. Cadres had been too rapidly produced; there was both inefficiency and misplaced zeal. There was also an evolutionary, rather than a revolutionary, attitude on the part of many of the inherited civil servants who had fallen into the error of believing that the adjustment from Kuomintang to Communist rule could be made painlessly. In addition to the accounts of the execution of landlords and counterrevolutionaries in the press and magazines there were now pages of confessions as businessmen, university professors, schoolteachers, civil servants and Party officials sought to expiate their crimes.

One way or another, most people in China were involved in these social reforms and purges. There was really no escape. The Marriage Law of the People's Republic, again foreshadowed by Mao in 1925, the Resist America and Aid Korea campaign, and the Germ Warfare campaign went on concurrently. These were also multiple-purpose campaigns. The Marriage Act was at once the fulfillment of Mao's earlier pledge and a thrust through the armor plating of Chinese society, the family system, which to so many Western observers was China's impenetrable protection against "going Communist." Women got equal rights with men, including the right to use their maiden names, or even the names of previous husbands. The law defined the equality of the sexes and granted women the right to free choice of occupation and to equal rights in the possession and management of family property. The village matchmaker was put out of business and the dowry system ended. Illegitimacy was legalized, divorce made easy; concubinage and infanticide were prohibited. And by raising the legal marriage age to twenty for men and eighteen for women, child marriages were finally eliminated.

The law released new social forces and caused new tensions. Hundreds of thousands of women flocked to the divorce courts in the first months of the new law. "Marriage" cadres encouraged women to drag errant husbands before the Courts. And slowly but surely the Communists made a breakthrough. China's social and ideological feet were unbound: a vast new reservoir of labor was added to the nation's resources; and the enthusiasm of many women for the Communist Party as a result of their greater freedom has been a considerable and continuing strength for the regime ever since.

Chapter II

HATE AMERICA

For two thousand miles the Yangtze River cuts through the heart of China, a brown swirling stream whose waters in this one valley mean life and livelihood to nearly half as many people as there are in the United States. Through centuries the pattern of life here had never changed. The people lived on the river in junks and by the river, some working like human horses, harnessed and bent as they struggled along the banks, towing the cargoes of rice that others grew so carefully in the bordering paddy fields.

Away to the north, beyond the Great Plain, China's Sorrow, the mighty and unpredictable Yellow River, brought its annual crops of fertility and floods and famine to other countless millions of Chinese. For almost all poverty, hunger, distress and overwork were day-to-day experiences that were accepted year after year as were the seasons of summer and winter, spring and fall.

Was it possible to dam and harness these rivers? To control their floods? To turn their destructive strengths into constructive power? And if this was possible, could not the humans who worked by their banks be changed, not merely physically but by nature, so that their senses, affections and passions changed and flowed like China's rivers between banks that man had devised? Mao had twin objectives: to turn all of China into a human wave, to mobilize the greatest mass movement in history, to storm and overwhelm the problems of economic development as the cities and their garrisons had been stormed and overwhelmed in the final phase of the civil war, to dam the rivers, harness the waters, build roads and railways, factories and blast furnaces; and to produce an entirely new Chinese society. The creation of an industrial State within the Confucian framework had not even entered into the calculations of the civilized and gifted Mandarins until late in the nineteenth century. The system produced scholarships but not smokestacks, intellectuals but not technicians.

The breaking of the chains that shackled the Chinese to past traditions, superstitions and loyalties was therefore essential; but it was only the first step. It was easy to destroy but difficult to create. The peasants had been the revolution's greatest strength: now they could constitute its most serious challenge. No amount of agitation would have roused them to revolt if they had been satisfied with their lot, if the oppressive burden of poverty had not created a target in landlordism against which their discontent could be channeled and inflamed. The revolutionary changes that merely began with land reform would also have been intolerable, in themselves a breeding ground for counterrevolution, if the regime had not persuaded the people of China that they were fighting for their lives—and peace.

The enemy now was the besieging forces of American "imperialism": and no single aspect of Peking's policy has served the interests of the regime better. As early as 1929 the Party with singular prescience had begun to channel its "anti-imperialist" policies against the United States, which it described as "wanting to suck the marrow of our bones and which is a hundred times worse than Great Britain or Japan." American aid to Chiang Kai-shek in the final years of the civil war provided demonstrable evidence of America's evil determination to enslave the Chinese people. It was now their arch-enemy, to be vilified constantly and discredited in every way. The last vestige of American influence, cultural, economic, religious and social, had to be stamped out.

The country had to grow strong quickly by sacrifice and endeavor to avoid falling prey to American imperialism. In June, 1950, just as Peking was preparing the land reform campaign and the campaign against the counterrevolutionaries, the North Koreans marched across the 38th Parallel and the United States, as the spearhead of the United Nations force, hurried to the aid of the South Koreans. In China this meant that every counterrevolutionary, every condemned landlord, every cheating businessman, gangster, pimp and prostitute could be linked either directly, or by implication, with America's determination to enslave and murder the Chinese people, or to corrupt and destroy them with its pernicious "yellow culture." The counterrevolutionaries were agents of the "bandit" Chiang Kai-shek, who was the "puppet" of the American imperialists, who were advancing north to the very borders of China and "invading" Taiwan. This was the stimulus so urgently needed to activate the new society. It was the justification for terror and for the campaign to mop up all surplus wealth.

With their emotions fanned by the widespread hate and fear of America that the propagandists generated, the Chinese people contributed enough money—voluntarily, according to Peking—to buy 3,700 jet fighters from the Soviet Union between June and December, 1950. Thereafter, when enthusiasm flagged, the Germ Warfare campaign stirred up fresh horrors. The population was mobilized to take preventive measures to kill flies, mosquitoes, fleas and rats, to clean up garbage, to destroy everything that might be a carrier or a breeding ground for America's filthy pestilences. In the first year of this campaign Peking listed the destruction of 120 million rats, and nearly 1½ million pounds weight of flies, mosquitoes and fleas. A hundred and sixty million tons of garbage, including some that had been there since Ming times, was carted away from the streets: 280,000 kilometers of drains and ditches were filled; 40 million cubic meters of earth were used to fill up stagnant pools. Big contingents of Chinese scientists went to Korea and came back laden with U.S.-made containers and "contaminated" insects. Brain-washed U.S. flyers added their depositions to the evidence. It was the greatest propaganda hoax in history: but that it succeeded in its purpose in China there is no doubt.

The Korean War became a rallying point, a call to Chinese nationalism, a justification for hard work. Thereafter, every new totalitarian innovation, every new call for austerity, was accompanied by a frenzy of hate against that "deadly enemy of the Chinese people," the United States. The back-breaking sacrifices of the "great leap forward" in 1958 had as their background the thunder of Communist guns against "American-occupied" Quemoy: the ideological battle with Russia on the inevitability of war coincided with an anti-American campaign that far exceeded in virulence everything that had preceded it.

It was all long planned and carefully thought out. In November, 1948, in an article in the now defunct Cominform journal, *For a Lasting Peace for a People's Democracy*, Mao had written: "Following victory in the Second World War, American imperialism and its stooges in various countries stepped into the boots of the German, Italian and Japanese Fascists, frenziedly prepared for a new world war and menaced the whole world. This mirrored the utter decay of the capitalist world and its fears on the verge of extinction. The enemy is still powerful. Hence, all the revolutionary forces within a country and the revolutionary forces of all countries must be united. An anti-imperialist front headed by the Soviet Union must be formed and pursue correct policy, otherwise no victory can be won. The foundation of the enemy is weak; it is disrupted inside and divorced from the people; it is confronted with unavoidable economic crises. Therefore it is conquerable. It would be a tremendous error to overestimate the forces of the enemy and to underestimate the forces of the revolution."

In so far as this was explicitly an ideological appeal to all Communists, it was fairly routine. What had not been fully comprehended at that time, however, was Mao's determination to use the United States as the principal "enemy" of the Chinese revolution. "Imperialism," Mao maintained, had turned China into a semicolony in the nineteenth century and had added the dead hand of exploitation to the cold precepts of Confucius. As such, it was an appropriate target for routine attack. But Mao intended to make it much more than that: hatred of the imperialism of the United States had to become an integral part of the revolution.

Years later, in a speech in February, 1957, he explained why. Dealing with the problem of conflict within a Communist society, he said: "These problems are new in Marxism-Leninism. Marx and Engels did not know about these problems for obvious reasons. Lenin mentioned them but did not enlarge upon them, because during his lifetime, as a result of foreign intervention, it was difficult to speak about internal problems only.

"As for Stalin, his opinions can be considered only negatively. The experience of the Soviet Union in this respect shows that Stalin made the mistake of substituting internal differences for external antagonisms, which resulted in a rule of terror and liquidation of thousands of Communists.

"In dealing with enemies it is necessary to use force. We in China have also used force to deal with enemies of the people. The total number of those liquidated by our security forces numbers 800,000. This is the figure up to 1954.

"Since then we are no longer using methods of terror. Instead we have substituted persuasion and education. If one persists in using the methods of terror in solving internal antagonisms, it may lead to transformation of these antagonisms into antagonisms of the nation-enemy type as happened in Hungary."

For Stalin's principle that the more internal enemies are eliminated the more bitter becomes the struggle with those who remain, Mao substituted external enemies, notably the United States, its allies, and, by logical extension, "counterrevolutionaries," "Chiang Kai-shek's bandits," and all other Western-associated external influences.

That this enabled the Chinese revolution to proceed—in relative Communist terms—without too frequent recourse to sanguinary methods is reflected in the durability of members of the Politburo and the Central Committee. Even Li Li-san, whose opposition to Mao Tse-tung's peasant-based revolution led to a disastrous attack on Changsha in 1930, and who has since admitted all sorts of serious errors of a "subjectivist nature" including "Leftist opportunism," has paid for his mistakes only by temporary demotion. In the past twenty-five years the only truly significant liquidation has been that of the former State Planner, Kao Kang, whose Communist leadership in Shensi, Kansu and Ninghai was already established before Mao Tse-tung and the survivors of the Long March arrived to find their sanctuary in Yenan in 1935: and even he is said to have died by his own hand and not by that of a Party assassin. Established, identified class enemies, and enemies symbolized by the United States, received no quarter: against others the weapon was persuasion. Instead of the terror within there was the terror without.

There have been peaks but no depressions in the Hate America campaign. It reached a high during the Korean War. It rose to another peak during the "great leap forward" of 1958, rose again during the "Camp David spirit" period, and in the months that led through the U2 incident, the summit conference collapse, the Eisenhower visit to the Far East, the crop failures of 1960, and the growing public ideological dispute with the Communist Party of the Soviet Union. At this time more than 3 million people at a mass rally in the People's Square in Peking heard Liu Ning-yi, chairman of the All-China Federation of Trade Unions, describe Eisenhower as a "bloodstained hangman and ringleader of bandits." China, he said, must thoroughly expose before the people of the world the true colors of the "U.S. imperialist bandits" and wage resolute, unremitting struggles against "imperialism." Chou En-lai, welcoming Belkacem Krim, vice-premier of the Algerian rebel government, called the United States the "arch enemy of world peace."

With the collapse of the summit conference in Paris the Chinese leaders exulted. In a speech of welcome to Haxhi Lleshi, chairman of the presidium of the People's Assembly of Albania—and China's one true friend among the European satellites—Chairman Liu Shao-chi said that "more and more people have now come to realize that although U.S. imperialism may make this or that change in its tactics at different times, and employ its two tactics—the policy of war preparations and 'peace' deceptions—simultaneously, or alternatively, its inherent nature and wild ambition to dominate the whole world and enslave its people will never change. The experience of the peoples of the world in their struggles against imperialism since the end of the Second World War has also proved again that no unrealistic illusions must be entertained about this most vicious enemy, U.S. imperialism, and that a struggle directed squarely against it must be waged. We must have the courage to rebuff U.S. imperialism and not be cowed by it when it threatens or launches aggressive war: we must be adept at seeing through and exposing its deceitful tactics and not be taken in when it plays with schemes of 'peace.' Only so can we put down the aggressive arrogance of U.S. imperialism." The *People's Daily* added: "Marxism-Leninism maintains that U.S. imperialism and its lackeys will never change their nature, that they are the most ferocious enemy of world peace and of the peoples of all lands."

Thinly veiled references to Khrushchev's obtuseness in failing to see through the American deceptions were now commonplace both in public speeches by the Chinese leaders and in press comments. Not everybody had seen through the U.S. duplicity, said the *People's Daily*. "The 'peace gestures' made by the U.S. imperialism and particularly Eisenhower as a fake 'peace lover' did indeed mislead some people and give rise to the illusion that U.S. policy had changed. These people failed to see that this U.S. imperialist wolf in the guise of a grandma was actually a man-eating beast."

Nothing that Communist China has seen in the past in the way of mass demonstrations, including even the mob psychology of the campaign to liquidate the counterrevolutionaries, matched the splenetic demonstrations that were now organized to vilify the United States. Sacrificing millions of man-hours in factories and paddy fields, the Communist Party organized gigantic anti-American rallies and mass demonstrations. In the three days from May 20 to May 22, 1960, 25 million demonstrators paraded in thirty-one cities. From Lhasa to Harbin leaders poured out their hymn of hate. Cadres composed special songs for the occasion. According to the *Peking Review*, demonstrators in the capital of Anhwei Province sang the following song:

> The hated U.S. imperialists plot war
> To bring disaster to the people.
> They wrecked the summit talks
> But try to shift the blame on others.
> Whatever their disguise the people know their
>   devil face.
> We'll never cease to struggle till their doom.

For more than a month the campaign continued, reaching its crescendo with the Eisenhower visit to Taiwan. "The whole nation went into militant action," said the *Peking Review*. "It was a national denunciation of U.S. imperialism, mankind's public enemy No. 1." Musicians, artists, poets, writers, actors and actresses, the newspapers, the radio, all were mobilized in the final frenzy of the campaign. In Peking during the official Hate America Week which began on June 22, 1960, every theatrical and operatic performance, movie show and public exhibition was devoted to the cause. The Modern Opera's principal attraction was *Hit the Aggressor Hard*, an opera "dedicated to the noble spirit of patriotism and internationalism of the Chinese People's Volunteers in the War to resist U.S. Aggression and Aid Korea." *The God of Plague*, a drama, showed "how the wrecking of the summit conference by U.S. imperialism and Eisenhower's gangster trip to the Far East rouses an anti-U.S. storm among the Asian peoples. U.S. imperialism is exposed as it was making the peace gestures while actually preparing for war." *Forward, Heroic Japanese People*, which showed to capacity houses, was produced by the China Children's Theater. It described the "nation-wide demonstrations in Japan against U.S. imperialism and the Kishi regime." *Fresh in Our Memory*, at the China Youth Art Theater, was about "the struggle of the Chinese people against U.S. imperialism and the Kuomintang secret agents during the War of Liberation."

Among the films, *Storm in Asia*, a documentary on "the struggles waged by the Asian Peoples against U. S. imperialism and its henchmen"; the *Battle of Sangkumryung*, a feature film based on the "famous battle of the War to Resist U.S. Aggression and Aid Korea, where the heroism and skill of the Chinese People's Volunteers in tunnel warfare put paid [finis] to all enemy attempts to take the height"; *Nameless Island*, a feature film showing "Chiang Kai-shek's forces taking a beating from the navy of the People's China"; and *Heroic Island*, which also involved defeats for the "U.S.-backed Chiang Kai-shek reactionaries," were the main attractions.

In the streets, squares, factories, mines and communes small groups put on such shows as *Get Out Ike, U.S. Imperialism Plays with Fire and Gets Burned*, and *Sunset of U.S. Imperialism*. In Peking alone, more than forty theatrical troupes and companies contributed to the campaign. At the Shodu Theater in Peking the cultural troupe of the General Political Department of the People's

Liberation Army sang a new cantata, "Down with Imperialism, Defend World Peace."

The Central Institute of Fine Arts specialized in a series of posters, cartoons, paintings, woodcuts and sculptures which "forcefully expressed Peking artists' indignation against U.S. aggression." A typical cartoon showed Eisenhower, the mask of peace fallen from his face and clutching a bomb in one hand and a banknote in another, hemmed in by the clenched and pointing fists of the people's world. "U.S. Imperialism Is the Most Vicious Enemy of the People of the World" was its title.

The Chinese People's Revolutionary Military Museum put on an exhibition of Korean War relics designed to demonstrate "that the U.S. imperialists with all their viciousness and ferocity are only paper tigers and to recall the brilliant example which the Koreans and Chinese peoples gave in dealing with these brigands."

With his poem, "The Hurricane," Kuo Hsiao-chuan, breathed the spirit of the week.

> The hurricane against U.S. imperialism sweeps across
>   heaven and earth:
> The God of Plague, the swindlers, the knaves
> Stand unmasked in all their vileness.
> The press secretary becomes the people's prisoner;
> The plague god's harbinger is stoned;
> The ambassador must creep stealthily to the back door,
> Whilst the once swaggering prime minister dares not
>   leave his mansion.
> The rat running down the street
> Comes face to face with the destroyers of the "four pests," *
> "Eisenhower, go home!" is his mildest greeting.

Under the circumstances, the conclusion reached by the magazine, *World Culture*, that "the poisonous influence of imperialism, particularly U.S. imperialism, which exercised through aggression the enslavement of the Chinese people for the past hundred years has been thoroughly wiped out," was scarcely a cause for surprise. It followed naturally that the "pro-America, worship-America and fear-

* Rats, sparrows, mosquitoes and flies.

America feelings have been completely blotted out and instead a gallant spirit—hate-America, despise-America, and belittle-America—has been established among the people of all China."

The theme in all this propaganda was that the United States, though dangerous, was weak enough to be beaten and destroyed. Eisenhower was often portrayed in cartoons as a germlike creature with the strong and healthy peoples of the world clustered around him ready to deliver the *coup de grâce*. In an interview with Anna Louise Strong in 1946 Mao Tse-tung first used the expression that the "imperialists" were "paper tigers." This was now seized upon to symbolize Communism's new strength. Mao saw the "east wind prevailing over the west wind" and said that "imperialists and all the reactionaries look very arrogant but they are outwardly strong and weak inside."

"Should the imperialists start a war of aggression, we, together with the people of the whole world will certainly wipe them clean from the surface of the globe," he said. Korea was not only a great victory over the United States, it was claimed, but an example of what China could do while it was still weak and before it grew strong industrially and militarily.

In a society which is denied any contact with external influences and subject, not merely for months but for years, to this venom, the hatred for the "war-mongering government of the United States" that all visitors to China report is readily comprehensible. Just as the campaign against the counterrevolutionaries engendered mass hysteria and thousands of decent Chinese people shouted for blood, the Chinese Communists have deliberately created a state of mind in which wars to be fought continuously in the campaign to isolate the United States and its allies are "just."

There was no break in this campaign after the American presidential election in November, 1960. On the contrary, Peking greeted the new administration in terms that had hitherto been reserved for Republicans. Mr. Kennedy, it said, had drafted reactionary anti-labor laws and had actively supported Senator McCarthy. He also had close connections with the Rockefeller, Morgan and other groups of monopoly capital. Vice-President Lyndon Johnson wore the mantle of his grandfather, who had fought in defense of slavery in the Civil War. Dean Rusk's appointment as Secretary of State meant that he would be a "yes" man for the Rockefeller dynasty of the Chase-Manhattan Bank and the Standard Oil Company, which were behind a militarist Germany and an unbending colonial policy. Douglas Dillon was an old hand at plundering other countries: the profits he had squeezed out of Africa were soaked in human blood. And so on.

No suggestion ever appeared that the Democrats might be interested in establishing a more favorable climate of relations between the United States and China. China's leaders neither wanted such a climate nor could afford to have one develop. The American embargo on trade with China, its "occupation" of Taiwan, its air and naval intrusions off the coast of China, the presence of American military aid and advisory groups on Quemoy and Matsu and the efforts made by the United States to discourage recognition of the Communist regime and its admission to the United Nations all fitted comfortably into China's own policy. For here was the "proof" it needed to convince its people of the aggressive intent of American "imperialism." Thus the normal enough function of recognition by the governments of underdeveloped countries was no longer a matter of diplomatic routine but a contest between the United States and China in which every new country "lost" to Taipeh—and therefore to Washington—was a "victory" for Peking. Kennedy, Mao solemnly told a large group of Afro-Asian visitors to Peking, was worse than Eisenhower.

Chapter III 𒀀𒀀𒀀𒀀𒀀𒀀𒀀𒀀𒀀𒀀𒀀

THE BITTER YEARS

MAO TSE-TUNG's decision to channel the emotions of the Chinese
people against American "imperialism" saved them from the bloody
excesses that marked the Stalinist period of industrialization in the
Soviet Union; it did not save them from hard work, hunger or the
precipitate leap toward Communism that Mao had seen as a natural
consequence of land reform.

About the middle of 1958 the Chinese press began to publish
long reports of Mao's journeys into remote country areas, of visits
of inspection to collective farms, and, especially, to the pilot commune which had been set up at Chilying in Honan Province early in
April.

The *Daily Worker* in Peking described the scene. "It was clearing
up on the afternoon of August 6. The showers had dispelled the
heat and the air was getting very fresh. The cotton, rice, corn, beans
and sweet potatoes were growing very well in the irrigated area in
Hsinhsiang hsien, auguring well for bumper harvests. . . .

36

"When a crowd started forming at the gate of the cooperative, Chairman Mao, accompanied by the secretaries of the Communist Party hsien committee and the Party cell in the cooperative entered the collective after taking a look at the signboard on the gate and bearing the characters 'Hsinhsiang Hsien Chilying People's Commune.'

"Turning to the Chairman, Secretary Wu said, 'This is the first commune in the entire hsien.' Chairman Mao nodded approvingly. 'This is a good name,' he said.

"Entering the courtyard, Chairman Mao noticed another two signboards hanging on the door of a house in the courtyard and bearing the characters 'Political Department.' 'What is this?' he asked.

" 'This is the Red and Expert University of the commune,' Comrade Ti Chi-chang, first secretary of the district committee, told the Chairman.

" 'Who is the president of this university?' Chairman Mao asked again.

" 'The secretary of the Party cell in the commune.' "

According to the *Daily Worker*, Mao was very concerned when he learned that the commune had 31,000 inhabitants. "It cannot be easy to manage such a huge cooperative," he said. "Do you have difficulties?"

"No difficulties at all," replied Wang Wen-shang, director of the commune.

Mao looked at the "happiness home" for the aged, children's nurseries, creches, mess halls, factories and cotton fields.

"On his way back to the village, Chairman Mao kept looking round with great satisfaction," the *Daily Worker* reported.

"Turning to Comrade Wu, he said: 'Secretary Wu, very promising indeed! What a fine thing it would be if all Honan were like this.'

" 'With a cooperative like this one, we need not worry about more and more similar cooperatives to come,' Comrade Wu said.

" 'You are right,' the Chairman said approvingly. 'With a cooperative like this one, many more similar cooperatives will come along.' "

This report is written in the wide-eyed, reverential manner reserved to describe all Mao Tse-tung's activities. It also presents a somewhat naïve Mao delighted by his discovery of this novel and spontaneous experiment in collective life, when, in fact, there is good reason to believe that the setting up of this guinea pig operation was his own pet scheme. Within a year most of China's 550 million peasants found their 740,000 collective farms merged into 26,000 (later 24,000) communes in which eating—and sometimes sleeping— was communal. In the most advanced communes, infants were sent off to creches, children to boarding schools and the elderly to "happiness homes." By the end of 1960 there were nearly 4 million commune creches for preschool-age children and a hundred thousand "happiness homes" for the aged. In some provinces 60 to 80 per cent of children were in nurseries; but throughout China generally there was little uniformity. Commune standards and people's reactions to the communes differed widely.

Since intensive rebuilding was required to bring the communes fully into operation, many of the more controversial aspects of the system, such as the boarding schools for all children, were tested only in pilot schemes. Peking having taken two steps forward was also prepared, as usual, to take one step backward and to meet, or to give the appearance of meeting, public criticism and resentment. It was also prepared, for both economic and psychological reasons, to take five or six years, or even longer, over the rebuilding program that would usher in the full communal life and to devote this period to educating the people in the virtues of the new system. This was not agreed to, however, without bitter and acrimonious debate within the Central Committee at a meeting at Wuchang in December, 1958, which decided, even against the firmly stated wishes of Mao Tse-tung, that the communes had gone too far too fast and were in urgent need of "tidying up."

The new policy was soon reflected in official guidance. In January, 1959, for instance, the *Changchun Kirin Jih-pao* answered criticisms that the rise of the people's communes spelled doom to the family institution. "Is there any foundation for this fear? 'There is,' they say, pointing out that living under one roof, commune members eat together at public service restaurants, children are packed off to nurseries and kindergartens, the old are sent to homes for the aged and primary school students are boarding in school. 'This amounts to a disintegration of the family, which is abolished as an institution,' they explain. Proceeding from this conviction, they surmise that the rise of the commune system means the end of the natural and kindred relationship of man."

This clearly was not the case at all, the newspaper explained. The only change in family life would be the elimination of the patriarchal system inherited from the past. In its place there would be "democracy and unity." That involved the destruction of the old family system and its replacement by a new one. No longer would the head of the house be permitted to practice "dictatorial rule" in family life, to have the final say in family problems. In abolishing the patriarchal rule and effecting the transformation of the old family, it would be necessary to eliminate the family as an economic unit of the society through the establishment of the largest possible number of public service restaurants, nurseries, kindergartens, homes for the aged, boarding schools and the emancipation of women "from the drudgery of domestic chores to enable them to gain economic independence by participation in social labor." Participation in social labor by all women was the prerequisite to their emancipation. To attain that aim, it was necessary to eliminate the family as an economic unit of the society.

But what would the new family life be?

The newspaper had the answer: "All able-bodied persons will participate in social labor. Women will be set free from the drudgery of domestic affairs in order to gain equality with men. The old, the young and the disabled will be provided for by society. Education will be a job for the society to handle. The consciousness of the people will be raised. And the people will be living as equals in a domestic, united friendly and happy life. At that time, the people will be happy to take part in labor, studies and other activities on week days, and to get together on holidays (there will be more holidays than there are at present) to enjoy their natural and kindred relationships.

"There is no ground, therefore, for the apprehension that in the new society there will be no parental or filial love. Not only will there be such love, but the relations between family members will be closer and more congenial than they are at present. In addition to the new small families, there will be the large family. The people's commune will be the large family where the people will labor, rest, study and recreate together as an economic unit in an atmosphere replete with democracy, unity, friendship and bliss. Living in such families, the people will be more broad-minded and think more in the collective way. They will love all members of the society."

The magazine *China Youth* was more explicit. "The family, as a state of communal life between the male and female sexes will definitely not be eliminated," it said. "However, the family of the future will be more rational than the family of today. Communal life between the sexes is for physiological reasons an indispensable human relationship. It must exist from the beginning to the end of humanity." Therefore under the commune system the family would never disappear. If the family was not to be marked by such a state of affairs as "five generations under the same roof," however, there should be real monogamy. Parentage would still be clearly distinguished and there would never be a return to the status of mass marriage and free mating.

Children would no longer be considered the private property of parents, for "today this theory is no longer tenable. The question is not whether the children should or should not be admitted to kindergartens and nurseries, but it is rather that parents find it most difficult now to bring up their children completely. So for parents to continue treating their children as private property is incompatible with the development of society. Generally speaking, children should be admitted to kindergartens and nurseries to be brought up, and to live the collective life from infancy, thereby cultivating the habit of loving labor."

There was to be no compulsion, only persuasion. "Generally speaking, the future direction to be followed is the operation of nurseries and kindergartens and though parents may have their choice of sending their children to these institutions, they should nevertheless understand their importance, and pleasantly and joyfully greet the new development." It was true, the magazine agreed, that the happiness homes, kindergartens and nurseries at the beginning might not be very satisfactory. But so long as the building of Socialism was proceeding successfully, they would at least prove better than reliance on the individual families concerned. "By that time, it is very possible, most of the old people will want to enter a happiness home and most parents will want to hand over their children to kindergartens and nurseries. In the leisure periods and festival days, the dear ones may regularly get together and truly enjoy the bliss of 'family life.'"

In this new family, the magazine continued, parents would rear children in a planned manner. That would be based on the material conditions of society and an attitude of responsibility would be assumed. The children born would be treated as people in society and not as private holdings. The rearing and education of the children would be coordinated with the needs of society, and there would not be instilled into them things which were not compatible with the age, or with the society, and which obstructed their over-all mental and physical development.

The pernicious influence of parents whose mental processes had not been fully redirected into the new channels of thought was constantly emphasized. If a student got Communist education in the school and received non-Communist education at home the result could not be satisfactory. The Peking newspaper *Kuang-ming Jih-pao* of October 24, 1959, made a special note of this point in advocating that all primary schools should become boarding schools. "Home education often breeds spoilt children, indisposed toward labor and selfish," it said. "Children finding no one to care for them at home begin to loaf and ramble and even contract bad habits. The boarding arrangement solves this problem. We all know that the further our society develops, the higher will be the degree of collectivism, and, consequently, the more important will be the education of our children in collectivism and having them live and eat together."

A woman who published a story entitled "Mother" was severely attacked for stressing "mother love" instead of "Communist spirit." In her story, a Mrs. Li had five children and loved them dearly. She loved other people's children, also, and became a nurse in a public creche, where she found great happiness and "mother love" in taking care of all the children in the creche.

The story was strongly condemned for lacking "class content." Mrs. Li thought only of "mother love" and did not care for "Socialist construction." "Mother love" was a "bourgeois concept" which was intolerable in a Socialist society.

An even greater crime was attributed to Pa Jen, the nom de plume of Wang Jeh-shu, a well known writer and former Chinese Communist ambassador to Indonesia, who committed the heresy of suggesting, like Shylock, that there are common human sentiments and feelings.

"In addition to social ideologies, there are general ideas among human beings," he said. "The pursuit of love, a longing for mother love, a joy of life, a dislike of death, a strong desire for happy life and respect for chivalry." It was human nature, he believed, that one could not wage a resolute struggle against one's own reactionary family.

China Youth called on the Red Flag Literary and Art Critique Group of the Chinese Department at the Peking University to compile a thorough denunciation of these ideas. "There is fundamentally no possibility for peoples of different classes to share common sentiments," the rebuttal began. Maternal love and the love men have for their children were inseparable from the economic life and ideas based on private ownership. In a feudal society family was the basic unit of production and life. The parents counted on their children's support and care when they grew old: and the children wanted to inherit the family name and property. That was the moral outlook of the feudal society and constituted the social foundation for maternal love.

The maternal love of the proletariat was also based upon its own moral standard. It "agreed entirely" with the proletarian struggle for the liberation of all oppressed people. A mother loved her sons in the same way as she loved 650 million people and found the greatest comfort in sending her sons one after the other on the revolutionary road.

"Pa Jen thinks that it is only human that one is unable to carry out a firm struggle against one's reactionary family," the report said. "Actually this is in every way the sign of vacillation in revolutionary stand. A loyal, heroic and stanch fighter is capable of drawing a line of distinction between himself and his counterrevolutionary parents."

As for bourgeois love, it was divided into two categories, the "love" that could be bought with money and "egoistic love," which was frequently looked upon as the sole purpose and the sole happiness in life. Some people publicized that love was above all, that it was greater than anything and sacred.

"On the face of it, this kind of extremely degenerate love outlook seems to be different from the bourgeois love which can be bought with money," the article declared. In essence the two were one and the same thing. It was just the individualist philosophy of life which gave chase to the fulfillment of personal desire expressed in another way. The writers used Anna in the novel *Anna Karenina* as a typical example of bourgeois love and a commune folk song to illustrate "lofty Communist morality": " 'The girl carries away the soil as the boy dredges the pond. Sweat drips from their bodies along with muddy water. The girl does not complain of fatigue although she has carried a thousand loads, nor does the boy feel the chill in the mud. It is not convenient to talk to each other because there are too many people, but they understand each other at heart. Both the boy and the girl are heroic fellows. They work until the stars disappear and the sun rises.' Can this kind of love engendered in common labor be found in the exploiting classes?"

Bourgeois friendship was inseparable from money and there was no possibility, therefore, of friendship existing between different classes. Pa Jen's view that all men loved to live and hated to die and had a craving for the happy soul merely exposed "the most dirty soul of the revisionists." "Joy of life" and "happy life" were built upon the blood and sweat and bones of the broad masses of the laboring people. The "joy" of the individual was the sole object of life. Consequently death was feared, for once the bourgeois died what they sought would come to nought. The proletariat held a completely different attitude toward life and death and happiness. "In the eyes of a proletarian revolutionary, the object of life is to work for collectivism and the realization of Communism and the greatest happiness is to labor, fight and work selflessly for this great undertaking."

To men and women who found themselves married to critics of the regime, the Communist posed the question: "What can you do if your spouse turns out to be a rightist?"

"First," said the answer, "you should take a correct, or proletarian stand, politically and ideologically draw a clear line of demarcation. If your spouse is a rightist, then the relationship between you and your spouse is no different from that between you and other comrades. As we understand, the following three kinds of attitude are taken by those whose spouse happens to be a rightist: (1) hate the rightist just as any other comrades do and politically draw a clear line against their spouse; (2) just listen but 'fail to feel any hatred' for their spouse; (3) refuse to admit that their spouse is a rightist, or even think that people do them wrong by branding their spouse as a rightist.

"The attitude in the first case is correct, but in the second case there lacks a firm political stand toward their spouse, hence shirking the responsibility of remolding the rightist and facing the danger of political fallibility unless they act resolutely. The attitude taken in the third case is completely incorrect."

With such contemplated—and partly effected—changes in social life went hard work, hard even by Chinese peasant standards. In an article written to celebrate the tenth anniversary of Communist rule, Chairman Liu Shao-chi admitted that in the mass campaign to make iron and steel during the first year of the communes "tens of millions of people neglected their sleep and meals and paid no attention to material remuneration." Ninety million women joined the labor force: school children from the age of eight were put to part-time work at manual labor. Teachers, civil servants, businessmen and women were driven from their desks into the fields and factories. Men, women and children worked till they fell exhausted, snatched a few hours' sleep in the fields or by their machines, and then rose to work again.

China became a battleground in which every able-bodied person was a soldier. Mao had prepared his base, assembled his armies and now in overwhelming strength thrust them into the battle. Shock troops attempted to take their assigned projects by storm, goaded, exhorted, cajoled, persuaded and sometimes forced.

The Communist Party decided that the forces of large-scale agricultural and industrial production constituted an industrial army. Factories and fields became "military camps" in which the "discipline for the worker standing before the machine should be as rigid as that in the army."

Proudly the *People's Daily* reported progress in the battle to change the face of China. In Shantung Province 15 million people were mobilized to deep-plow 13 million acres of land. In one Manchurian region more than 4 million peasants formed up into divisions, regiments, battalions and companies and platoons on another massive deep-plowing operation which tore up nearly a million and a half acres of land in a week.

Here, according to an account which appeared in the Shanghai newspaper, *Wen Hui-pao*, is how it was done: "At 6:30 A.M. the duty officer blew the whistle to tell everybody to get ready. At 6:45 A.M. he blew the whistle again for all women with young children to send them to the nurseries. At 6:55 A.M. he blew the whistle once more for all commune members, male or female, to pick up their farming tools, turn their name plates upward, line up and march to the fields to begin a day's work. In the evening, under the bright moonlight, many people continue to work in the fields. They are prepared to keep on working without any rest for four days and four nights."

By day and by night bugle calls roused men and women to get on with the battle. There were plowing armies, transport armies, road and railway building armies, bridge building armies, dam building armies, armies for the production of coal, iron ore and steel and even armies for the destruction of graveyards. In the municipality of Changchow in Kiangsu a fifth of the population were mobilized to work without relief for five consecutive days and nights to transport minerals, using wheelbarrows, baskets, soapboxes, sieves, flour bags and even straw hats. One army of 120,000 workers mined 800,000 tons of iron ore in six days: another of 200,000 sowed 630,000 acres of wheat in twenty days. And so it went on until men and women collapsed and the Party realized that there was a limit to human endurance. Something approaching a standard for hours of work and pay was now laid down. Again conditions vary from commune to commune, but twenty-eight days' work each month is fairly general for men and twenty-five for women. Five hours a day are set as the minimum rest period. Wages are paid on the basis of full attendance and on the grade of work and an effort is made to keep "duty" hours down to twelve a day, of which two are devoted to study and militia training. A worker who fails to reach the required number of days of attendance loses wages according to the number of days of absence. Extra wages are paid to those who exceed minimum attendance days.

Grades are established on "attitude toward labor, quality of work and number of days of attendance." A worker who is chosen as "one pressing forward consistently" for three consecutive months is entitled to an advance in grade. Those who fail to reach the basic working days not only lose pay, but are subjected either to group criticism and education, or are fined, either in money or food, "according to circumstances of each case after discussion by the masses." Work and eat: loaf and starve. Those are the alternatives. Most people work.

An Indian social scientist inspected the communes and came to the conclusion that their inhabitants had been reduced to the level of inmates in a zoo, but a zoo with a difference. "In a zoo the animals do not have to work hard, and, what is more, they do not have to listen to the quasi-compulsory radio. This lack of privacy and solitude is to me more terrifying than all the other hells put together. Such is the triumph of a tyranny that crushes the human spirit, destroys the home and reduces its subjects to subanimal robots."

The communes, as we have noted, were also the subject of serious attack within the ranks of the Chinese Communist Party. But whatever the early doubts among some of Mao Tse-tung's lieutenants, the official conclusion at the end of the first two years was that this was the most successful and important of all mass movements initiated by the Party and that though "tidying up" would need to continue, the system should not be abandoned.

"Tidying up" was a rational process. In their early form the effective management of the communes would have been beyond the capabilities of the most highly skilled administrators. It proved a nightmare for unsophisticated peasants and Party hacks who found themselves not only obliged to direct manpower on a huge scale but to conduct highly complex organizations that included agriculture and industry, unprecedented social problems on a mass scale and problems of supply, and to set—and to fill—unrealistic production quotas. They had to create industries with which they were unfamiliar and to train workers for enterprises which they themselves did not understand. To add to their problems, the early organization of the communes, with the emphasis on mass control and action, precluded specialization and reasonable delegation of authority. Some communes were like armies in which there were only generals and recruits, who, in many cases, interpreted the communes as Communism, and, on the principle of "each according to his needs," expected that they would work on a "free supply" system.

Each commune has about five thousand families divided into production brigades. These are about the size of the two-hundred-family agricultural cooperatives which they replaced. At the lowest level are production teams of about forty families each. With command coming from the top many inexperienced cadres interpreted the call for mass labor too liberally. Vast armies of workers with flags and bugles created an impression of efficiency and effort that often failed to show up in results.

"Tidying up" has brought decentralization and greater emphasis first on the production brigades and more recently on the production teams. This has not eliminated the capability for quick mobilization of mass forces for specific projects: but the emphasis is on the production team, the platoon, rather than on the commune, the division. "Free supply" was not intended to operate and has been eliminated. To provide extra incentive only 30 to 40 per cent of wages are in kind: the rest is paid, or is supposed to be paid, in cash.

All this is an ideological step backward: but it is made with the clear intent of taking another two steps forward. No one was allowed to forget this. Despite the Central Committee's decision at Wuchang not to rush the formation of urban communes, there was little surprise when Li Fu-chun, the State Planner, announced at the 1960 National People's Congress that China was in the process of organizing urban communes "in a big way." During the early part of 1960 community dining rooms, service centers, creches and laundries had been established in most cities and a prolonged period of "study" had been followed through to ensure acclimatization of outlook. Shift workers were uprooted from their homes and concentrated in zones in which they lived among workers on the same shift, thereby simplifying transport problems and ensuring rest for night workers. Small workshops called "street factories" were established to provide centers of "social labor" for housewives now liberated from cooking and the care of their children.

To those who hoped that the communes and the leap forward meant that better times were soon to come, however, the message was that the building of Socialism and Communism involved "complicated, violent, protracted, arduous struggle," which would "cost inestimable labor and energy and involve unavoidable sacrifice of lives."

A young married woman who wrote to *China Youth* inquiring whether some day she and her husband and child would not be able to relax and enjoy a happy family life, was answered by Wu Chih-Pu, first secretary of the Honan Provincial Committee. Pleasure and happiness could rest only on the spirit of uninterrupted revolution, he said, on the well-being of mankind and on the noble concept of social reform and self-reform. "Do we want enjoyment?" he asked. "We should go after it in these respects, for such an enjoyment is then saintly and divine, the richest, most superior and inexhaustible. Many martyrs who struggled for Communism were exemplary in seeking such enjoyment from which they drew strength and found pleasure and happiness beyond the imagination of some people. Such a concept of enjoyment is part of the world outlook to be established by the Chinese youth of our time as well as a moral quality which the youth of our great era must acquire."

The communes have invoked expressions of distaste, even horror, outside China. But they are an essential part of Mao's social revolution. In many ways, and partly because there has been greater flexibility in their application than in their theory, they have been extremely successful. They have dealt another blow at the patriarchal family system. They have strengthened Party control. They have released huge new labor forces. They have made possible the creation of task forces for use in such emergencies in the 1960–1961 famine and flood control. They have resulted in huge savings—much bigger than were ever collected from the cooperatives that preceded them. They have accelerated the final collapse of inherited wealth and privileged classes in rural society. They have facilitated the diversification of rural industries. They have contributed heavily to improved rural health and education, and they have played a considerable part in the great, if extremely uneven, progress made by China since 1958.

It is also true that there have been glaring weaknesses in the system. Commune blast furnaces, for instance, produced more than a third of the 1958 output of steel, but its quality was so poor that it could not be used even for the manufacture of simple agricultural tools. Raw materials were squandered, and, more importantly, millions of man-hours wasted. The latter was especially important since a substantial part of the potential agricultural force was diverted to nonproductive industrial effort which clogged the still inadequate road and rail systems.

On many specific projects the ready mobilization of millions of men and women resulted in spectacular successes. The system was much less successful, however, in food production. The *Agricultural Almanac*, the Mrs. Beeton's cookbook of peasant China, was laid aside by the Communists as based on superstition—and because it provided for twenty-four annual festival holidays. But the ill equipped cadres who directed the communes knew less than the *Almanac* and the peasants about how to produce food from the good earth of China. Too much arable land was used for roads, industry and mining. Many water conservation projects were haphazardly undertaken, and, because they were not properly coordinated with neighboring communes, failed in their objective.

It took the droughts and other natural disasters of 1959–1960 to convince Peking that mass labor did not hold the solution to all its problems.

On balance, however, the commune credits are higher than their debits. By the only comparison that is relevant, most Chinese commune dwellers are certainly no worse off in material terms than they were before, and, partly because of the communes, China's huge, ill balanced economy is moving ahead.

Nevertheless, the regime did attempt to go too quickly and it paid bitterly for its errors. As early as October, 1958, for instance, the *People's Daily* claimed that work on irrigation and water conservation projects had made the country drought-free. As the 1959–1960 drought revealed this was a gross overestimation. By the middle of the year widespread doubts had begun to creep into the Communist newspapers about crop prospects for the year. On July 31 the *People's Daily* said that "if the summer harvest equals that of 1959, or is a little bigger, or even smaller, it will be, nevertheless, a great victory for China's agriculture." By October 1, the Chinese people were being prepared for the worst. More than 60 per cent of China's total sown area (264 million acres) had been damaged by natural disasters, it was said. Crops had been seriously affected on between 50 million and 66.6 million acres of farmland and general "natural adversities were without parallel in the past hundred years." For more than forty days in the months of March and June the flow of water in the Yellow River was interrupted, or nearly interrupted, and the river could be forded on foot. Typhoons—eleven from June to October—were the most numerous in fifty years; large areas were afflicted by locust and other insect plagues (perhaps caused by the earlier destruction of the sparrows); and elsewhere there had been serious frosts and hailstorms.

An urgent quest for wheat and barley in Canada and Australia early in 1961 underlined the gravity of China's food situation. Food served in commune restaurants had frequently been a source of irritation. Now, to charges of bad cooking, were added complaints of inadequate food. The shortages were clearly acute.

In Peking grain was rationed to thirty-three pounds of wheat and rice a month for each adult; vegetables, formerly sold in unlimited quantities, were reduced to a pound a day for a family. Milk and eggs were available for babies only—and on doctor's orders.

Tea and tobacco were replaced by substitute leaves, with a ration of one cigarette a month of good tobacco. The cotton clothing allowance was reduced to just over five yards a person a year and socks and underwear were included in the list of garments requiring ration tickets.

Elsewhere, but especially in South China, the situation was much more serious. In Kwantung Province the daily rice ration was cut from six ounces a person a day to two ounces, while the cadres tried to push production of sweet potatoes, a highly unpopular food usually given only to pigs. The *People's Daily* prescribed the use of a combination of wheat and rape stalks, explaining that they could be processed into starch which, with the addition of a little wheat or rice flour, could be used to make steamed bread.

With shortages in grains went shortages also in meat and poultry. A huge pig-breeding plan produced pigs which died of insufficient food; and vegetables, following the temporary prohibition of private plots, were in shorter supply than ever. To meet the deficiencies, the regime, even before the end of 1959, found itself obliged to take an ideological step backward and once again to promote private pig raising and gardening on individual plots beside the commune houses.

The sum was a picture of rural distress. The *People's Daily* admitted frankly that twice the amount of grain needed to be produced and three times the amount of cotton if the people of China were to receive their needs in food and clothing.

There were administrative, technical and even strategic failures. The cadres lacked the skill, and sometimes the will, to direct the peasants in all the multi-faceted aspects of commune activity. In addition to droughts and floods and pests, crops had failed because of inadequate and incorrect fertilization, or because seeds had been planted too close together in a fruitless and unscientific effort to increase production. "Bad elements" and counterrevolutionaries had crept into the Party and "were attempting to stage a comeback." Up to 10 per cent of officials and a similar proportion of the population were regarded as either disloyal or dangerous and an immediate rectification campaign was ordered to weed them out and to bring them under control.

Early in April, 1960, before the second crop failure, Li Fu-chun had emphasized that agriculture was the foundation for the development of the national economy and that agricultural production therefore had to be placed in the foremost position. He criticized many aspects of China's leap forward. "Not merely has agriculture been neglected to promote heavy industry," he said, "but, also, in all sectors of the economy, there has been a waste of men, materials and money. There has been inefficient planning, concentrating too much on a few large industrial centers and at the other end of the scale too much localism with a lack of regard for the interests of the country as a whole."

Writing in *Red Flag* a few months later he proposed a really draconian step backward. Manpower would have to be concentrated on agricultural development, especially on grain production, he said, and all other enterprises should not increase the number of workers during the next three years. His statement followed the second session of the National People's Congress, which, on April 10, had approved a ten-year national agricultural and development program, calling for a wide range of measures designed to increase productivity. These included the further construction of water conservation projects; the rapid expansion of fertilizer supply; improvement of old-style farming tools and the popularization of modern farm tools: the use of higher yielding seedling strains; soil improvement; pro-

tection and breeding of draft livestock: further work on the extermination of pests and plant diseases; the reclamation of wasteland
and the expansion of cultivated acreage.

In the struggle to improve tools in the ricelands and to mechanize
agriculture in wheat, cotton and vegetable fields and to build new
chemical fertilizer factories, agriculture received an allocation in
1960 of 1.1 million tons of steel, or double the 1959 allocation. This
envisaged the production during the year of 22,000 tractors, 2,000
combine harvesters, 8,000 trucks, 10 million rubber-tired handcarts
and 2.8 million tons of fertilizer. Shock brigades and mobile teams
stepped up their work on water conservation, with the object of
trebling by 1967 the irrigated area, including sandy wastelands, barren
lands, short frost-free areas, and mountainous and reclaimable wastelands.

Mao Tse-tung had predicted three bitter years for the Chinese
people when the "great leap forward" began in 1958. Now, with
three years passed, the fourth promised to be the most bitter year
of all. Agriculture had failed to make expected progress; industry
was obliged to steady its pace; and each year at least 13 million new
mouths had to be fed. Was there any way out of this impasse?

Chapter IV ꙮꙮꙮꙮꙮꙮꙮꙮꙮꙮ

PEACEFUL COEXISTENCE

To THE Chinese leaders the assumption that there must be a contradiction between rising population and industrial and agricultural growth inside China is a denial both of the ideological framework of the revolution and of the "world outlook" that the people are constantly urged to acquire. They are told to consider events in China as they fit into that great "life and death struggle" with "imperialism." The great natural resources of Southeast Asia, Africa and Latin America must be denied to the imperialists: they must also be used to the advantage of all peoples. Just as the "little family" is merging into the "big family" of the communes, the "little family of China" will merge into "the big family of the world."

There are numerous, sometimes apparently contradictory but, in fact, complementary, paths to this goal. Peaceful coexistence means nothing more than the temporary alliance with all (usually weaker) nations, parties and peoples willing to be allied with. It does not mean toleration of imperialism and its allies.

53

As the Moscow Conference of Representatives of Communist and Workers Parties defined it on December 7, 1960: "The policy of peaceful coexistence is a policy of mobilizing the masses and launching vigorous action against the enemies of peace. Peaceful coexistence of States does not imply renunciation of the class struggle —[it] is a form of class struggle between Socialism and capitalism.

"In conditions of peaceful coexistence favorable opportunities are provided for the development of the class struggle in the capitalist countries and the national liberation movement of the peoples of colonial and dependent countries. It implies intensification of the struggle of the working class, of all the Communist parties, for the triumph of Socialist ideas."

The People's Democratic dictatorship peacefully coexisted with many people in China: it destroyed its enemies violently. When the appropriate time came, the businessmen, the peasants, the intellectuals and the bureaucrats no longer found themselves coexisting with the system but assimilated by it. On the much larger world canvas, this is also how Chinese Communist policy functions. The principal "counterrevolutionary" is the United States, which must be first isolated by depriving it of allies and friends, especially among the underdeveloped countries of Asia, Africa and Latin America, whose peoples Mao regards as historically destined to fulfill the role of the Chinese peasant in the world revolution, and then brought to its knees by the greater strength of the Communist world. This is in the great tradition of his guerrilla warfare. The United States is a "city" to be surrounded: the underdeveloped world is the "countryside" in which the revolution must be built. Those unwise enough to seek the protection of alliances with the United States are naturally added to the lists of the counterrevolutionaries and marked for liquidation. Others who seek to follow the path of peaceful coexistence may be maintained like the puppet political parties and bourgeoisie of China—useful for purposes of the united front but ultimately destined for eclipse in the Communist embrace.

Nowhere is this tactic of peaceful coexistence better illustrated than in Peking's approach to its minority areas. Thirty years ago when they were establishing their Soviets in Kiangsi, the Chinese Communists recognized the "right of self-determination of the national minorities in China, their right to complete separation from

China, and to the formation of an independent State for each national minority." All Mongolians, Tibetans, Miao, Yao, Koreans and others living in the territory of China were promised the full right to self-determination. It was firmly stated that they could either join the Union of Chinese Soviets or secede from it and form their own State as they preferred.

Tibet provides a case study of the application of these principles and an example of how they may be applied elsewhere. Late in 1950 the People's Liberation Army marched in to "liberate" the Tibetans from "imperialism." Organized resistance was short-lived, and, after unsuccessfully appealing to the United Nations for assistance, the Tibetan Government agreed to Chinese occupation. For their part, the Chinese promised in a 17-point agreement signed on May 23, 1951, that "in accordance with the policy toward nationalities laid down in the common program of the Chinese People's Provisional Consultative Committee, the Tibetan people have the right of exercising national regional autonomy under the unified leadership of the Chinese People's Government." This was interpreted by the Dalai Lama as meaning that Tibet had the right to self-government in internal affairs, and it was on this understanding that the God-King prepared to coexist with Peking.

By 1954 it was apparent that Peking's emphasis was less on autonomy and much more on the "big family" concept. Speaking at the National People's Congress on the new Constitution, Liu Shao-chi said: "All people in our country, and among the minorities, who support the people's democratic system and are united in the big family of the motherland have a bright future in the Socialist system."

What this unity meant was made clear on the eve of the Second Five Year Plan by Prime Minister Chou En-lai, who said: "We used to say that our nation is large in area, rich in materials and has a large population. However, all the large areas and rich materials are in the minority population areas, and the Han people have only the densely populated areas. The future expansion of industry and agriculture will take place mostly in the minority nationality areas. From the standpoint of the entire nation, amalgamation benefits both sides and division hurts both."

Huge areas and considerable numbers of people were affected by this decision. At least sixty races, some of them quite distinct from the Chinese, with their own languages, religions and cultures are included in the minorities. Their numbers are variously estimated from 30 to 40 million. They extend along all China's inland borders and occupy substantially more than half of the entire area of the country. Along with the Tibetans they include Uighurs, Kazakhs, Kirghiz, Uzbeks, Turkmen, Mongols, Russians, Manchus, Thais and many others. A substantial number are Chinese Moslems, or Huis, a name used to describe ethnic groups who are followers of Islam.

Among most of these people, but especially among the Tibetans and the Moslem Huis, what Mao regarded as feudal "theocratic authority" was an immediate barrier to Communist plans. In February, 1955, Mao told the Dalai Lama in Peking that religion was "something bad" and that because of it Tibet's progress would be set back and the population would decrease. He considered that a "poison" had been instilled into Tibet by the propagation of religion.

To counter the effects of this "poison" the Chinese set up Communist schools in Lhasa and other Tibetan towns. From about 1954 they took thousands of Tibetan children below the age of fifteen to China. They warned the parents that this was Mao's order and that the penalty for refusing was execution.

Mao's object was twofold: to remove the children from the parents' influence and to exclude them from religious instruction which was inhibiting all Chinese efforts to indoctrinate and to "educate" the Tibetan population. The policy was bitterly opposed by the Tibetans, and, in 1955, while the Dalai Lama was in Peking, the Khamba tribesmen rose in revolt.

In his speech at the Supreme State Conference in Peking in February, 1957, Mao said that "because conditions in Tibet are not ripe, democratic reforms have not yet been carried out there. It has now been decided not to proceed with democratic reforms in Tibet during the period of the Second Five Year Plan, and we can only decide whether it will be done in the period of the Third Five Year Plan in the light of the situation obtaining at that time."

This ideological delay did not imply a similar approach either to the military situation in Tibet or the material exploitation of the country. Between 1950 and 1957 the Chinese, largely with the labor of tens of thousands of conscripted Tibetans, had pushed a series of highways from China into the Tibetan plateau. Three main roads linked Sikang, Chinghai and Sinkiang with Tibet. These new roads extended for more than 4,000 miles and brought into Tibet not only large units of the People's Liberation Army with orders "to put down the counterrevolution thoroughly" but many Chinese immigrants. The flow of trade between Tibet and India began to recede. Chinese geological teams tramped over the Roof of the World in the first organized look at Tibet's riches: small-scale factories appeared in the towns; and, but for the ruthless Chinese military action in Lhasa in 1959 and the flight of the Dalai Lama to India, Tibet's final acquiescence to Chinese Communist rule might have seemed reasonably painless.

It was anything but that, as the report to the International Commission of Jurists by its Legal Inquiry Committee on Tibet subsequently revealed. The Commission is a nongovernmental organization which has consultative status with the United Nations Economic and Social Council. Its members are distinguished international lawyers and jurists of the highest probity: and the committee selected to inquire into events in Tibet was no less distinguished. Its members included, Purshottam Trikamdas, senior advocate of the Supreme Court of India, who was chairman; Arturo A. Alafriz, attorney-at-law and President of the Federation of Bar Associations of the Philippines; K. Bentsi-Enchill, Secretary of the Ghana Bar Association; N. C. Chatterjee, Vice-President of the Supreme Court of India Bar Association; Rolf Christophersen, Secretary-General of the Norwegian Bar Association; Mr. Justice T. S. Fernando, Judge of the Supreme Court of Ceylon; E. Maung, former Justice of the Supreme Court of Burma, and former Minister for Judicial and Foreign Affairs in Burma; R. P. Mookerjee, Dean of the Faculty of Law in the Calcutta University and former Justice of the Calcutta High Court; Ong Huck Lim, member of the Bar Council of the Federation of Malaya; M. R. Seni Pramoj, attorney-at-law and former Prime Minister of Thailand; and Lord Shawcross, Q.C., former Attorney-General of England. Lord Shawcross resigned in October, 1959, due to unforeseen personal and professional commitments, and Dr. E. Maung resigned in May, 1960, on becoming a member of the Government of Burma.

The committee met in New Delhi and Mussorie in northern India in November, 1959, and subsequently in Geneva in June, 1960, to prepare its report. It was the committee's view that throughout a thirty-year period prior to the Chinese Communist invasion in 1950 Tibet had exercised exclusive authority in domestic affairs within its territory, that it had successfully defended its territory against attack under color of a claim to sovereignty and that vis-à-vis the Republic of China no act was committed or declaration made that compromised its internal independence. In other words, there was effective government which owed no subservience whatsoever in internal affairs. During this period, the committee concluded, Tibet also conducted its own foreign relations. It was therefore "at the very least a de facto independent State" when it signed the Agreement on Peaceful Measures with China in 1951, and the repudiation of this agreement by the Tibetan Government in 1959 was fully justified.

The committee found that the Chinese in committing the crime of genocide, had systematically set out to destroy Buddhism in Tibet. "In the pursuit of this design they have killed religious figures because their religious belief and practice was an encouragement and example to others," their report stated.

The Chinese regarded the Tibetan lamas as the root of all evil, and as the core of the counterrevolution. Like the landlords and counterrevolutionaries of China proper, they had to be hounded out and destroyed. Lamas who had taken vows of continence and chastity were given the alternative of marriage or of imprisonment to reform through labor. Others were forced into sexual intercourse under threat of death. Some were buried alive, burnt alive, hanged, shot, crucified, stoned and dragged behind trucks. Sometimes heavy stones were put on their heads, making their eyeballs start from the sockets, others were dragged apart by trucks. One man was tied to a pole, beaten and ridiculed and finally forced to eat his own flesh. "The Chinese soldiers mockingly said that this was the punishment for those who seek help from boastful Americans," one witness reported. Another saw five lamas strangled by a rope, with a heavy image of Buddha providing the necessary force.

On the question of the forcible transfer of children to China, the committee reported: "There is no doubt on the evidence that large numbers of children, many being babies, have been taken under force, or the threat of force, from their homes and transferred from Tibet to China. In other cases children have been taken probably in accordance with their own wishes but contrary to the wishes of their parents."

And the evidence?

From Jeuba, Ba, in 1954: "Forty-eight babies below the age of one year were taken to China, in order, the Chinese said, that their parents would do more work. Many parents pleaded with the Chinese not to take the babies. Fifteen parents who protested were thrown into the river by the Chinese and one committed suicide."

From Doi-Dura, Amdo, 1956: "From 1956 onwards all babies were to be taken away ten to fifteen days after birth."

Tatsang, Amdo, 1951: "Beginning in 1951 children from eight to fifteen were sent to China."

Tatsang, Amdo, 1956: "The Chinese began to take away newborn babies, telling the people that babies would interfere with their work. Anyone who refused would be executed. The brains of the parents were rotten and the children's brains should not be the same."

Do, Rigong and Maharka, Amdo, 1956: "The Chinese announced that all the babies would be taken away so that the mothers could work and would have sufficient to eat."

Derge, Kham, 1956: "About three or four thousand people between the ages of fifteen and fifty were sent to China from Derge district. Only about thirty or forty returned and these were apparently well trained and well trusted."

Floggings, public degradations and starvation for the purpose of showing divine failure to provide nourishment were used repeatedly against the lamas. And while the committee remained unconvinced that the Chinese had in fact attempted sterilization in an attempt to prevent them from propagating their own faith, it noted that this belief was widespread among Tibetans.

The Dalai Lama was one who had no doubts. In a statement to the committee at Mussorie, he replied as follows to a series of questions on this point:

Question: "Was there mass sterilization by the Chinese?"
Dalai Lama: "Yes. In 1957."

Question: "Where can we have information about this?"

Dalai Lama: "The information is being kept in a statement and will be sent to you."

Question: "Was it on a large scale?"

Dalai Lama: "Yes. On quite a large scale. Two or three villages were completely sterilized."

Question: "Was it because of any bad diseases like leprosy or venereal disease?"

Dalai Lama: "No, not for any such reason."

Communist assertions that the Tibetans enjoyed no human rights before the entry of the Chinese were found to be based on distorted and exaggerated accounts of life in Tibet. "The material condition of the people compared very favorably with that of most other Asian countries and even with that of some European countries," the report said. "In the basic needs of food, housing and clothing the Tibetans were well provided on simple lines. An underfed Tibetan was practically nonexistent. Houses were solidly built. Clothes were made of excellent homespun, warm, hard-wearing and pleasant to see."

The People's Liberation Army killed men, women and children, singly, in one's and two's and in thousands. And thus, by the dual process of stamping out religion and liquidating counterrevolutionaries, it prepared this frontier region for extensive Chinese settlement and the exploitation of Tibet's newly discovered deposits of coal, iron, copper, salt and alkali and its rich forest reserves.

In his report to the Legal Inquiry Committee at Mussorie, the Dalai Lama said that large-scale settlement of some 5 million Chinese had already taken place in eastern and northeastern Tibet, and that millions were proposed to be settled in U and Tsang provinces in central Tibet. Migration began in 1950 and became mass migration into eastern Tibet in 1956, where eventually there were twenty Chinese for every Tibetan. "It was clearly stated to me while I was in Peking in 1955 that Tibet was a vast country with scarce population and China has a large population with insufficient land, so land and people should be exchanged," the Dalai Lama said. "I understand that during the past few months this is being done on a considerable scale in Central Tibet. Once this is achieved my people will become a hopeless minority in my own country."

Many Tibetan children removed from their parents' control went to the Central Institute for Nationalities, which was set up in Peking in 1951, and now has branches in many parts of China. The institutions serve as "schools for training Communist cadres of the minority nationalities." The cadres' task after graduation is to convince the minorities that assimilation within the cultural, religious and ideological framework of the Han empire is the only proper course.

The fifth session of the National People's Congress in March, 1958, was liberally sprinkled with such expressions of opinion by trained groups from the minority areas. One composite group of Thai, Nung, Yi, Lahu, Yao, Hani, Nahsi, Tibetan, Hui, Pai, Miao and Kawa people said that "under the new situation of the struggle, local nationalism has become a dangerous tendency that cannot be ignored. Some schemers within the national minorities, taking advantage of the comparative weakness of the economic, class and ideological basis of the Socialist system, are openly selling capitalist poison under the cloak of nationalism."

Nationalism and Communism were utterly incompatible with each other, they declared. Any nationality that broke away from the "big family of the motherland" and the unified leadership of the central authority would necessarily turn away from the smooth road of Socialism and back to the old road of oppression and enslavement.

A representative from Inner Mongolia revealed that his region had "accommodated a great number of resettlers" and that other settlers from China proper would continue to be made welcome. "We oppose the idea of each nationality working on its own and separation among the nationalities," he said. "Such separation is in substance the disruption of the solidarity and unity of the big family of the motherland, which, while it helps imperialism and capitalism, is harmful to the nationalities and Socialist construction."

During 1958 and 1959 the Party made urgent calls on the youth of China to "volunteer" for service in the border regions of minority areas. There were references in the press to the "tons of minerals" including petroleum, lead, zinc, copper, iron, coal, manganese, chromium, aluminum, antimony, gold, silver, mercury and quartz that had been discovered. Remote Chinghai, Sikang, Sinkiang and Kansu were all marked down to become major industrial bases.

Early migrations were on a fairly small scale. In October, 1958, Chu Teh revealed that 1.38 million had gone to the northwest, the northeast and Inner Mongolia. Later the numbers increased substantially. The population of Inner Mongolia, for instance, was revealed in March 13, 1959, at 6,700,000—an increase of 600,000 in six months. After allowing for a 2 per cent natural increase, this means that nearly half a million immigrants flocked into the region during this period.

Next to the Tibetans, Peking encountered its greatest difficulties with the Huis, whose religion was closely interwoven with their way of life. For centuries there had been little or no intermarriage between Hui and Han. By discrediting Muslim religious leaders with charges of immorality and counterrevolutionary activities, however, Peking appears to be slowly consolidating its control in these areas. This has not been accomplished without bloodshed, and as late as December, 1959, the Chinghai Provincial People's Congress continued to report opposition and resistance in the border areas.

The breaking down of the traditional leadership exercised by the mullahs, and obligatory intermarriage between the Hui and the Han settlers, and the decision to ban the use of Arabic all produced natural tensions which reached a peak with the establishment of the communes. Muslims in Chinghai late in 1958 were reported to be holding mass grievance-airing meetings directed, under Party control, against the "counterrevolutionary elements under the cloak of religion and reactionary cattle owners."

Fear of assimilation by the Hans has always been acute among the Mongols, who are now outnumbered by seven to one in their own region. It is even stronger in Sinkiang, where an uprising in 1958 on the borders of the Kazakh and Khirkiz republics lasted for two months and was put down only after the arrival of substantial military reinforcements. In March, 1959, reports appeared again of counterrevolutionaries who were opposing Communist reforms and trying to find pretexts for leaving the communes.

Though there has been this resistance, the Party has advanced a long way in the ideological and cultural assimilation of the minorities. It has also opened up new industrial and, to a much lesser extent, agricultural areas far removed from the militarily vulnerable coastal areas. This development will predictably increase during the next two decades and will absorb part of China's excess population while contributing both to its industrial development and to its security. Climatic conditions, and, in particular, water shortages will nevertheless place a relatively low ceiling on the population.

What, then, is to happen to China's mounting millions? The idea that China might look beyond her big and underpopulated minority areas toward other lands as a dumping ground for excess population was advanced as early as 1952 by Professor C. P. Fitzgerald in his book *Revolution in China* (The Cresset Press Ltd., London). He suggested that a solution which would be easy for China would be a constant flood of emigrants into Siberia in the north, and into the islands and Southeast Asia in the south.

Extremes of heat and cold make no difference to Chinese capabilities. Alone among the peoples of Southeast Asia they retain their capacity for hard work even in the tropics. China's periods of greatness have always been marked by a heavy emphasis on expansion and colonization. And, finally, as Fitzgerald notes, if the Communists believe in the world Communist community, they may see no reason why the process should be halted in the minority areas at the present frontiers of China, for between fellow Communist States frontiers should be unreal.

This is not an argument calculated to appeal strongly to the Soviet Union if it involves the settlement of Siberia by Chinese. Moscow might also be expected to resist a major move into Outer Mongolia, where Peking has recently become extremely active. But there are other contiguous areas where resistance to "big family" concepts is likely to prove much weaker.

In the books that came from the Foreign Language Press in Peking during the first years of Communist rule maps of the border regions followed lines long accepted both by the Nationalist regime and the West. By 1954, however, significant changes had begun to appear. China, it now appeared, was entitled not only to Tibet but to large chunks of Kashmir, Nepal, Sikkim, Bhutan, India, Pakistan, Burma, and Indo-China. In some maps even Korea appeared as Chinese territory, a painful reminder of Mao Tse-tung's lament of 1939 that China had "lost" Korea, Taiwan, the Ryukyu Islands, the Pescadores and Port Arthur to Japan; Burma, Bhutan, Nepal and Hong Kong to Britain; Annam to France and Macao to Portugal.

Speaking to the House of the People in New Delhi on May 11, 1959, Mr. Nehru said: "The Chinese look down upon every country other than their own. They consider themselves as a Middle Kingdom, as a celestial race, as a great country. . . . " By the end of the year he was speaking much more harshly. In Mr. Nehru's view, the difficulties he encountered over the borders of northeastern India and in Kashmir spring directly from Chinese chauvinism, from the tradition of the Tang dynasty and Genghiz Khan, under whom China formed the strongest continental empire the world has ever seen, and which sought to impose its rule and its standards on all with whom it came in contact.

That Mao Tse-tung is steeped in the history of China is clear from his writings: but Marx has added to his thoughts a new dimension for conquest in which borders are dissolved, not crossed. South of China, underdeveloped, by Chinese standards underpopulated, and even partly unexplored, are the countries of Southeast Asia. They are rich in natural resources, in food and in food potential. Burma, Thailand and South Vietnam are the rice bowl of Asia. The mighty Mekong has huge power and irrigation potential; Malaya and Indonesia are the world's top producers of rubber and tin; and Indonesia, in particular, has uncounted natural wealth, especially oil and hydroelectric potential.

Chapter V 🝔🝔🝔🝔🝔🝔🝔🝔🝔🝔

REVOLUTION BY EXPORT

As EARLY as 1948 a series of Soviet-inspired revolutions had begun in the dependent territories and newly independent states of South and Southeast Asia. One uprising had been quickly suppressed by Indonesian nationalists in the Netherlands East Indies, where all Indonesians were fighting to throw out the Dutch. Another had proved unsuccessful in India, which had just won its freedom from Britain. In Burma, Malaya and the Philippines, however, Communist forces, with weapons mostly left over from the Second World War, were on the rampage: and, in the Indo-China States, the veteran Communist leader, Ho Chi-minh, was locked in a bloody struggle with the French.

Ineptitude characterized all these first postwar Communist revolts. Badly planned, inadequately prepared, often poorly led, unwisely conducted and with no thought of securing the sort of political bases from which Mao Tse-tung had operated in China, their wanton and indiscriminate acts of terrorism alienated the peoples on whom their success or failure depended: and this despite the existence of local conditions which should have provided exceptional opportunities for Communist exploitation.

With the exception of Thailand, which owed its escape from colonialism to its value as a buffer between British interests in Burma and Malaya and the French in the Indo-Chinese states of Laos, Cambodia and Vietnam, all of Southeast Asia before the Second World War had been under colonial rule. Britain, though moving intelligently to meet the national aspirations of its dependent peoples, maintained its colonial grip on Malaya, the Crown Colony of Singapore at the tip of the Malay Peninsula and its Borneo territories; the French and the Dutch in their areas thought they could turn the clock back.

In the reservoirs of anticolonialism thus replenished, in the backwardness of the rural communities and the availability for fifth column purposes of some 12 million Overseas Chinese, who owned the tills and dominated the trade of almost every Southeast Asian state, Peking saw unique opportunities. Every area had its own special possibilities. Singapore, with a population of 1,200,000, of whom five-sixths were Chinese, had been a traditional center of Chinese Communist activity in Southeast Asia. Vietnam, Laos and Burma shared borders with China; and, in Vietnam, especially, there was a widespread inclination among the nationalists to regard the French as a much greater evil than the Communists.

Malaya's plural society with about 3 million Malays, who, under British rule, enjoyed special rights and privileges that were not shared by about 2½ million Chinese, raised incipient communal problems which were clearly within the Communists' powers to exploit. Better still, from the Communists' viewpoint, Malaya was plagued by Chinese subsistence farmers who had squatted on land to which they had no title. Since four-fifths of Malaya is jungle, there was no lack of virgin land: but good arable soil exists only in small and isolated pockets, which the shrewd and able Chinese searched for diligently, though this often meant establishing themselves in remote and isolated areas far from the centers of population and the government's writ. The first squatters appeared during the depression in the thirties, and their numbers grew rapidly during the Second World War, when tin mines and rubber estates closed down and thousands of people fled from the towns to grow their own food. By the beginning of 1948 it was estimated that there were half a million squatters. They seemed to be everywhere—along the main roads, on side tracks, even deep in the jungle. Sometimes they acted as useful market gardeners; but in the more remote areas they scratched out a beggarly living, growing rice where they could and tapioca and relying on a couple of yellow-backed sows and half a dozen pepper trees to provide them with their cash crops. They lived in huts hewn from jungle logs and thatched with palm and had no contact with the indigenous Malays.

They were an obvious recruiting ground and source of food for the Communists. While the harassed British authorities struggled to cope with the squatters and to regroup them in new villages that had to be something better than concentration camps and yet guarded and surrounded with barbed wire to prevent the continued flow of food into the jungle, Communist guerrillas had their opportunity. They wasted it by methods and tactics that were often barbarous, and paid no attention either to the well-being of the squatters or to the mass of the population. They behaved like gangsters. They stole and shot and intimidated. In the first two and a half years of the campaign, or the "Emergency," as the uprising was known in Malaya, they killed 1,275 members of the British and Malayan security forces; during the same period they killed 1,828 civilians and abducted 491 others; the overwhelming majority of these were Chinese. If some were informers and "running dogs of the imperialists," many more were not. A squatter family that held out against Communist demands for food went in peril of its life. The roads and railways were unsafe not merely for Europeans and members of the security forces but for all people. Rubber and mine workers died hideous deaths as the Communists sought to gain power by indiscriminate bloodshed.

These excesses were common to all the Southeast Asian Communist revolts of the time. Communism became another word for brigandage and dacoity in Burma. In Indo-China Communist rebel leader Ho Chi-minh's guerrillas kept all people in a state of nervous tension with indiscriminate attacks and pointless bloodshed. Night after night Saigon used to rock as Communist mortar bombs exploded in the city. It was all frightening enough, but also futile. Not by these methods could Southeast Asia be won.

No one appreciated the futility of these tactics better than Mao Tse-tung. In territories still under colonial rule there were peasant and other forces, both passively and actively anticolonialist, that merely needed direction and Communist leadership. In countries which had already secured what Mao regarded as nominal independence, enduring links with the colonial Powers indicated that economic domination continued and that true freedom had yet to be won by bloodshed and the destruction of the last vestiges of "imperialist" rule.

China moved swiftly to pass on its formula. In November, 1949, at an Australasian Trade Union conference, sponsored by the World Federation of Trade Unions, Communist delegates from all parts of Asia and Australasia gathered in Peking to learn the lessons of the Chinese experience.

Liu Shao-chi was the Chinese spokesman. His speech, broadcast by Peking Radio on November 24, 1949, set the Asian revolutions on an entirely new course. He borrowed from Lenin in describing the colonies and semicolonies as "reservoirs of world imperialism on which it relies for its existence." The so-called "civilization" of imperialism was built up on its criminal rule over the colonies and semicolonies, he said; the building up the happiness of the minority on the unhappiness of the more than a billion in the colonies and semicolonies was the essence of imperialist civilization. It was therefore necessary for the colonial and semicolonial people and the working people in the imperialist countries to unite to fight together against their common enemy—imperialism.

He listed Vietnam, Burma, Indonesia, Malaya, the Philippines and India as countries where national liberation movements and armed struggles for emancipation were taking place, or had taken place. In Japan, he said, the progressive labor movement and the progressive people's movement against the conversion of the country into a colony of American imperialism were developing. The movement of the Korean people against Syngman Rhee and for the establishment of a unified, popular democratic republic of Korea could not be halted. With the backing of the Soviet Union, he predicted, it could be fully expected that these movements would persist, develop and attain full victory. "Their struggles are entirely righteous," he said. "They should and will win victory. The great victory of the Chinese people has set them the best example. . . . It is wholly justifiable for the colonial and semicolonial peoples to conduct armed struggle for their own national independence against imperialist attacks. In resisting imperialist attacks, the armed struggles of the colonies and semicolonies to win national independence are a mighty force in strengthening and defending world peace. . . .

"The path taken by the Chinese people in defeating imperialism and its lackeys and in founding the People's Republic of China is a path that should be traced by the peoples of various colonial and semicolonial countries in their fight for national independence and people's democracy."

Then followed four simple rules for revolution. They were:

(1) The working class (that is, the Communist Party) must unite with all other classes, political parties, or groups, organizations and individuals who are willing to fight imperialism;

(2) The nation-wide united front must be led by and built around the working class and its party, the Communist Party, with the latter at its center. It must not be led by the wavering and compromising national bourgeoisie, or the petty bourgeoisie;

(3) In order to enable the working class and its Party, the Communist Party, to become the center for uniting all forces working against imperialism and competently to lead the national united front to victory, it is necessary to build up through long struggles the Communist Party, which is armed with the theory of Marxism and Leninism, which understands strategy and tactics, practices self-criticism and strict discipline and is closely linked with the masses;

(4) It is necessary to set up wherever and whenever possible a national liberation army, which is led by the Communist Party and is powerful and skillful in fighting its enemies. It is necessary to set up bases on which the liberation army relies for its activities and to make the mass struggles in the enemy-controlled area and the armed struggles coordinate with each other. Armed struggle is the main form of struggle for the national liberation struggles of many colonies and semicolonies.

Explanatory details included elementary Maoist guerrilla theory, such as: "Armed struggle is to be carried on in the countryside, while in the enemy-controlled cities and areas other legal and illegal mass struggles should be conducted to coordinate with it."

Within months the new tactics swept into Southeast Asia changing overnight the war in Indo-China from one of fruitless attrition and terror into a war of annihilation. The Chinese Communist forces which reached the Indo-China border late in 1949 quickly established contact with Ho Chi-minh—who once served as a cook's assistant to Escoffier at the Hotel Carlton in London—and his highly intelligent commander-in-chief, General Vo Nguyen Giap. French fears that the Chinese might just keep rolling south did not materialize. Instead, under the direction of General Ho Lung, one of the oldest and most distinguished of the Communist military leaders, the Chinese "borrowed" tens of thousands of Vietminh guerrillas, took them into South China for political indoctrination and military training and sent them back late in 1950 to shatter the line of French forts guarding the porte de Chîne.

Ho Chi-minh built up political bases among the peasants, thereby confining the war to the countryside, reserved his élite regular army for major assaults, created regional battalions from among the guerrillas and without a plane or a tank to support him prepared the way for victory.

The French struck out from the Red River delta to cut the Vietminh's main supply route from China. Instead, they found their own supply lines cut while other Vietminh forces pushed their way into the delta. The Vietminh came in two's and three's at night, formed up into sections, platoons, companies, battalions and finally even into regiments and divisions. They wanted rice and recruits and the salt and machine and consumer goods that the French had to provide to maintain the economic life of the millions of peasants in the delta. They tore up the roads and carried them away in baskets, isolated the hundreds of little blockhouses the French had built and destroyed them one by one.

The French came back from their ventures into the jungles and turned to mop up the delta. But the Vietminh slipped through the net and struck hard against the French at their weakest point, the mountains of the northwest. Blindly the French hit back against an enemy that refused to fight but now turned again to move into the delta.

The French again countered and the Vietminh swept into northern Laos, established their Laotian satellite, Prince Souphanouvong and his Pathet Lao "government" in the little village of Sam Neua and began to sow those seeds of revolutionary war that flourished years later among the fearfully neglected villagers of this poverty-stricken little Southeast Asian rural slum.

"Just give us a set-piece battle and we will finish the Vietminh for ever," the French used to say. They flew their forces to exposed positions deep in Vietminh country and dared the enemy to attack. The Vietminh probed and tested, and, when they found they lacked the overwhelming strength that Mao's formula called for, pulled back. Late in 1953, however, the French presented the Vietminh with their main chance. Into the valley of Dien Bien Phu, far from the defense perimeter in the Red River delta, the French dropped their paratroopers, and then reinforced them with the élite of the French Expeditionary Force. They flew in tanks in pieces and assembled them in the middle of the broad valley. They dug gun positions, and tunneled underground to build hospitals and command posts. They surrendered to the Vietminh the high jungle-clad hills that surround the valley: and they prayed for an attack.

The Vietminh took three months to prepare. They cut a new road through the jungle, recruited a huge force of porters and on the long haul from China brought artillery and antiaircraft guns. Four divisions of regular forces closed in on the French. On March 12, 1954, they opened fire. Fifty-six days later the garrison surrendered. In 1949 one French battalion, supplied from the air, had been strong enough to go anywhere; now sixteen battalions had perished in the first—and last—set-piece battle of the war. The French lost their Indo-China territories, and Vietnam was divided in two, with Ho Chi-minh's Communists in possession of the North.

With victory won in Tongking the North Vietnamese and Peking regimes combined to rebuild the railway linking Hanoi and the port of Haiphong with Canton. An outright gift of 800 million yuan ($335 million) by China in 1955 helped to lay the foundations for North Vietnam's industrialization, the grant envisaging the construction of eighteen industrial projects by 1961. To this considerable gift Peking in 1959 added another 300 million yuan ($126 million) in a long-term, low-interest loan plus an outright grant of 100 million yuan ($43 million) and, in 1961, another loan of 141,750,000 rubles (about $160 million). The loans bear interest at the nominal rate of 1 per cent, with repayment in goods over a ten-year period, beginning in 1967: the grant, given "without compensation," is to be used for the construction of forty-seven industrial and communication enterprises, including iron and steel plants, coal mines, textile mills, electric power stations and the extension of railways.

From this Southeast Asian beachhead and using the Lao Dong (Communist) Party of Vietnam as a principal agency, Peking worked south through Laos and South Vietnam. Just as the Chinese took Vietminh guerrillas into South China and turned them into regular forces to annihilate the fixed French positions in Tongking, and eventually to sweep the French out of the country, the Vietminh (now called Viet Cong) used similar tactics in Laos. North of the little kingdom's two wild jungle provinces of Sam Neua and Phong Saly in North Vietnam are two Communist army bases, one at Dien Bien Phu, the other at a village named Yen Bay. Here dissident Laotians and the tribesmen who inhabit the untamed uplands of Laos, the Meos, the Khas, the Black Thais, the White Thais and the Red Thais, their separate identities established by the color of their clothing, were trained, armed and equipped to provide military support for the Pathet Lao leader, Prince Souphanouvong. With the exception of Prince Souphanouvong, whose children go to school in Moscow, all the leading members of the Pathet Lao and its political offshoot, the Neo Lao Hak Xat Party, are members of the Lao Dong Party of North Vietnam, from whose political schools mobile Communist groups moved into areas under the nominal control of the Royal Laotian Government, spreading through the entire countryside to organize Communist cells.

After a bloody land reform campaign the North Vietnamese began to exercise much greater moderation in their own areas. With landlords and counterrevolutionaries effectively disposed of, Ho Chi-minh now used Mao Tse-tung's concept of persuasion and external antagonisms (again the U.S. "imperialists" and their "puppets") as the substitute for Stalin's force and internal antagonisms.

Many wishful-thinking Westerners have curiously identified this with what they regard as Ho Chi-minh's Russian orientation: but it is, in fact, specifically Chinese. Ho Chi-minh, one of whose earliest Comintern tasks was to act as an interpreter for Michael Borodin, Sun Yat-sen's Russian adviser, personally translated Mao's *On Practice* and *On Contradiction* into Vietnamese and published them for the guidance of the Lao Dong Party. By copying Mao's methods of persuasion he hoped to portray life in North Vietnam as attractive enough to induce the Southerners to welcome unification. The policy is both expedient and popular. The army, which was expanded to some fifteen divisions after the fall of Dien Bien Phu, has always felt cheated of total victory. The non-Communists see a coalition government as the one hope for the future. And the masses generally have not found that Chinese and Soviet economic aid makes up for the rice that once came from the richer South. One difficult and even dissident group is the 750,000 Catholics who remained in the North after the exodus of another three-quarters of a million to the South in 1954 and 1955. They have been spared the more shattering attempts at brain-washing that Peking has applied to its Christians, and especially to the Catholics, but they have not responded with any warmth to Ho Chi-minh's overtures. In compensation, however, there are now many in the South who wonder unwisely whether the difference between controls in the Communist North and anti-Communist South is only a matter of degree. The forces favoring unification are much larger than they are in South Korea, where the war left bitternesses that do not exist in Vietnam.

A nucleus of three to five thousand armed Communist guerrillas permanently active in South Vietnam was heavily reinforced by Vietminh cadres in 1960 and set off a campaign of assassination and intimidation against unpopular officials in the Ngo Dinh Diem regime. Leading pro-Diem figures and civil servants were marked down for attack and killed in hundreds. Communist propaganda concentrated on the law enforcing stronger security measures in South Vietnam and against the agrovilles, or newly created rural towns, in which isolated peasants were resettled in new villages as a priority task in separating them from the Communist guerrillas. As the British and Malayans discovered during the Communist insurrection in Malaya, such a resettlement program can succeed only with the cooperation of the peasants. They must be convinced that their living conditions, economically, and in terms of security, will be improved; and they must be encouraged (by all means, including secret payment for information) to be primarily responsible for their own village defense.

Neither condition was properly fulfilled in South Vietnam. The peasants, who were not only obliged to leave their own homes but also to work hard in building the new towns, hated the program. They felt they were inadequately recompensed for their inconvenience and labor; and they showed little interest in offending the guerrillas by attending to their own defense. Thus, by a typical Maoist tactic, the Communists succeeded in building up significant peasant resistance against unpopular governmental measures made necessary in the first instance by Communist activities! Instead of isolating the guerrillas from the rural population, the agrovilles tended to exacerbate peasant grievances and to provide the Communists with further recruits among whom they could create the political bases demanded by Mao as the essential requirement for effective guerrilla action in the countryside and the isolation of the towns and cities.

Before leaping too far ahead, it should be pointed out that success in Indo-China in the war against the French in the early fifties did not blind the Chinese to the dangers of provoking armed revolt elsewhere before conditions were suitable. The Indian Communist Party, for instance, made the error of interpreting the decisions of the Peking conference in 1949 as a clarion call for armed action in complete disregard of circumstances and consequences. In June, 1950, therefore, the *People's Daily* explained that though armed struggle was essential for the "liberation" of many colonies and semi-colonies, the time and place for coordinating this kind of revolutionary armed struggle had to be decided according to concrete conditions. "It can by no means be conducted in any colony, or semicolony, at any time without the necessary conditions and preparation," it said. In December of the same year the Indian Communists called off their futile acts of violence and stopped referring to Mr. Nehru as a "lackey of the imperialists." In a statement of policy issued some months later the Party made public its errors with a reference to its "wrong understanding of the lessons of the Chinese revolution."

In Malaya, where the Chinese Communist Party had always maintained close relations with the Malayan Communist Party, local Communist leaders made a determined effort to graft the Maoist sapling on the dying roots of the Stalinist uprising. A fifty-page directive entitled "Working Directions of the Execution of the Party's Urgent Tasks" admitted the errors of the past, ordered the immediate cessation of all indiscriminate acts of terrorism, set political activities on the highest plane and called on the regular armed forces to conduct themselves as élites.

The bomb explosions and the bus and taxi burnings in Singapore soon ceased. Unarmed civilians in Malaya no longer traveled in peril. The night mail train between Kuala Lumpur and Singapore, which had been previously driven off the line by repeated Communist attacks, resumed its normal schedule and the roads became more or less safe for normal civilian travel. Sometimes the Communists erred and shot the wrong man, but they were always willing to apologize for mistakes. A distinguished London barrister, wounded and captured in an ambush, was released as soon as he had established his identity. A white ant exterminator, whose jeep and khaki shirt and shorts had led the Communists to believe that he was a policeman (and therefore a legitimate target), received first-aid attention from a medical orderly before he, too, was sent about his business. But the change came too late. Its campaign of terror, murder and plunder had alienated too many of those who were once prepared to accept on its face value the claim of the Party to lead a movement for the "liberation" of the people of Malaya from colonial domination. Faced with the prospect in 1955 of independence won by negotiation and not by the gun, the Communists first attempted to reach agreement with Tengku Abdul Rahman, Malaya's first Prime Minister, and with the political leaders of Singapore. When this failed, they made their own little Yenan in the jungles on the Thai side of the Malayan-Thailand border and set about the penetration and subversion of Malayan political, labor, social and youth movements. "It [the Malayan Communist Party] is trying now to regain lost ground by reverting to the longer-term methods of bringing about a united front, through which, by secret infiltration, it can prepare the way for another bid for power," said the Government of the Federation of Malaya in the White Paper entitled "The Communist Threat" published in 1959. It also made the specific charge that the "Chinese Communist Party is attempting to persuade the peoples of the Federation of Malaya, in particular the so-called 'Overseas' Chinese, to look to the Communist regime in China for inspiration and guidance."

In all plans for Communist domination in Southeast Asia the Overseas Chinese figure largely. A Thai Government report dealing with the internal Chinese problem declared that of the estimated 3 million Chinese living in Thailand (half a million are in the capital, Bangkok), 60 per cent could be described as having become "more or less sympathetic" to Communist China, 30 per cent supported the Nationalists and 10 per cent were not interested in politics. Though other observers tend to list the genuinely apolitical Chinese, and those who still prefer to be noncommittal as forming a substantially larger proportion, the ratio of two to one favoring Peking over Taipeh represents a fairly accurate picture of Overseas Chinese sympathies and political thought in Southeast Asia. The anti-Communists among the Overseas Chinese are being reduced to a hard core, resistant to subversion and able to withstand such shocks as the admission of Communist China to the United Nations.

Though the Kuomintang has tried to maintain a beachhead in the area by sending out approved textbooks registered with the Overseas Affairs Commission in Taipeh, it is in the schools that the Communists have had their greatest success. The usually poorly paid Chinese schoolteachers in Southeast Asia are either indifferent to Communism, or in sympathy with it, and the Communists therefore have had little difficulty in implanting their cells and branches in the Chinese schools and securing a firm base among the literate Chinese youth. Their massive publishing efforts swamp the market. Taipeh can neither cope with the demand for books of all types among the Overseas Chinese, nor match the Communists' propaganda skill.

The degree of awareness of the problem among Southeast Asian governments and the actions they have taken to prevent the open subversion of their Chinese communities depends in large part on their attitude toward Peking. In Malaya possession of such publications as the works of Mao Tse-tung is an offense punishable by detention, though textbooks in arithmetic, famous Chinese novels written centuries before Marx and other works were once permitted to enter the country in an unrestricted flow. Thailand, Vietnam, the Philippines and the British Borneo colonies have restrictive regulations: Indonesia and Burma make no discrimination between political works and works which, on the face of it, have no political bias.

Malaya soon learned that in the hands of a Communist propagandist even arithmetic was not safe and Confucius could be made to read like Marxist dialectics. Of the 36,000 book and magazine titles that streamed into the country from China in 1958 at the rate of more than a million a month, only eight hundred were found to be innocuous. A work entitled *Interpretation and Notes of Confucius' Analects* by Yang Pa-chuen, published by the Classics Publishing House, Peking, gave a precise account of how the Communists were determined to make even the classics serve Communist ideology. "We have to assess Confucius correctly and we must differentiate the effects in history created by others who have utilized him," Yang wrote. "We have to understand the *Analects* correctly. We have to eliminate the influence caused by distorted quotations, especially those quoted by idealists in the past. At the same time, we must also eliminate all ill influences impressed on us by corrupt, feudalistic moral concepts. First of all, we should search with a fact-finding effort for the real meaning of the original text, and then analyze it from the viewpoint of Marx and Lenin, using their method of thinking, historical materialism and dialectical materialism. We may assess it, discard it, or accept it. It is only in this way we can draw a fair conclusion on Confucius, give him a proper assessment, and really inherit the excellent cultural legacy of China. . . ."

In thousands of such books Peking managed to insert the concept of class struggle. A dictionary, published by the New China Book Store, Peking, and designed for use by Chinese school children in Southeast Asia managed to give even the most innocuous words an Orwellian twist. The example given for the word "all" for instance, was: "The American imperialists must be held responsible for *all* the consequences of their crime of scattering germs." The example for "join" was: "I have already *joined* the Chinese New Democratic Youth Corps." In another dictionary for school students published by the Tung Fang Book Company, Shanghai, "the Communist Party" was defined as "the vanguard of the pro-letarian rebellion. It is the political party of the workers' class. The aim of Communism is the realization of a Communist society in which there is no fleecing of some persons by some other persons. In this kind of society, everyone does the job he can do best, gets what he needs and leads the most reasonable and happy life." In the New China dictionary, produced by the People's Education Publishing House, Peking, "capital" was "a fixed quantity or amount of productive materials or money which capitalists utilize to fleece workers." "Liberate" meant "to overthrow the reactionary ruling classes so that the great masses of the people may shake off the oppression of imperialism and of the reactionary classes."

To the newly independent Malayan Government, the World Knowledge Publishing House's book, *Malaya* by Lin Fang-sheng, which referred to the "discounted independence which the British imperialists have been compelled by circumstances to promise," served as a further reminder of how Peking interpreted "peaceful coexistence."

The government stripped the bookstalls of the offending Com-munist literature and took pains to ensure that when its Chinese children sat down to learn arithmetic they did not do it in the way prescribed by the arithmetic textbook for Junior Middle School, Volume I, published by the People's Education Publishing House, Peking, which stated unexceptionally that the "method of finding out the sum of two known numbers is called addition," and then proceeded to present a problem in addition in terms of the number of industrial plants which Russia had built for China.

Here, and elsewhere, ten years of this sort of indoctrination have left roots that are not easily destroyed. "As each month goes by, Communist activities become more frequent and more blatant, and the power of persons known to be Communists grows," re-ported the Singapore Government in a White Paper on August 23, 1957. "Once again the aim is to bring about a united front of workers, farmers and students supported by a favorable press and by political sympathizers. The gravest developments have been among the workers. A determined and successful bid for controlling the People's Action Party has been the second feature of recent months. Here the Communists have worked through the cultural, educational and propaganda groups in the People's Action Party and through them have gone far to obtain domination of the party." Since so many of Singapore's inhabitants are Chinese, and the Malayan Communist Party's recruits come from this section of Singaporean and Malayan society, Peking's influence is understandably greater here than in other parts of Southeast Asia where the Chinese are in a minority.

Population statistics in Southeast Asia are no measure of Chinese influence, however. The squat junks that sailed from the Fukien coast of China laden with Chinese for Southeast Asia carried industrious, intelligent and hard-working men who came in the first instance only to make money. Very few wanted to remain peasant farmers: instead they moved into the cities, towns and villages, quickly filling in colonial societies an essential middleman role between the Europeans and the indigenous peoples. Their importance was always far out of proportion to their numbers.

In Thailand, where there was no European middle-class élite, they not only became owners of the rice mills and principal shops but acted as financiers to Thai police and army leaders who shared and contested power after 1947. Chinese intelligence and skill generated much of the power for Thailand's momentum: indeed, but for the Chinese there would have been little real progress of any sort in this country and much less than there was in other countries of the region. Nor could the Chinese be altogether blamed for their clannishness. In Indonesia and Malaya the Muslim religion, which imposes on its adherents a strict way of life, was a constant barrier to assimilation.

Nowhere was there any real attempt to make the Chinese feel part of the community to which they now belonged. In 1954, when I was living in Singapore, I tried on behalf of my Chinese cook to have his children admitted to a government-subsidized school where the medium of instruction was English and there seemed a reasonable hope that Mao and Marx would not be included in the homework. Despite my representations at high level, I could find no subsidized school in which there was a vacancy, and off went the children to one of the Chinese-language schools described by the Special (Political) branch of the Singapore Police as "little Marxist academies."

President Ngo Dinh Diem, who inherited with independence in 1954 a Chinese population of nearly a million in South Vietnam, was confronted with a situation in which the Chinese, under treaty rights granted by the French in 1946, enjoyed the privileges of living in Vietnam with none of the responsibilities. Like the Chinese in Thailand, they owned most of the rice mills and ran the principal shops. In August, 1956, in an effort to eliminate the Chinese problem at one stroke, Diem granted the right of Vietnamese citizenship to all Chinese born in Vietnam and two weeks later issued an ordinance barring Chinese nationals from trading as fishmongers, butchers, retailers of products in common use and operating a large number of other businesses traditionally in the hands of the Chinese. Much earlier, the Philippines had barred the Chinese from the retail trade: and in 1958 Indonesia began to take heavy action against them.

Clipping the wings of the Overseas Chinese, whatever their political hue, does not meet the challenge posed by China's growing strength, however, or even its fledgling activities in Southeast Asia. For reasons associated with economic survival, anti-Chinese measures cannot be too draconian since, in the present stage of the area's development, the Chinese, as Indonesia has discovered, are almost indispensable. Moreover, the Overseas Chinese are not the problem but only one of its symptoms. If all countries were to follow Indonesia's example and send the Chinese back to China, Southeast Asia would, like Indonesia, fall apart economically: it would also be confronted, as it is today, with the problem of living in the shadow of the giant.

Chapter VI ▭▭▭▭▭▭▭▭▭▭▭

WIDER HORIZONS

A NOTABLE change of emphasis in China's foreign policy became apparent in 1954. China had already succeeded in extricating itself from the Korean War on terms that it subsequently interpreted as a major victory over the U.S. "paper tiger." Now, when Ho Chi-minh with Mao Tse-tung's politico-military tactics and material aid seemed headed for much more than a limited victory in Indo-China, China puzzled some Western observers, and deluded many Afro-Asians, by suddenly emerging as an avowed champion of seemingly genuine peace.

There were cogent reasons for this. Of all the early Communist revolts in South and Southeast Asia, only that in Vietnam had succeeded. With the continuing failure of the insurrections in Malaya, Burma and the Philippines, it was obvious that less emphasis would have to be placed on military operations and more on the preparation of political bases. To have required local guerrillas, even in Laos and

Cambodia, to push on militarily would have been "left adventurism," or trying to do too much too quickly without adequate preparation. During the early years of the civil war in China, Mao repeatedly, if not always successfully, attempted to persuade the Party that the revolution was essentially long-drawn-out, that it had to pass through the process of developing from small to big and from the countryside to the cities. Disaster inevitably occurred when he was overruled. He had similar views now about Southeast Asia. South Vietnam excepted, the rest of South and Southeast Asia needed much political preparation before it would be ready for a renewal of armed revolt: and the very real prospect of war with the United States in the event of overt aggression either by China, or by North Vietnam, ruled out any more direct form of action.

In the case of Vietnam, Hanoi and Peking had every reason to believe that the provisions of the Geneva Agreement, which ended the Indo-China War, assured Ho Chi-minh of full control over all the country without further recourse to arms. This was a major, but understandable, error. Few who knew the situation in South Vietnam between the fall of Dien Bien Phu and the beginning of the battle between President Ngo Dinh Diem and the exotic religious sects and the vice lords of Saigon early in 1955 doubted that the Communist assessment was correct. Diem had to fight not only the Bao Dai loyalists and the sects but the political intrigues of the French and British who wanted to dislodge him. Diem's dogged resistance upset all this; and while his stubbornness and myopia are helping to produce a similar result today, he must be given credit for causing its postponement for several years.

This could not have been predicted in Peking, or anywhere else. And there was a great deal of sound sense in the Chinese plan to create firm political bases for future action and to unite with all forces willing to be united with. The objectives were unchanged—to achieve ultimate Communist control; but they were pursued in two different ways: the peaceful, instead of the military, elimination of Western influence from the region, and the subversion of indigenous nationalist elements in preparation for renewed military action.

Instead of continuing its denunciation of non-Communist Asian leaders, Peking looked for friends. They were not difficult to find at first. China's rapidly increasing strength had had a powerful impact on Asia. Like a massive furnace glowing at the entrance to a small room, its hot glow penetrated to all parts of the area. And Asia, anti-colonialist and anti-imperialist, by no means accepted the Western lead in regarding the theory and even the practice of the Chinese experiment with opprobrium. To the contention that Communist China was an unprovoked aggressor in Korea, it was argued that China did fear the United States, and that there was real concern in the minds of the Peking leaders as General MacArthur approached the Yalu River in 1950. That the United States had no intention of attacking China, and was, in fact, intent only on the halting of an obvious Communist aggression, may have been clear to the Western world, but it was much less clear to many others. For if Communist China had committed aggression in Korea, was it not patent also that the United States had intervened in China's civil war and was still intervening in its defense of Chiang Kai-shek on Taiwan? Given the isolation of the Chinese leaders from external contacts and their tendency to regard themselves as ringed by hostile, potentially aggressive foes, many Asians believed there was a large field of human relations to be explored here by Powers not too closely allied with the West.

Choice, necessity and opportunity led Mr. Nehru into the role of explorer. He was angered by the American attitude toward the Indo-China War and inclined to be petulant and irritated by the United States. "Offer an American a cigarette and he will immediately say, 'No, thanks, I prefer my own,'" he remarked to Sutan Sjahrir, the Indonesian Socialist leader, during a visit to Indonesia in 1954; and he often repeated at this time the story of a Washington dinner party at which his host told him, no doubt with some naïve pride, that every man at the table was a millionaire. To the sensitive, unmaterialistic Nehru these were examples of American arrogance: they colored his judgment; but they nevertheless helped to lead him into an experiment of far-reaching importance, which established, more than any other event or combination of events, the ambitions and chauvinism of Peking.

These approaches by Mr. Nehru were based neither on ignorance nor naïveté. When, in 1950, the West was preoccupied with the Korean War, his reproaches on the question of the invasion of Tibet gave expression to his worries in forthright terms. Three separate notes delivered by India declared that the "invasion by Chinese troops of Tibet cannot but be regarded as deplorable," that it had "no justification whatever," and that the Indian Government deemed it "most surprising and regrettable." They warned Peking of the consequences of its act, stressing that it would "give powerful support to those who are opposed to the admission of the People's Government to the United Nations and the Security Council," that it might "prejudice the position of China in the eyes of the world," and that it had "greatly added to the tensions of the world and to a general drift towards war."

Just as it had been clear at the time of the 1950 invasion that the ill equipped Tibetan forces lacked the means of resisting the Chinese armies, reports from Lhasa in 1954 indicated that the Tibetans' hopes of autonomy under the terms of their agreement with China were rapidly being dispelled by the influx of Chinese troops and cadres. The urgent need, therefore, was to persuade Peking that the hope for friendly relations between India and China, and, in the wider view, for relations between China and Asia, lay in the degree of sincerity attaching to the assurances that Tibetan autonomy within the general framework of the People's Republic would be respected.

Mr. Nehru's opportunity to get through to the Chinese came during a break in the 1954 Geneva conference, when Chou En-lai paid a brief visit to New Delhi. The two leaders spent ten hours together in Mr. Nehru's sitting room: when they emerged Mr. Nehru believed that the prospect for future relations between Communist China and the non-Communist states of Asia were much less bleak than the pessimists had predicted. Mr. Nehru had conceded Peking's claim to suzerainty over Tibet, a country in which India had considerable traditional and strategic interests, while Chou was especially reassuring on Tibet's rights to autonomy within the framework of Communist China. In the five principles of peaceful coexistence,* which they adopted as governing principles for their future conduct and relationship, Mr. Nehru saw the possibility of enduring peace in Asia.

The closing months of 1954, therefore, found India working to

* Mutual respect for each other's territorial integrity and sovereignty, mutual nonaggression, mutual noninterference in each other's internal affairs, equality and mutual benefit, and peaceful coexistence.

break down the barriers between Communist China and the rest of Asia while the West endeavored, through SEATO, to create new ones. Mr. Nehru's approach made no concessions to Communism, as such. He spurned the totalitarian approach to his own internal difficulties and, internationally, looked for the "toning down" of Communism. First Chou En-lai, and later Khrushchev, convinced him that neither China nor the Soviet Union had any particular desire to "push Communism" in other Asian states. Even if they had so wanted, he did not believe that it was possible to keep a revolutionary sentiment such as Communism at high pitch for years. Communism succeeded, he felt, only when it was allied to nationalism, as in China. When it was imposed, from outside, as in Hungary, it failed. It had failed in South Asia, even in the weakest country, Burma, because it was directed against the nationalist movement. Precisely because it could succeed only with nationalist backing, it had to tone down as a world crusading movement: just as the evil of the French Revolution fell away, leaving only the good behind, so would the evil of Communism fall away, leaving only the good. Thus, such tensions as existed could be reduced by outside contact and China could take its place in the Asian family without prejudice to its neighbors' peace, or peace of mind.

This was to be the spirit of the Afro-Asian conference at Bandung, in 1955. The bamboo curtain was to be torn down, dispelling the doubts and fears. While the United States and its Western allies, Britain, France, Australia and New Zealand, prepared their "hard" approach at Manila by creating SEATO (in which they enlisted the support only of Pakistan, Thailand and the Philippines), Nehru and the other Colombo Powers' Prime Ministers set their "soft" approach in train at Bogor in Indonesia. Among the twenty-nine invited countries to the Afro-Asian conference Communist China was notable for its inclusion, Nationalist China for its exclusion. The conference was anticolonial, though friends of the West were at pains to make clear that there were new forms of colonialism as well as old. It was, in a sense, antiwhite. When a correspondent asked Sir John Kotelawala, the Prime Minister of Ceylon, why Australia was not invited, he replied, "To hell with Australians. They don't want us. Why should we want them?" But above all, under the guiding hand of Mr. Nehru, it was an effort to remove the barriers that existed between the newly independent states of Asia, to broaden their leaders' understanding and knowledge of each other and to establish the five principles of *panchsheel* as the basis for future Afro-Asian amity and accord.

Mr. Nehru's plans for Bandung did not always run smoothly. The Turks, the Filipinos, the Thais, the Pakistanis, the Ceylonese and others had their own apprehensions. "Communism confronts the world with a new form of colonialism much deadlier than the old one," said Fadhil Jamali, of Iraq. "Under the old form, there was at least some chance of hearing the cries of pain." And Sir John Kotelawala felt so strongly that he called a special press conference to denounce the Cominform.

Through the cyclone that sometimes blew so violently around his head Chou En-lai was correct and urbane. Outside the conference hall, in colonial times a Dutch club, crowds of eager Indonesians gathered each day to watch the delegates arrive and depart: always the biggest cheer was reserved for Chou.

In his opening address he made a telling point among the Buddhists, Hindus, Muslims and Christians of the twenty-eight other nations assembled at the conference by emphasizing such points as China's devotion to religious freedom. "Freedom of religious belief is a principle recognized by all modern nations," he said. "We Communists are atheists, but we respect all those who have religious belief. We hope that those with religious belief will also respect those without. China is a country where there is freedom of religious belief. There are in China not only 7 million Communists, but also tens of millions of Muslims and Buddhists and millions of Protestants and Catholics. Here in the Chinese delegation there is a pious Eaman of the Islamic faith. Such a situation is no obstacle to the internal unity of China. Why should it be impossible in the community of Asian and African countries to unite those with religious belief and those without? The days of instigating religious strife should have passed, because those who profit from instigating such strife are not those among us."

At successive private dinner parties, many of them organized by Nehru in his self-appointed role as Chou's sponsor, he strove to dispel Asian fears about China's intentions. To nations with Chinese minorities, he announced that he was ready to conclude dual nationality treaties. He assured Prince Norodom Sihanouk of Cambodia that China had no intention of interfering in Cambodian affairs; and to doubting Carlos Romulo of the Philippines he issued an invitation to inspect the coastal areas of the Fukien coast to see for himself if there was any offensive build-up of military forces. Reporting after the conference ended to Parliament in New Delhi, Nehru declared optimistically: "It would be a misreading of history to regard Bandung as an isolated occurrence and not part of a great movement of human history."

During the latter part of 1955 and 1956 the barriers tumbled. Bandung had destroyed the inhibitions and aroused the curiosity of many Asians and Africans. Khrushchev and Bulganin visited India, Burma and Afghanistan, proclaiming the era of "competitive coexistence" with substantial grants of economic aid. Chinese delegations led by the smooth and diplomatic Chou En-lai, Madame Sun Yat-sen (Madame Chiang Kai-shek's elder sister) and others made good-will trips to many parts of the Southeast Asian area. Even Pakistan, which had flown in the face of the Colombo Powers by joining SEATO and which had outlawed the Communist Party in 1954, became the center of great goings and comings. It was host to three major Chinese delegations in 1956, and in turn Prime Minister Suhrawardy made a state visit to China, the first by a Pakistani prime minister to any Communist country. Prime Minister Souvanna Phouma, then Prime Minister of Laos, went off to Peking: so did Prince Norodom Sihanouk of Cambodia and U Nu of Burma and Sukarno of Indonesia.

To emphasize this new sense of "big family" Peking spent millions of dollars encouraging the peoples of Asia and Africa to increase their cultural, economic and political contacts with China. It declared that the "area of peace" had been enlarged by the acceptance of the principles of peaceful coexistence and showed its good will by grants of economic aid. The first Chinese grant to a non-Communist neighbor ($22.8 million to Cambodia) was small, but there was the promise of more to come in the statement by Finance Minister Li Hsien-nien in June, 1956, that 2.17 per cent of the total state expenditure for the year, amounting to $268 million, had been earmarked for foreign aid.

Results of the new policy were sometimes highly gratifying to Peking. While the United States was maintaining the Cambodian Army and police force and contributing to small-scale economic projects a total sum of about $32 million a year, the Chinese began a series of cheap impact projects, including the construction of paper and plywood mills, a cement factory and a textile factory. They also embarked on a campaign to establish control over the economically important local Chinese community, numbering about half a million people. This was a slow and patient campaign which began by eliminating the use of Hong Kong as a channel for family remittances to China and ended with the establishment of a tax described as a "contribution to the national cause," through which the economic mission, and subsequently the Chinese Embassy, financed subversive activities in Cambodia.

These included subsidies to the vernacular Chinese and Vietnamese newspapers published in Phnom Penh, the Cambodian capital, and a cash distribution of between $600,000 and $700,000 to the fourteen provincial governors for any works they considered "desirable." Chou En-lai made a personal gift of a radio station to Sihanouk: next to Radio Hanoi it has the most powerful transmitter in Southeast Asia.

One single American project, the Phnom Penh–Sihanoukville highway connecting the capital with the new (French aid) port of Sihanoukville cost more than all the early Chinese projects put together. In terms of winning friends and influencing people, however, the Chinese were a long way in front. To many Cambodians even the American highway was of dubious worth. The Communist propaganda that it was built only as a means of rushing tanks and troops into the country in the event of war was given verisimilitude by the seeming lack of other uses to which it might be put. The Cambodians believed that it was uneconomic to move rice, the principal export crop, by road and that in any case to do this would tie up the country's entire fleet of trucks. In the months after the United States handed over the road to the Cambodians in July, 1959, the Communists performed an extraordinarily good job of verbal sabotage on it. Landslides and unexpected sinkings and shiftings of the highway surface were the foundation for their stories that it was unsafe for travel and that the Americans had saddled the Cambodian Government with a potentially dangerous white elephant whose crippling maintenance it could not afford. Amid general doubts and confusion over the road, the Chinese made a telling psychological offer to build a light railway connecting Phnom Penh with Sihanoukville over which the export rice crop might be moved without undue cost. The Chinese also offered to take over from the Americans the maintenance and from the French the training of the 31,000-man Cambodian Army. They were anxious to provide two thousand technicians to help in rural districts, to step up rice production, to take Cambodians for training in Chinese technical schools and to get a foothold in Cambodia's own schools.

Sihanouk hesitated about some of these projects. He had no wish to see the Chinese meddling with the army or in the schools, and he had long been alert to Communist activities among the younger intellectuals, the schoolteachers and the teacher trainees. He did not care for Chinese Communist cadres wandering about unsupervised in every district: and he took a long time to make up his mind about accepting the railway. Yet by 1960 some hundreds of Chinese experts were scouring the country for oil, coal and iron ore. Others were working on simple irrigation schemes and small rural projects designed to increase productivity—and to bring them into contact with the Cambodian people.

Privately, Sihanouk admitted that he believed the Chinese would eventually dominate all Southeast Asia. He copied from Mao and Chou En-lai the idea of going out to build roads and to participate generally in manual labor. He sent some of his thirty children off to school in Peking, and sometimes threatened to scrap American military aid and to take it from China instead.

Tremendously popular, he moves about Cambodia in a manner reminiscent of the travels of a Renaissance Court, complete with courtesans, all his Ministers and the diplomatic corps. He is not a Communist and undoubtedly views with distaste the prospect of Communist rule. He also realizes the dangers of flirting with the Communists: but such are his fears of his non-Communist neighbors, Thailand and South Vietnam, that his suspicions of SEATO exceed those he bears for Peking.

President Sukarno of Indonesia was another who carried back to his own country the idea that Communist China had found the solution to the problem of economic development in underdeveloped countries. Long after the achievement of independence in 1949 at the end of a bitter struggle with the Dutch, Sukarno continued to act and to speak as if he believed that colonialism was a greater threat to his country than Communism. He watched with no apparent concern while the Communists reestablished their political bases and in ten years, partly with the aid of funds received from the Indonesian Chinese community and the Chinese Embassy, became the biggest political party in Indonesia. China gave Indonesia a $16.4 million trade credit to buy 45,000 tons of rice and 35 million yards of textiles and another credit of $30 million to build three textile mills and soda and cement factories. Through a rice-rubber pact signed in 1952, it had already become Ceylon's largest supplier of rice, and, acting as an agent for the Communist bloc, also the largest buyer of Ceylon's major exports, rubber and tea.

This new tactic of Peking's was closely coordinated with similar Russian moves. Though apparent quite early in the fifties it did not begin to gather momentum until the Khrushchev and Bulganin tour of India, Burma and Afghanistan. Bloc aid to South and Southeast Asian countries since 1952 now totals about $2 billion—most of it devoted to "impact" projects, of which the Bihlai steel mill in India is the outstanding example, or in the form of low-interest-bearing credits to stimulate bilateral trade. Loans, which are invariably given on better terms than the West has so far matched, are usually repayable in goods. In the extreme case of Afghanistan, this approach has resulted in a major reorientation of trade away from the West and toward the Soviet Union. Elsewhere, if not so spectacular, the results have also been worth-while in both economic and political terms. Between 1952 and 1957 Soviet trade with underdeveloped Asia increased by 500 per cent. It has been going up ever since. Peking's part has been smaller than Moscow's, but in recent years, despite its own food problems and capital shortages, it has been rapidly expanding its "people's diplomacy" and aid-and-trade program to all parts of the underdeveloped world.

By 1960 an early trickle of delegations to China from Africa and Latin America had become a flood. Mao was an urbane host and an ardent proselytizer. To one group representing fourteen countries, he said: "Our common enemy is U.S. imperialism. We all stand on the same front and need to unite with and support each other." To another group of Africans from twelve different countries he promised that the world would "witness an even greater upsurge against imperialism," and predicted that "ultimate victory will certainly be won in the common struggle against imperialism and colonialism." To

Latin American groups, he said, "the struggles of the people of Cuba and other Latin American countries have helped the Chinese people and the struggle of the Chinese people has helped the people of Cuba and other Latin American countries." To a mixed group of Japanese, Cubans, Brazilians and Argentinians, he said, "We should unite and drive U.S. imperialism from Asia, Africa and Latin America back to where it came from."

The whole underdeveloped world had now become his guerrilla battlefield, rich in resources, filled with people who could become allies, anticolonial, anti-imperialist and, in many areas, ripe for revolution. Again, the first essential was to work through new-found friends to establish political bases. From isolated village bases his forces had once spread out over the countryside of China, linking up with other bases, encircling cities and towns and finally overwhelming them. From these new bases in far-off lands the forces against imperialism could spread out, link up, encircle the imperialists and finally overwhelm them. Their methods, as Lu Ting-yi, the Communist Party's propaganda chief, proposed, were to include "the legal and illegal, extraparliamentary and parliamentary, sanguinary and bloodless, economic and political, military and ideological."

Circumstances dictated the action. The Suez crisis in 1956 and intense anti-British feeling in the Arab states provided an opening first with Egypt and subsequently with the United Arab Republic, and even Yemen, a stronghold of Muslim conservatism. Egypt rejected an offer of troops but gladly took a gift of $5 million in Swiss francs. In January, 1958, China signed a treaty of friendship with Yemen in Peking and pushed into the willing hands of its crown prince a $17 million loan for building a textile plant and a modern highway. Soon three hundred Chinese technicians turned up to help the Yemenis on their anti-imperialist way.

Peking had a hand in stirring the revolution that took Iraq out of the Bagdad Pact. It offered volunteers to fight the imperialists during the Sjafruddin revolt in Indonesia, and again when United States forces landed in Lebanon. Within ten days of the American landing at Beirut, 164 million Chinese had participated in organized demonstrations of protest. The demonstrations began in the People's Square in Peking, but quickly switched their focal point to the office of the British chargé d'affaires following the news that British paratroops had landed in Jordan. In an unbroken file demonstrators marched past the British building for thirty-four hours. They included students, housewives, factory workers, peasants, teachers, doctors, scientists, poets and artists. They covered the long wall of the building and all nearby trees and lampposts in the neighborhood with streamers. "Within a few hours, only the British emblem over the gateway was left uncovered," said *China Reconstructs*. "Out of the gateway marched over a hundred members of the Chinese staff to join the demonstration too."

In twenty-four days the *People's Daily* carried twenty editorials "condemning the aggressors and calling for support for the Arab people." The New China Printing Press turned out a million copies of pamphlets and books on the Middle East. Along the walls and hoardings of every city huge posters appeared denouncing the United States and Britain. The Central Academy of Fine Arts and the Academy of Chinese Traditional Painting were both mobilized to draw cartoons to match the violence of the spoken campaign. Groups of workers, students, civil servants and others produced "living newspapers" and performed them in factories, parks and at street corners.

Two revolutions—in Algeria and in Cuba—and Guinea's differences with France provided the principal stimulus to Peking in its campaign to carry the struggle into Africa and Latin America. In January, 1959, the Party took over the gymnasiums in the capital to set in train this new "liberation" campaign. Politburo member Mayor Peng Chen, who is also Teng Hsiao-ping's deputy in the Secretariat, was the keynote speaker. Latin America was no longer the "backyard" in which the U.S. imperialists could do as they liked, he said. The 200 million Latin Americans had awakened. Their indignation against the U.S. aggressors had grown to such an extent that it had become irrepressible, and in this the victory won by the people of Cuba was proof. The whole of Africa was astir. For the imperialists and colonial rulers, from Cairo to Accra, from Tangier to the Cape of Good Hope, there were volcanoes everywhere. Some had already erupted. Others were threatening to erupt.

"The 650 million people of the Chinese People's Republic stand on the same front with all the peoples fighting for independence and freedom in Asia, Africa and Latin America," Peng said. "Their enemy is our enemy; their struggle is our struggle. In our common struggle against imperialism, we shall always stand united. Victory will finally be ours."

Peng ended his speech with a series of slogans which were soon to be hammered into the Chinese people by all the mass communications media and at rallies in which millions, and tens of millions, participated.

"Let us hail the new victories won in the struggle against colonialism!

"Support the national and democratic revolutionary movement in Cuba!

"Support the people of the Congo in their struggle for national independence!

"Down with the imperialist-colonial system!

"Oppose the U.S. imperialists' interference in Cuba's internal affairs!

"Oppose the slaughter of the people of the Congo by the Belgian colonial authorities!

"Belgian colonialists, get out of the Congo!

"Imperialists, quit Latin America!

"Imperialists, quit Africa!

"Peoples of Asia, Africa and Latin America, unite!

"Long live the victory of the national liberation movement!

"Long live the great solidarity of the peoples of the world!"

At Peking's invitation, and with all expenses paid, delegations of trade unionists, students, teachers, Communists, non-Communists, cultural groups, politicians and others swarmed into China. Many were impressed with China's material development: some were appalled by the totalitarian methods by which it was achieved. But since all were carefully shepherded away from regions and projects that Peking preferred them not to see, the majority went home believing that the Chinese model contained much that was worth-while.

Peking's anticolonialism was an unqualified success. To the Africans emerging, or about to emerge, from colonial rule, Peking impressively catalogued their continent's resources and how imperialism had exploited them in the past and planned to exploit them in the future. "As everyone knows," said the *Peking Review,* "the important mineral resources in Africa account for a major portion of those found in the capitalist world. For instance, it accounts for 99 per cent of the columbite; 98 per cent of the diamonds; 80.1 per cent of the cobalt; 47.7 per cent of the antimony; 24.4 per cent of the copper; and 29.4 per cent of the manganese ore. Africa's output of uranium exceeds the combined production of the United States and Canada; and between 60 per cent and 80 per cent of the total output in the capitalist world is produced in the Congo. To a considerable extent, the major imperialist countries, such as the United States, Britain and France, depend on Africa for the raw materials in their manufacture of weapons of mass destruction."

The material wealth of Africa and the backwardness of its people provided irrefutable evidence, Peking said, of the retarding effects of contemporary colonialism. Here were vast, untapped possibilities for rapid economic development and prosperity by the application of methods which the Chinese Communists were themselves employing and would be glad to teach the Africans. Why, in hydroelectric potential, the Congo alone could produce 240,000 million kwh of cheap power annually, or more than the current consumption of thermal and hydro power in West Germany, France, Italy, Austria, Belgium, the Netherlands, Luxemburg, Switzerland, Denmark, Greece, Ireland, Iceland, Portugal and Turkey combined. Power plus people equaled Communism: in Africa it also meant abundance for all. With power there could be great aluminium plants in central Africa, fertilizer and cement factories and factories using the rich deposits of uranium for the peaceful development of atomic energy.

But first of all colonialism and neocolonialism had to be abolished. It was not merely enough to get rid of the British, the French, the Belgians and all the other exploiters of the past. In their stead were coming the neocolonialists, the imperialists of the United States, who were penetrating Africa under the guise of "aid" and "development" but with the intention of using Africa's resources to "support dirty colonial wars and for the plunder of strategic raw materials." Aid was merely a weapon of the U.S. imperialists to further their expansion. It was a new form of colonialism in action. But it was a colonialism more ferocious, more treacherous and more skillful in self-camouflage than the old.

U.S. foreign "aid" was brutal plunder imposed on the recipient countries. More often than not they found it impossible to extricate themselves from this quagmire. To obtain military "aid" from the United States, they had to defray huge expenditures for militarization and make appropriations several times greater than the amount of U.S. aid for arms expansion. The inevitable result was runaway inflation, currency devaluation, drastic reduction of foreign exchange reserves and soaring costs of living. As a result of American dumping, industrial and agricultural production in countries receiving American aid declined rapidly.

Imperialists would never quit by themselves. When they had no other way out, the imperialists would retreat in order to prepare for a further advance, and so they might agree to grant nominal independence to certain countries while still retaining their political, economic and military control. Therefore, as *Red Flag* summed up on November 1, 1960: "At present the primary task of the peoples of the various countries of the world is to form the broadest united front against imperialism headed by the United States, resolutely oppose the U.S. imperialist policies of aggression and war, firmly oppose colonialism, promote the growth of the national liberation movement and stimulate the development of the revolutionary struggle of the working people in the imperialist countries against the bellicose groups and monopoly capital."

As early as September 22, 1958, the Chinese Government recognized the Provisional Government of Algeria; in October, 1958, it recognized the Republic of Guinea. At Peking's invitation an Algerian military delegation arrived in China early in 1959. It received a substantial gift in cash, tactical military advice, and further tangible evidence of its hosts' solidarity when millions turned out to celebrate "Algeria Week."

At this stage, however, the Algerians seemed hesitant about accepting Peking's offers of direct military assistance and more than a year passed before Belkacem Krim, the rebel vice-premier, turned up in Peking to carry the negotiations a stage further. After talks extending over a period of several weeks, during which he also visited North Vietnam and North Korea, Krim put his signature to a joint communiqué with Marshal Chen Yi, the Foreign Minister. They noted that "as long as colonialist oppressors and imperialist aggressors were not eliminated . . . genuine and permanent peace will be impossible." The communiqué also reported that the two parties had studied various ways to enhance friendly cooperation between Algeria and China.

Four months later Ferhat Abbas, the premier of the Algerian provisional government, arrived in Peking. Chou En-lai was at the airport to greet him and to ride with him in an open car through the streets to the official guest house. The crowds waved Chinese and Algerian national flags and bunches of fall flowers, beat drums and let off firecrackers as Chou and Abbas made their triumphal drive into the city.

In his speech of welcome Chou said the Algerian people had set a brilliant example to all the African peoples and had won the profound sympathy and firm support of the peoples of Asia and of all the world. The Chinese people had always regarded the Algerian people's victory as their own victory and as a great victory for the world's peoples in their struggle against imperialism and colonialism. "We will do everything we can to support the Algerian people's struggle for national liberation," he said. "We have done so and will continue to do so in the future."

Ferhat Abbas, in a speech at a banquet given in his honor, revealed that the rebels had shed their doubts as to the wisdom of accepting Chinese military aid. He blamed the French for "chloroforming" international opinion on Algeria and de Gaulle for refusing to negotiate. "It was under such conditions that the Provisional Government of the Algerian Republic made an important political decision during its recent deliberations," he said. Renouncing the making of peace through direct French-Algerian talks, Algeria had decided to "internationalize" the Algerian problem. After denouncing NATO countries "led by the United States, which helps in permitting a war of colonial reconquest to be carried on within the framework of the Atlantic Pact," he ended on a dramatic note: "The hour of active solidarity has struck, the Algerian people will remain in the fight, and it is not in vain they appeal to the Chinese people to put an end to a war of extermination of a people determined to win its independence."

The details had all been taken care of. All that remained now was to put the seal on the Chinese aid program. Enthusiastic references to the "militant" Sino-Algerian friendship and the inclusion of such people as Marshal Ho Lung, a vice-premier, who ten years earlier had led the Chinese military mission to Ho Chi-minh's headquarters in Tongking and General Chang Ai-ping, fifty-three-year-old deputy chief of the General Staff of the Chinese People's Liberation Army, left little doubt as to the nature of the talks. In Moscow, on his way home, the Algerian leader was explicit. The "active solidarity" agreed to in Peking, he explained, meant "total aid" for "the intensification of the armed struggle in Algeria."

In the case of Guinea, different techniques were clearly indicated. Guinea's decision in 1958 to opt for independence instead of remaining within the French Union led de Gaulle to retaliate by withdrawing French civil servants and technicians. Lacking its own trained bureaucrats, Guinea stood in urgent need of help from abroad. It got it swiftly—from the Communist bloc. China contributed an initial gift of five thousand tons of rice, and a second larger shipment of ten thousand tons early in 1960. The Soviet Union contributed a $35 million, low-interest loan and Communist technicians moved in as the French moved out.

In October, 1959, Mr. Diawandou, the Guinean Minister of Education, visited Peking and signed a cultural cooperation agreement under which China provided ten scholarships for Guinean students to train in China and for a Chinese acrobatic troupe to visit Guinea. Some months later this agreement was renewed and extended, this time opening the way for an exchange of teachers and students and the direct penetration of Chinese Communist ideas among Guinean students in their own environment.

Relations between the two countries took a step back early in 1960, when Peking threatened to break relations because the Guinean Government received a Nationalist Chinese delegation. Guinean protestations of friendship healed the breach and to show there was no ill will China sent a further gift of ten thousand tons of rice and invited President Sékou Touré to Peking to receive an interest-free loan of $25 million and to put his signature to treaties of friendship and trade under which the two countries will exchange 1.2 billion Guinean francs' ($4.92 million) worth of goods each year. The nature and the terms of the loan, the agreement on the provision of technicians and other specialists and the conditions under which they will live in Guinea were all carefully designed to underscore the advantages that flow from association with altruistic, humanitarian China by way of contrast with the implicit evils and designs of American aid.

Despite the threat of famine, at the head of the list of Chinese exports was rice, a staple item in Guinea's diet. An even more interesting item, "educational and cultural supplies," was tucked away among textiles, building materials, agricultural machinery and implements and medicines, all well calculated to reflect China's growing industrial strength. In return, China will receive coffee, industrial diamonds, rubber and other raw materials.

The $25 million loan was not only interest-free, it was also "without any conditions or privileges attached." Guinea will have the use of the full amount for ten years and thereafter will repay the loan, either in goods or in the currency of a third country agreed upon with China, in ten annual installments. China will send experts, technicians and skilled workers to Guinea, provide complete equipment, machinery and materials and assist in the training of Guinean technicians and skilled workers. All traveling expenses, going and coming, of the Chinese experts will be met by China. Their living expenses will come out of the loan, but "their standard of living shall not exceed that of personnel of the same rank in the Republic of Guinea."

In case that sort of innuendo went over anyone's head, the joint communiqué was much more explicit. "At present, all threats and obstacles to world peace come from the side of imperialism," said President Sékou Touré and Liu Shao-chi. "Therefore the two parties solemnly declare their resolute support for the just struggle of national liberation of the peoples of Algeria, the Congo, South Africa and other countries. They condemn the schemes of imperialism as interfering in the Congo's internal affairs and encroaching on its territorial integrity. . . ."

At the state banquet in Peking to celebrate the new accord, Liu Shao-chi left no doubt as to the identity of the "imperialists." He accused the United States of supporting both the French in Algeria and the "colonialist authorities of the Union of South Africa in their barbarous policy of racial discrimination." Under the flag of the United Nations, the United States was also "invading the Congo on a large scale, committing intervention and creating division there in an attempt to realize its scheme of swallowing up the Congo." Should it succeed, he added, it would "unfold its schemes against the other independent African countries."

Sékou Touré, in turn, demanded that "ideological, economic and cultural imperialism be brought to an end." He expressed his "warmest thanks" for all the contributions China had already made to the struggle of the African people. He reassured his listeners that "even though many slanders have been directed against your people, whom the imperialists wish to isolate from African political consciousness, we can assure you that the Africans know where the truth lies. . . . They know also the lesson they can draw from your history—to unite more effectively in the anti-imperialist struggle." The note of jubilation in the *People's Daily* editorial summing up the results of the Sékou Touré visit and the signing of the first treaty of friendship with an African state was understandable. "It is a momentous event not only in the history of Chinese-Guinean relations but also in the history of relations between China and Africa," said the newspaper.

Mali, which had agreed earlier to exchange diplomatic missions with Nationalist China while still federated with Senegal, opted for Peking when the federation broke up; and none of the other newly independent African States, on whose support Taipeh had been counting to keep the Communists out of the United Nations, were prepared to vote against Peking when the question of discussing its membership came before the United Nations in 1960.

The National Afro-Asian Solidarity Committee in Peking and the Chinese-African People's Friendship Association, under the presidency of Liu Chang-sheng, who began his career with the Communists as a member of the Russian Youth Corps in Vladivostok, coordinated support in China for the African peoples in their "struggles against imperialism and colonialism." These bodies, and related organizations, sponsored twenty-six major Chinese delegations to Africa during 1959 and the first six months of 1960, and during the same period they entertained about a hundred African delegations in China. The New China News Agency established permanent offices in Cairo, Conakry, Rabat and Accra. Peking Radio increased its broadcasts in English to Africa to thirty-five hours a week. Seven hours were broadcast in Chinese for the Chinese communities in East Asia. French, Arabic and Turkish broadcasts were also beamed to the Middle East and

Africa. A special broadcast of seven hours a week was devoted to the Congo. And one day Portuguese officials in Africa found that Peking had included Portuguese in their broadcast lists. They sensed trouble: and their senses were keen. The establishment of an underground Communist Party in October, 1955, was the first step. Fourteen months later the Party took the lead in forming the Popular Movement for the Liberation of Angola. In 1959 this new organization set up a coordinating center called the Revolutionary Front with headquarters in Conakry, where Chinese, Russian and North Vietnamese aid and advice soon led to a full-scale revolt in northern Angola.

Latin America received similar treatment. "The struggle of the peoples of Asia, Africa and Latin America for national independence and against colonial oppressions has become an irresistible torrent," said Chou En-lai in celebration of Castro's entry into Havana in January, 1959. "The overthrow of the U.S.-sponsored regime by the Cuban people and the angry roar raised by the people of the Congo against colonialism are indications that these struggles will continue to develop vigorously this year." To help these struggles Peking beamed twenty-one hours of broadcast time to Latin America each week. And it overflowed with enthusiasm when Blas Roca, general secretary of the People's Socialist Party of Cuba, brought the tidings that Castro himself needed no prodding to use the Cuban revolt as the point of departure for revolutions everywhere in Latin America. In a speech in Peking on April 28, 1960, Blas Roca said the American imperialists were angry because Cuba had set the example for the rest of Latin America.

"Since Cuba can have a sovereign revolutionary government neither at the beck and call of, nor subservient to, Washington then why cannot Argentina, Brazil and Colombia have the same?" he asked. "Since Cuba can carry through a thoroughgoing land reform, develop multiple production, transform its economy and, casting aside U.S. monopoly capital investors, proceed with its own industrialization, then why cannot Ecuador, Bolivia, Chile and Peru do the same? Since Cuba can overthrow a regime of terror and dictatorship, which was armed to the teeth and had the active support of the United States and the U.S. Military Advisory Group to the last minute before its, downfall, then why cannot the Dominican Republic, Nicaragua and

Paraguay also be liberated from similar dictatorships?" Such expressions of opinion found ready listeners in China. The *People's Daily* followed the speech with an editorial in which it said that until American imperialism had been dealt crushing blows by the people of the whole world, until it had suffered a crushing defeat, it would never give up its ambition to dominate the globe and enslave the world's people. Chou En-lai promised that the United States for its crimes of aggression would be "dealt doubly powerful counterblows by the iron fist of the mighty Socialist camp." And on June 2, 1960, Liu Shao-chi, speaking at a state banquet in honor of a visiting delegation from Albania, called on the "peoples of the world" to carry on "persistent struggles against U.S. imperialism, to strike incessant blows against its scheming activities and to isolate it to the greatest possible extent."

The China-Latin American Friendship Association was formed in Peking on March 16, 1960, amid the usual mass publicity and the launching of "support the Latin American People's Week." One out of every five delegations that visited China during the first six months of 1960 was from Latin America. Brazil sent eleven delegations, Cuba eight, Chile seven and Argentina five. So great was the flow of delegations that it became difficult to keep the score card. The flow was two-way. A Chinese trade union delegation left for Cuba on April 15, 1960; a Cuban trade union delegation arrived in Peking two days later. On July 23, 1960, China and Cuba signed a trade and payments agreement on scientific and technical cooperation (under which China will train Cuban technicians) and an agreement on cultural cooperation. The establishment of formal diplomatic relations was announced two months later, and by November nearly 10,000 tons of Chinese rice and beans were unloading at Havana. Before the end of the year 350,000 tons of Cuba sugar had arrived in China, and flowing back to Havana from Chinese ports were machine tools, trucks, motors, internal combustion engines, machines, scientific research instruments, steel and chemical products, flour, edible oil, clothing and industrial raw materials.

One notable visitor at this time was Major Ernesto "Che" Guevara, the Argentinian Left-wing adventurer, whose previous failure in an attempt to organize a Communist take-over in Guatemala has been more than compensated for by his successful partnership with Castro.

At the usual state banquet Chou En-lai gave Guevara an enthusiastic welcome. "What the Chinese people particularly admire is that the Cuban people have displayed dauntless bravery in face of threats and intimidation by U.S. imperialism and have again and again defeated its subversive plots and disruptive activities," he said. "The Cuban people have been waging a struggle directed squarely against that most vicious U.S. imperialism, which is in close proximity to Cuba. They have answered the U.S. economic blockade by ridding Cuba of the economic influence of U.S. imperialism and are ready, by organizing a militia, to repulse at any moment armed provocation and attack by the enemy. The Cuban people's struggle shows that an awakened oppressed people, so long as they can correctly assess the enemy strategically and are tactically skillful in handling the struggles against the enemy, will grow from weak to strong and will certainly be able to win and consolidate their victories. The struggle and victories of the Cuban people have become the hope and example of the other Latin American peoples. They have greatly inspired all the oppressed peoples of the world in their struggle for national independence and made important contributions to the cause of defending world peace." The Chinese people had given and would continue to give resolute support to the Cuban people in their "anti-imperialist revolutionary struggles." His toast to the "militant friendship of the Chinese and Cuban peoples" left no doubt that here, as in Algeria, Chinese revolutionary tactics and material would have a big part to play.

By coincidence Guevara arrived in Peking on November 17, 1960, the day the United States sent its air and naval forces to the Carribean to prevent landings in Guatemala and Nicaragua. It was no coincidence, however, that rebel groups in these countries had already revolted, or that seeds of incipient revolt were visible in Nicaragua, Costa Rica, Honduras and Panama. The activist slogan of the day in Latin America was "Cuba Si; Yanquis No." It was also the slogan with which the usual crowds with their streamers, flags and banners greeted Guevara when he landed at Peking airport. "A cornered dog trying to jump over a high wall will only break its head," said the *People's Daily*. "The doom of U.S. imperialism in Latin America is drawing nearer and nearer." Once again Mao Tse-tung had found the material for revolt and was beginning to put it to use.

Chapter VII

PARTY, PEOPLE AND PROSPECTS

The previous chapters have dealt with method and intention. What matters is not what Mao Tse-tung wants to do but the success or failure likely to attend his efforts. How firm is the Chinese Communist base? What are the chances that it will be overthrown by internal revolt, or by an invasion by Chiang Kai-shek? Do these extraordinary efforts to leap from the carrying pole into the nuclear age hold significant prospects of success? Is there any danger that the United States will be isolated by this extension of Maoist guerrilla warfare into the realm of international politics?

In considering whether the Chinese Communist regime has the capacity to survive there are three major factors to be taken into account: the Party, the army, and the Chinese people, in particular the peasants. The Party is the State and the army is the principal organ of state power: the peasants are the "ocean" in which the Party "swam" to victory. The strength, cohesion and dynamism of the

Party and its control over the army are vitally important. Just as the Party must control the army's guns, the army must also be capable of controlling the peasants, who, having been hoodwinked into communes, overworked and underpaid, must be considered at least as potentially counterrevolutionary.

Both the internal Chinese revolution and the external world revolution, as it is seen in Peking, draw their inspiration from Mao Tse-tung. Mao was the true creator of the peasant uprising that threw Chiang Kai-shek out of mainland China. His were the guerrilla skills that used inferior forces to beat superior forces. The nature and the scope of the social revolution in China have Marxist and ultranationalist goals but Maotian subtleties. But since the Soviet Union modified some of its more bellicose and repressive policies after Stalin's death, is it not logical to suppose that China will also change after Mao, who is now nearing his seventies, passes from the scene and younger Chinese leaders, with closer contacts with the non-Communist world, take over?

The answer lies largely in the difference in character and influence of the two men. Stalin, the absolute and ruthless dictator, was cordially detested by his closest associates. Under Mao, the Chinese Communist Party and the Chinese people have been spared the Stalinist blood baths both in the struggle for power and the struggle to industrialize. Many of Mao's subordinates have differed with him—over the early rash and headlong excesses of the communes in 1958, for instance, and on other major decisions. The more sophisticated technocrats have sometimes been dismayed by his habit of treating economic problems as merely another facet of guerrilla warfare. The essentially business-like and pragmatic Chou En-lai who, as Prime Minister, is concerned more with results than ideological pipe dreams, is sometimes impatient of Mao's theorizing; and there are other lesser critics, among the economists and especially within the army, who have not always taken kindly to the multipurpose role Mao designed for them. The fact remains, however, that never in the history of revolution have so many revolutionary leaders remained firmly united for so long as they have in China under Mao Tse-tung.

All members of the all-important Standing Committee of the Politburo—Mao Tse-tung, Liu Shao-chi, Chou En-lai, Chu Teh, Chen Yun, Lin Piao and Teng Hsiao-ping—took part in the Long March.

All were members of the Politburo in 1945, and four—Mao, Liu, Chou and Chu—were members in 1934. Only four of the nineteen members of the Politburo missed the Long March and all had good Party reasons for their absence. Peng Chen, for instance, was serving a six-year jail term as the guest of Chiang Kai-shek. He went to Yenan as soon as he was released and is now deputy to Teng Hsiao-ping in the eight-man Secretariat, which serves as the general staff of the Party, providing the Politburo and the Standing Committee with the intelligence on which decisions are based and transmitting the orders to the lower echelons. Two other members of both the Secretariat and the Politburo are Tan Chen-lin, who was in a high Party position in Fukien Province when the Long March began, and Li Hsien-nien. Li couples these two posts with a seat in the National Defense Council. He is also a vice-premier, Minister of Finance and director of the Office of Trade and Finance. Now only fifty-three, the highest positions in Party and government seem likely to be his within the next decade. Two other younger members of the Politburo are Li Ching-chuan, secretary of the Szechwan branch of the Party and Ko Ching-shih, who replaced Marshal Chen Yi as Mayor of Shanghai. Li Ching-chuan is fifty-three and Ko two years his senior.

Among the members and alternate members of the Politburo and the Standing Committee, the men who really count, there is no real evidence today of what could properly be described as factionalism. At the top the Party is firm, firmer without doubt, than any other major Communist Party. This is true also of the government, for the top posts are interlocking. In addition to his senior Party positions, Liu Shao-chi is chairman of the People's Republic, chairman (ex-officio) of the National Defense Council, and, as such, commander-in-chief of the People's Liberation Army. Prime Minister Chou En-lai is third in the Party hierarchy (ranking before Marshal Chu Teh, now seventy-five). Chen Yun ranks fifth in the Party, is first vice-premier and chairman of the State Capital Construction Commission. Only fifty-five, he is also a man to be watched, as is Marshal Lin Piao, who despite his long and distinguished military record, is only fifty-four. He is Defense Minister, a vice-premier and a vice-chairman of the National Defense Council. Marshal Chen Yi is Foreign Minister, a vice-premier and a vice-chairman of the National Defense Council. Li Fu-chun combines his chairmanship of the State Planning Com-

mission with another vice-premiership. And so on. Every major decision of government is, *ipso facto*, a major Party decision. And this
web of Party-bureaucratic control extends through the entire society.

This current concentration of power in the hands of a few men
does not necessarily mean that the stability will of certainty be pro-
jected into the immediate future. Whether it will persist during the
next decade depends in large part on the leaders who will succeed
Mao and his principal lieutenants, Liu Shao-chi and Chou En-lai,
both of whom are now in their middle sixties. In this connection the
composition of the Chinese delegation to the 1960 Moscow conference provided some strong clues. It was led by Liu Shao-chi, included
fifty-nine-year-old Teng Hsiao-ping and Peng Chen, both Politburo
members and the two top men in the Secretariat, and Li Ching-chuan.
Others who went along were Lu Ting-yi, the Party propaganda chief,
and Kang Sheng, former chief of the Secret Police, two of the six
alternate members of the Politburo. Lu was born in Kiangsu in 1907.
Kang Sheng is three years older.

The remaining five members of the delegation were Yang Shang-
kun, alternate member of the Secretariat and deputy secretary-general,
who was born in Szechwan in 1907; Hu Chiao-mu, the sixty-year-old
vice-director of the propaganda department of the Secretariat; Liu
Hsiao, who was born in Hunan in 1907 and has been ambassador to
the Soviet Union since 1955; Liao Cheng-chih, who was born in
Tokyo in 1908 and is chairman of both the Commission for Overseas
Chinese Affairs and the Chinese Committee for Afro-Asian Solidarity;
and Liu Ning-yi, who was born in Hopei in 1905, organized the
Communist underground in Shanghai in the forties and is now chairman of the All-China Federation of Trade Unions.

This is a typical cross section of the next decade of Chinese Communist leadership. With the exception of Chou En-lai, it includes
the men with the broadest international experience in the regime.
Teng Hsiao-ping is perhaps the most efficient man of all. Small, brittle
and slow of gait—he walks with a stick—he is also brilliant, pains-
taking and ruthless. He prepared the report that sent former State
Planner Kao Kang to his suicide's grave. At the Moscow Communist
parties' conference, Liu Shao-chi, though leader of the Chinese delegation, left much of the burden of the blistering battle with Khrushchev to Teng. Long an associate of Chou En-lai, with whom he

joined the Party in Paris in 1921 during his nine-year stay in France,
Teng has both the revolutionary distinction of having participated
in the Long March and wide administrative experience in financial
and economic matters. Kang Sheng spent six years studying in Moscow; Liao Cheng-chih was educated at Waseda University in Tokyo
and during the late twenties visited Germany, Belgium and Holland
before going to the Soviet Union to study. He was twenty-six years
old before he returned to China in time to take part in the Long
March. He led the Chinese delegation to the Afro-Asian People's
Solidarity Conference at Conakry in April, 1960. Lu Ting-yi and Yang
Shang-kun both studied in Moscow. Liu Ning-yi has many international contacts through his chairmanship of the China-Iraq Friendship Association and his position as secretary-general of the Peace
Liaison Committee of the Asian and Pacific Regions. He went to the
Conakry conference with Liao Cheng-chih and habitually bobs up
in the pictures showing Mao with guests from the underdeveloped
world.

These men not only represent the next generation of leadership,
they are also the most articulate spokesmen of the hard Maoist line.
If Mao and Liu Shao-chi are the architects of the Chinese revolution,
these others are the practicing builders—at home and abroad. Almost
all of them are keynote speakers for the great mass demonstrations
by which Peking whips up hysteria for the world revolution. Liao
Cheng-chih, for instance, is a frequent leader at rallies dealing with
peace and Japanese and Overseas Chinese affairs. He has given the
Party line at antibomb rallies and at "support Laos" and "support the
Congo" rallies. He is usually on hand, gracious, courteous and smiling,
when Mao Tse-tung receives guests from Africa, Asia and Latin
America.

Liu Ning-yi, who called President Eisenhower a "bloodstained hangman and ringleader of bandits," is a leading hater in the Hate America campaign. Lu Ting-yi proposed that the United States should be
isolated by all means including the "legal and illegal, extra-parliamen-
tary and parliamentary, sanguinary and bloodless, economic and
political, military and ideological."

These are "just" wars men, "the east wind is prevailing over the
west wind" men. These are the men, in short, who want to push on
rapidly with the world revolution. They want to dissolve the borders

that separate the Middle Kingdom from Southeast Asia, to isolate the United States to the greatest possible extent, and to maintain the flow of poison and hatred against it among the Chinese people and the people of the underdeveloped world.

Even among such men, united as they are in revolutionary purpose, the possibility of a divisive struggle for power after Mao's death cannot be entirely dismissed. But the current checks and balances within the Party organization are heavily against it. Mao has stamped his personality and his views heavily through the vital departments in the Party Secretariat. Tung Pi-wu, one of his oldest associates, is the Party watchdog at the head of the control committee. An Tzu-wen, for many years Mao's confidential secretary, directs the organization department, which is responsible for planning national movements and campaigns. Lu Ting-yi and Chen Po-ta, Mao's ghost-writer, are associated in the propaganda department. And, finally, Teng Hsiao-ping, who is both a Mao man and a close confidant of Liu Shao-chi, exercises the widest power through his job as secretary-general of the Secretariat. Teng is much more than a post office for the Party. He is in a unique position to guide decisions at the top and to supervise and interpret the execution of directives below. He represents non-military Party authority at the highest levels of the National Defense Council, and commands a key team of Party brain trusters, including Li Fu-chun, the State Planner; Li Hsien-nien, the Minister of Finance; Li Hsueh-feng, the director of the Party's industrial works department; Peng Chen, his immediate deputy; and General Tan Cheng, who is director of the General Political Department of the People's Liberation Army. Teng is, in fact, the spider at the center of the web of Party control. Though he has been reported as brittle-tempered, his friendship with Liu and Mao does not appear to have inhibited his relations with Chou En-lai. In importance even now he is second only to Mao Tse-tung into whose shoes he seems certain to step. And a formidable leader he will make, too. Mao need have no fears that his plans will fail from any lack of dedication and determination on the part of Teng. The group immediately junior to him, including those five or six years younger, are also steeped in the Mao tradition. Nor is long-range leadership training neglected. The Young Communist League has its own department in the Secretariat and its first secretary, Hu Yao-pang, is also a member of the Central Committee.

The rank and file of the Party are neither so firm nor so efficient, however. In the post-mortems on crop failures in 1959–1960, for instance, some inglorious examples of inefficiency among the cadres were revealed. To give the show window effect by which they hoped to win the acclaim of their seniors, many cadres concentrated on roadside rice and wheat fields, using excessive labor, fertilizer and water to create the desirable effect on areas they thought likely to be subject to higher inspection, while neglecting the rest of the land.

Such irresponsible behavior led to the reestablishment early in 1961 of the six Party bureaus, under the control of leading members of the Central Committee. The bureaus will act for the Central Committee in strengthening leadership over the Party committees in the various provinces, municipalities and autonomous regions. This decision was a measure of the Party's concern with rural leadership, since an earlier experiment on these lines led to the first and only serious split in the top leadership, when in March, 1955, Kao Kang, a "ring-leader of the anti-Party faction," and the "incorrigible renegade," Jao Shu-shih, were expelled on charges of attempting to create their own little Communist kingdom in Manchuria.

The revival of the bureaus at this time suggested that the Party was now less fearful of personal ambitions at the top than it was of discontent and inefficiency below. The new bureaus had in their immediate sights not only inefficient Party officials but the disaffected 10 per cent of the population who had not been satisfactorily "remolded" and others in calamity-stricken areas who were showing signs of being discouraged and disillusioned.

Considering its rapid expansion—from fifty-seven members in 1921 to 13,960,000 in 1959—the Party has nevertheless succeeded in maintaining a fairly high level of zealotry and loyalty in its lower ranks. Frequent rectification campaigns, and the more drastic controls envisaged in the reestablishment of the Party bureaus, are designed to ensure this. According to Liu Lan-tao, alternate secretary of the Secretariat, "we have purged from our glorious Communist Party tens of thousands of counterrevolutionaries, class enemies, bourgeois rightists, elements guilty of grave breaches of law and violations of discipline and other bad elements who have infiltrated our Party. In this way we have purified and consolidated the organization of Party to an unparalleled degree, tremendously increased the Communist consciousness of the great masses of our members and raised our Party to a high level of Marxism-Leninism." The Communists have also created a huge number of basic-level Party organs to ensure that ideological control is widely exercised. These organizations totaled more than a million in 1959, or one for about every six hundred of the population. After the publication of Mao's fourth volume of selected works in October, 1960, they were reported by the *People's Daily* to have "sprouted like dandelions in a spring lawn." With a significant section of the population still regarded as hostile to the regime, this constant vigilance is clearly needed to guard against the possibility of counterrevolution and to maintain a high standard of indoctrination and enthusiasm among the cadres, who are in turn responsible for maintaining the required discipline and tempo of production in agriculture and industry.

All members are not willing and obedient tools of the Party. At the same time, the continuing breakdown in traditional Chinese society, the example of what happens to "enemies" of the regime, the repeated rectification campaigns and Mao's success in inspiring a fairly widespread revolutionary dynamic have combined to produce a high degree of effective centralized control. That control is not all the Party would like it to be—but, provided the instruments of Party authority are firm, it is enough.

Of these, the most important is the People's Liberation Army on whose power the Communist authority rests. It has sometimes seemed less than enchanted with Party policy. There were serious defections to the Nationalists among prisoners-of-war in Korea, for instance, and during the first months of the "great leap forward" a large number of officers became openly hostile toward Party interference in military affairs. Professional officers believed that the system of Party committees through the army impeded command decisions and the concentration of command. They were equally opposed to the Party conclusion that "the army should not be only a combat group but at the same time a work team and a production team."

This crisis received almost no public attention inside China and very little outside it. But from such publications as the *Liberation*

Army Daily and other journals with fairly restricted circulations, it is possible to piece together some of the details. Between May and July, 1958, leading members of the Party and senior army officers met in conference so secret that its existence was revealed only after it had broken up. Mao Tse-tung and all the country's top revolutionary leaders addressed it. What they said has not been revealed; there has been less reticence about why they said it. The *Liberation Army Daily*, for instance, reported that an apparently significant section of the army leadership had "neglected the revolutionary nature of the people's army and neglected Chinese Communist Party leadership," stressing modernization and standardization, unification and centralization and the "part of atomic weapons and modern military techniques." The officers were half-hearted in their support of the view expressed by Marshal Chu Teh that "policies, political systems and the inclination or disinclination of people's hearts, not technique, finally decide victory or defeat in war."

Many officers, who had grown up in a much more powerful and essentially different army from that which Mao and his old-line commanders had known, scoffed at such archaic ideas. By rectification they were taught to understand their errors. The Military Academy was reorganized to secure the dominance of Party commissars. No less than 150,000 of these special Party agents, including 160 generals, were deployed to serve for a time in the ranks, and before the end of the year Major-General Tseng Hsiang-huang, a leading political officer, reported that the army once again had become a "university of Communism."

His optimism seemed somewhat premature, and both to strengthen Party controls within the army and to accommodate the professionals' desire for modernization, Marshal Lin Piao was appointed Minister of Defense in place of Marshal Peng Teh-huai; General Lo Jui-ching, formerly Minister of Public Security, who played the leading role in the suppression of counterrevolutionaries, became Chief of the General Staff. "No personal ambitions are allowed," Lin insisted. "Discipline should be strictly observed. Importance should be attacked at all times and in all places to the unity of the Party and nothing should be done behind the back of the Party." He concluded by quoting Mao: "Our principle is that the Party commands the gun and the gun will never be allowed to command the Party."

He instituted an intensified indoctrination campaign within the army while deploying units to serve in the communes. Troops did not abandon their guns, but they were required to spend much of their time in production and on internal security. During 1958 they helped to build more than 20,000 water conservation projects and contributed some 59 million man-days to industrial construction, agricultural seasonal work, including plowing, harvesting, and calamity and relief work.

As China's leading strategist, however, Lin Piao had no intention of destroying the fighting force of the People's Liberation Army. He shared the view that the army needed to modernize and that the advent of nuclear weapons had necessitated changes. He promised that the army would not lag behind. One of his closest associates, Senior General Liu Ya-lou, the air force commander, who served as a political commissar with Lin's forces on the Long March, framed the new military policy in terms of the Party slogan, "walking on two legs." Writing in the *Liberation Army Journal*, he said: "American imperialism is nothing. Its only advantage is to have more tons of steel. If we catch up with Britain and then the United States in industrial and agricultural production and in the fields of science and technology, in terms of modernized equipment our army will certainly catch up and surpass them. China's working class and scientists will certainly be able to make the most up-to-date aircraft and atomic bombs in the not distant future. By that time, in addition to the political factor in which we always occupy an absolutely predominant position, we can use atomic weapons and rockets made by the workers, engineers and scientists in our country in coping with the enemies who dare to invade our country and undermine world peace."

Demonstrable political advantages and military disadvantages have flowed from the army's participation in manual labor and the "great leap forward." Unlike the Nationalist armies, however, and the armies of the war lords, the People's Liberation Army is disciplined and respected and, despite occasional rumblings of discontent, now firmly under Party control. It is better cared for, better fed and better dressed than the rest of the population. It is an élite; but the Party will have to take care that it does not stagnate. In common with all other sections of the Chinese community its morale demands a continuing concept of struggle, and in this the preparation for war (even if war is not intended), modernization and Hate America campaigns are vital. So long as this dynamic and Party controls can be maintained, the army is unlikely to play any role in a counterrevolution other than that of Party bulldog.

On Taiwan the Nationalists argue that the preconditions for revolt in China exist today just as they existed in Hungary in 1956; that whereas the Hungarian uprising failed because of the lack of effective, indigenous external support, a Chinese uprising could succeed because of the availability on Taiwan of a well trained and well equipped army of more than twenty divisions and an air force, which, though numerically inferior, has proved itself materially superior in action with the Communists.

The argument is plausible. Even before the bitter years of the "great leap forward" Mao Tse-tung's seemingly liberal doctrine of letting a hundred blossoms bloom produced a sufficient crop of poisonous intellectual weeds to establish that the seeds of disaffection clearly existed in that class. But the conception of the intellectuals leading a counterrevolution is unconvincing. They turned somersaults to purge themselves of their "rightist misconceptions" during the rectification campaign; these slender reeds are not the stuff that counterrevolutionaries are made of. Nor is the Hungarian analogy really apposite. In Hungary, Communist authority was installed and maintained by the Soviet Red Army. In China, the revolution began in the grass roots, moving from Mao's mountain hideout in South China to Yenan and then back again until it embraced the entire country. Though the ideology was alien, the Chinese people sowed the wind that swept the Kuomintang out of China. The Kuomintang asserts that they are now reaping the whirlwind and that the peasants, if not the intellectuals, will prove the regime's undoing. Undoubtedly, many peasants have many reasons to be hostile. Land reform was the reward for service in beating Chiang Kai-shek. But instead of enjoying landownership, the peasants were driven through two other revolutions—collectivization and communization—in which all they had won they now lost. Compensations were few. The early increases in grain did not go to fill their bellies. Bumper crops did not mean full rice bowls, since there were now millions of new mouths to feed each year and agricultural products constituted China's only initial means of capital accumulation for industrial development.

From the published treaties and agreements concluded between Moscow and Peking, it is clear that until 1961 large quantities of military and industrial aid from Russia were being paid for in foodstuffs. Apart from any shipments to the Soviet Union which have not been disclosed—and discrepancies between crops claimed and food eaten suggest they may be considerable—China is known to have exported 1,850,000 tons of grain to Russia in 1958, and to have averaged shipments of about a million tons a year. Rice paid for the rubber China got from Ceylon, for Cuban sugar and for imports from North Korea and the satellites of Eastern Europe. It won friends in Guinea and Cuba.

Official Party explanations of the continuing shortages have generally avoided reference to export needs. Natural calamities, such as the droughts, typhoons and plagues of 1960, and sometimes the admission of unwise planning, inefficiency and "bad elements" have been blamed. Until the really acute shortages became apparent in the winter of 1960–1961, however, the Party generally continued to insist that the masses of poor and lower middle peasants were better off, that they received more food and clothing than they had in the past, and that in the general leveling off it was proper that the rich should suffer by their down-grading. Vast quantities of grain were diverted to industrial purposes, it was said, and the expansion of urban and mining populations by more than 20 millions in three years had caused increased consumption in the cities; in fact, because everyone was working harder there was a natural and inevitable demand for more food.

The peasants are not well off, but their lot is in many cases better than it has been in the immediate past, or even for hundreds of years. Chinese peasants have always worked hard. They have always been desperately poor. And very frequently they have died of hunger. As early as 400 B.C., a Minister in the State of Wei described farmers as living in a perpetual state of poverty. That was their accustomed lot until 1949. Droughts and floods brought repeated famines. Infanticide was an economic necessity. The only periods when the peasants were relatively better off were periods of regimentation.

Mao's success in consolidating his rural holds stems as much from the Chinese tradition, therefore, as it does from Marx. The Chinese people are heir to a great civilization; they are also heir to a tradition of authoritarian controls. Mr. Nehru calls it the "inner self-discipline" of the Chinese people; but it is, in fact, a discipline imposed by a system which, whether Confucian or Communist in its authority, demands order.

For all the repressions, restrictions and tyrannies that their rule implies, however, the Communists, in addition to order, brought the first real promise of better things to come. They roused the passions of the people against the United States by the Germ Warfare campaign and by subsequent campaigns designed to picture the Chinese people as besieged by the American "imperialists"; but they also stamped out plague, cholera and smallpox. Chinese cities were filthy; now they are almost antiseptically clean. The country swarmed with flies; now there are no flies. Rats ran rampant in the refuse that filled every back street; rats and refuse have gone. Chinese who became sick, especially those living in the countryside, either cured themselves with herbal medicines, or died; now there are more than a million doctors, nurses, midwives and pharmacists, and the communes stock the latest drugs. China was corrupt; some corruption still exists, especially among lesser officials, but it is being ruthlessly stamped out. Cities such as Shanghai swarmed with prostitutes; they have all disappeared. Most children automatically go to school. The illiterate are learning to read and write. Infanticide, and the circumstances which made the practice necessary, have both been eliminated. The idle work. Gambling is a forgotten evil. Many women enjoy their emancipation and probably work no harder now than they worked in the past. The rich have disappeared. The new level of society is desperately low for those who once enjoyed a higher standard of living, but the leveling off process, at least until the 1960-61 famine, dragged up millions to a higher level than their parents knew before them.

However much we Westerners with our libertarian instincts may deplore this new China, however much it may seem to reek of the concentration camp, we must remember that it is evaluated against very different standards by the people most concerned—the Chinese. Rectification campaigns, campaigns against counterrevolutionaries and all the other campaigns designed to secure obedience and control are not nonstop sessions. They are applied judiciously and periodically. Peking "yells" at the people every now and then to administer Mao's "shock." In between, though they work bitterly hard, most people accept their lot stoically and sometimes even with cheerfulness.

Mao Tse-tung is a great leader; he is also a shrewd psychologist. The people do not suddenly start such schemes as the communes by themselves, as the regime attempts to imply. But by constant contact with the people Mao finds his ideas, which are presented to the masses as their very own. Land reform, the peasants were told, was their idea. They also "spontaneously" decided to root out counter-revolutionaries and to proceed through collectivization to the communes. All this is fraudulent. But we delude ourselves if we think it is entirely unsuccessful and imagine that most Chinese people are waiting to be "liberated." The Communists' blunders are apparent enough to the Chinese people, but their capacity for progress is also apparent.

When the Communists took over in 1949 after the years of war with Japan and the civil war they inherited a legacy of agricultural neglect. Rice production was less than 50 million tons a year, wheat less than 14 million. Total production, including potatoes, soya beans and other "grains" was 113,181,000 tons from a cultivated area of 244,702,000 acres. In 1957, on the eve of the Second Five Year Plan and the "great leap forward," another 20 million acres had been brought under cultivation and production increased, so Peking claimed, to 192,820,000 tons. The Second Five Year Plan envisaged a final output at the end of 1962 of 270 million tons. By the end of 1958, however, enthusiastic and unskilled Party officials reported from the communes that their quotas had been overfulfilled. Grain production was officially stated to have totaled 375 million tons, and in a fever of excitement the goal for 1960 was increased to 525 million tons. The 1958 figures were grossly exaggerated. Undoubtedly even the final figure of 270 million tons and the 1959 figure of 275 million tons were also exaggerated, since such production would indicate the feasibility both of substantially higher rations than the Chinese have received in recent years and larger exports than have ever been disclosed.

When the Party talked of the Yellow River almost drying up, however, of the typhoons and locusts, the peasants knew it did not exaggerate. These were calamities which they had seen with their own eyes. Nor can they have failed to be conscious of the tremendous effort that the Party began to make in agriculture in the closing months of 1960 and early in 1961.

What are its prospects of success? On this point experts differ greatly. Lord Boyd Orr, former head of the Food and Agriculture Organization of the United Nations and one of Britain's leading specialists in agriculture, says there are nearly 200 million acres of virgin land which can be brought to the plow. W. W. Rostow, in *The Prospects for Communist China* (The Technology Press of M.I.T., 1954) put the figure at 20 to 30 million acres in northern Manchuria, 25 million acres occupied by family shrines and graves, another 10 million acres for wheat growing in northern and central China, and an unspecified area which is suitable for the cultivation of cotton.

Boyd Orr, on the basis of his figures and his enthusiasm for the achievements he saw in agriculture during his visit to China during 1958, the first year of the "great leap forward," came to the conclusion that China's prospects for agriculture were favorable: but Rostow, writing in 1954, doubted that farm output could be raised by more than 10 per cent within five years and 20 per cent in a decade.

China's capacity to use mass labor to bring new areas under cultivation has been noted. But because of the demands of industry and the need for new roads and railways, the net increase in cultivated lands has been slight. Excluding the 25 million acres devoted to graveyards and family shrines, most of which are now being cultivated or used for factories or commune buildings, production from new areas is unlikely to be constant and will prove even more subject to natural disaster than the traditional agricultural areas. Even so, Rostow's estimates of arable land appear too low. At the same time, it is difficult to credit the accuracy of Boyd Orr's estimates, or the sweeping claims of Chou En-lai that 500 million acres can eventually be cultivated. Even the most optimistic estimate indicates that an absolute maximum of 350 million acres are likely to be cultivated in the next twenty years.

Despite strenuous efforts to increase the output of chemical fertilizer, its use is still meager and mobile teams including farmers, factory workers, school children, housewives, and even regular army units have been employed on mass manure collection drives. Nothing that can be used for manure is neglected. "Manure can be found everywhere and fertilizer can be made from almost everything," the *People's Daily* said. In this, the human body still has a considerable part to play—and not merely in the production of excrement. One young refugee in Hong Kong described how he had been assigned to work in a detail where fresh corpses were put in shallow trenches for a few days. The worms from the decaying bodies were used to feed chickens and the decomposing flesh stimulated plant growth.

In 1949 there was no factory in China for producing synthetic ammonia fertilizer, and the yearly output of nitrogenous fertilizer was only 26,000 tons. By 1957, the production of synthetic ammonia totaled 150,000 tons and that of sulphate of ammonia 630,000 tons. A slight increase raised the combined output to 811,000 tons in 1958, and a huge leap forward for 1962 of from 5 million to 7 million tons is contemplated. Another leap in the Third Five Year Plan is expected to raise the output to 15 million tons. Even if these figures are reached, however, China's supply of fertilizers will be less than half the amount necessary to achieve maximum results from farm lands already under cultivation.

There are tremendous plans on the drawing boards for dam construction and water conservation, bigger by far than anything yet attempted. The drawback is cost. Professor Ma Yin-chu, formerly President of the Peking University and one of China's leading economists, lost his position at the university for expressing qualified doubts about the wisdom of current Party policy, especially in relation to agriculture and population. He pointed out that works at the Three Gorges in Szechwan Province, as a solution to the Yangtze floods and the harnessing of the waters for electric power, would cost 60,000 million yuan, or more than double the annual budget, and inundate some 250,000 acres of cultivated land. Cost, he believed, was also a major factor against the rapid production of chemical fertilizers.

If China's population were relatively static, however, the resolution —and flexibility—of the Party, improved transport (and therefore better distribution), more fertilizers and more common sense would seem to indicate more food for the peasants and a general rise in living standards. Unfortunately for China, and for the rest of the world, China's population is far from static. The end of the civil war and vast improvements in medical welfare brought a baby boom comparable with that which Japan experienced between 1945 and 1950. In the first eight years of Communist rule 1.95 million births were registered in Shanghai against only 400,000 deaths. In 1949 only 30,000 babies were born in Tientsin; in 1958 the figure was more than 100,000. Despite the land reclamation projects, population growth and industrialization actually cut the amount of cultivated land per head of population from .462 acres in 1953 to .429 acres in 1958. In the following year sown acres decreased and, while the communes concentrated unsuccessfully on productivity, and futile backyard steel production, population shot up again.

Since labor means productivity, and people mean victory in war, it is a primary heresy in China now to believe that large numbers of people are a liability. "China's population is a very good thing," Mao said on the eve of victory in the civil war. "Even if it is increased by a number of times, we still have the ways and means to solve it. This is production. The ridiculous theory that the increase in subsistence cannot catch up with the growth of population propounded by Western bourgeois economists such as Malthus has not only been frustrated by the Marxist theory but has been entirely crushed by the events in the postrevolution Soviet Union and China's liberated areas."

In 1957 he had a temporary change of mind. Reporting that births had risen by millions a year, Mao said this was "a sign of great progress made in medical services and the general rise in living standards, especially in the countryside and of the faith people have in the future. But this figure must be of great concern to us all," he added. "I will quote two other figures. The increase in grain harvest for the last two years has been 10 million tons a year. This is barely sufficient to cover the needs of our growing population. The second figure concerns the problem of education. It is estimated that at present 40 per cent of our youth have not been placed in primary schools. Steps must, therefore, be taken to keep our population for a long time at a stable level, say of 600 million. A wide campaign of explanation and proper help must be undertaken to achieve this aim."

With this official seal, birth control practices were widely recommended, not because of any need to restrict the level of population, it was said, but because too frequent births affected the output of work and the health of women workers. In the early stages of the campaign, women were encouraged to eat tadpoles and to use pastes made from flour as a means of preventing pregnancy. Neither proved efficacious. Efforts were made to persuade young people that their duty to the State demanded that they should not let early marriage interfere with duties to society. "The best method is to organize them [youth] for cultural and recreational activities and widely promote physical culture among them," said Shanghai's *Wen Hui-pao*. "In the age bracket of eighteen to twenty-five, which is the best time for study and work, marriage will affect both. However, at such ages, it is easiest to have babies." As the newspaper noted, however, it was common to find women in their early twenties with two or three children—and this, in turn, led to ill-health and decreased efficiency.

Soviet population figures and methods were analyzed and some comfort was found in the decrease in the birth rate there from 3.63 per cent in 1920 to 1.94 in 1955. The fulminations against Professor Ma Yin-chu for stating that the population was growing too fast and capital accumulation too slowly, however, and the cold-blooded official belief that China could lose 300 million people in a nuclear war and still win, marked the end of any serious effort to introduce a crash birth control program. Man was now said to be the most precious thing on earth: miracles could be wrought in China as long as there were enough men. "Facts prove this is so," said an article in *New Construction* in May, 1960. "Our revolution has changed everything. Today we have no problems of unemployment but feel no surplus of manpower. On the contrary, we feel a shortage of manpower."

This is true. China does not have enough hands for all the tasks it has set itself. That many of these tasks, such as the production of steel by homemade blast furnaces, should never have been set is immaterial. Even if these millions of man-hours had not been diverted from agricultural production and wasted, however, China would not have been able adequately to feed itself and at the same time to use agriculture as a means for capital accumulation in preparing for its economic take-off. Nor is it conceivable that even the new emphasis on the importance of agriculture will be the means of providing sufficient food from indigenous sources for the tens and hundreds of millions who will take their place in Chinese society in the next twenty-five years.

Official Chinese estimates of the annual rate of increase vary from

2 per cent to 3 per cent a year, with 2.2 per cent often stated as a more precise figure. Assuming that 2 per cent is correct—it was cited by Chou En-lai in an interview toward the end of 1960—and that the population in 1961 is 670 million, the following table indicates the population pattern that China may expect to follow:

1962—683 million		1970—	800 million
1963—697 "		1975—	884 "
1964—711 "		1980—	976 "
1965—725 "		1985—1,078 "
1966—739 "		1990—1,189 "
1967—755 "		1995—1,312 "
1968—770 "		2000—1,449 "
1969—785 "			

If the rate of growth is 2.2 per cent, the population by the end of the century will be substantially more than 1,500 million and there will be many more Chinese in the world in the year 2000 than there were people in 1960. Whatever the current rate, the probability is that improving health services will cause it to increase before the decline that customarily occurs in industrial societies sets in. A population of a billion by 1980 is therefore not only possible but probable.

Peking does not intend to allow this to stand in the way of its plans. Nor does it intend to allow peasant tensions—and what it regards as the potentially hostile strength of about 10 per cent of the population, or 67 million—to explode in counterrevolution. At the time of the establishment of the communes in the summer of 1958, Mao Tse-tung, always conscious of the need both for military discipline and military control, issued his call for the formation of militia divisions on such a scale that everyone would become a soldier. By 1959 there were references to militia divisions totaling between 20 million and 60 million men: the following year militia representatives spoke in terms of "we hundreds of millions of militiamen," and the speeches of the Party leaders indicated that China was now fully mobilized.

"Red and expert" youths of both sexes got their guns at ceremonial rallies. The *People's Daily* described the scene in one village where "more than four hundred women warriors were specially well dressed, most of them wearing jackets of red cloth with pink flowers, or white cloth with blue flowers. They did not bother with the oil stains from their rifles. Cheng Hsiu-ling, who received a rifle, felt that her pigtail was interfering with her movements, and she had it cut off right away."

The day after the guns were issued, the correspondent of the *People's Daily* found the militia carrying out military drill in a "spirited manner" early in the morning before going to work, and in the evening after returning from the fields. During production hours, the rifles were stacked on the ground "and some of the men even shouted drill commands, 'one, two, three, four' as they worked."

Coming home in the evening, the militia carried their hoes over their shoulders and their rifles in their hands. One militia battalion of a thousand proceeded on the double to the production front and in two and a half hours plowed sixty-eight acres of land, weeded another fifty-six acres and applied fertilizer to sixteen acres.

Like so many of Mao's other plans, the decision to turn every Chinese into a soldier had many purposes. The basic rule was that the militia division was a military organization, labor organization, educational organization and athletic organization combined in one. The militia élite included a hard core of regulars. These were all trusted men and women qualified as "red and expert." They were charged with giving the general masses some basic military training, inculcating the military spirit and the coupling of this with the propaganda about the ever-present threat of American imperialism. They were also the shock troops of the great battle of the "general line," the men with the trumpets and bugles and flags.

General Fu Chiu-tao, Director of the Conscription Department of the People's Liberation Army and a member of the National Defense Council, speaking at the National People's Congress in April, 1960, said that the building of the people's militia divisions was an important element of Mao's military thinking. The militia were a "powerful assistant and mighty reserve for the People's Liberation Army." They were also a powerful instrument for defending the revolutionary regime and consolidating the people's democratic dictatorship. The militia were the "ears and limbs and most reliable reserve of the armed forces." In the era of peaceful construction the most basic activity of the militia was production, for militiamen were both civilians and soldiers. For that reason, militia work should be carried out centering around production. In order to raise labor productivity, it was necessary to have better work organization, discipline and order.

The militia are, in fact, the custodians of the regime at the lowest levels of both agriculture and industry. Their tasks are to increase production, to challenge and inspire the advanced workers while assisting backward ones, to serve as shock workers themselves, to pep up the campaign against "American imperialist warmongers," and to suppress counterrevolution. In any less well regimented country they would in themselves constitute a threat to the regime. In China, however, they are at once an insurance that the peasant does not neglect his duties, guards for the granaries and an effective barrier in the way of counterrevolution.

Of all the possibilities in store for China, prospects of a large-scale successful revolt by the peasants are the most remote. The controls are adequate and effective and, whether we like it or not, the people of China are inevitably becoming more closely identified with the regime. This has been brought about largely by "brain-washing." On the one hand, many Westerners deplore this as evil and hateful and cite in example the cases in which Allied prisoners-of-war in Korea denounced their countries and swore they had participated in germ warfare. On the other hand, they express the gravest doubts whether the Chinese people could have been persuaded to give their allegiance to a regime which fails to recognize the basic dignity of man and has turned the country and its people into a maddened ant heap. This is curious logic. If adult, educated Westerners, some of them of quite senior military rank, could be persuaded in a matter of weeks, or months, to believe that black is white and to put their signatures to the most spurious, and damaging, of confessions, why on earth should anyone doubt that illiterate peasants or children reared in a society in which they have no external contacts and no means of escaping from years of indoctrination, should not be just as sensitive to "brain-washing"?

Political indoctrination in China is not merely a matter of political discussions, of public criticism and the confession of wrong acts and thoughts, or rectification, or Hate America campaigns. The entire culture is now part of it, the wall newspapers, the living newspapers, the drama and opera groups, the choirs and folk orchestras, the poetry

reading associations, the clubs devoted to ballad singing, all the art
and music and literature of the day. Painting is political—with a
commune, or a smokestack habitually tucked away in the corner of
a landscape, or picture postcard stuff of Chairman Mao talking to
happy and smiling peasants, or happy smiling Africans or Latin
Americans. All writing is political. All music and drama is political.

Culture is the glorification of the communes because of the rich
life they will one day make possible, and of industry because of the
goods people will ultimately receive in return for work and sacrifice.
It is all a delusion; but it is the only reality many people in China
know. Because of it, and because of the controls which now watch
every garden patch for every poisonous weed of independent thought
that may foolishly appear among the good Communist blooms, we
may rest assured that Chiang Kai-shek will wither on his Taiwan vine
long before mainland China falls to internal revolt.

Chapter VIII   🬀🬀🬀🬀🬀🬀🬀🬀🬀🬀

THE DRAGON CLOSE BEHIND US

PEKING attributed China's failure to achieve an economic break-through in the nineteenth century and before the advent of the Communist regime to the nature of traditional Chinese society, Western imperialism and the absence of a Communist vanguard to provide adequate leadership. There is some validity in the first two beliefs. China was a peasant society in which 90 per cent of the population received little or no education and exercised even less influence on government, which was the exclusive responsibility of the scholar-gentry class. The family system, with its lack of primogeniture and its emphasis on costly ceremonial, such as marriage feasts, denied the opportunity for capital accumulation. Bureaucracy disdained anything smacking of industry and commerce.

While traditional Chinese society had a highly inhibiting effect on industrial growth, the West in search of trade undoubtedly exploited China for its own ends. Some significant industrial development occurred in the treaty ports, and the Communists inherited the major industrial complex created by the Japanese in Manchuria during the first part of the twentieth century; but, generally, resistance to Western and Japanese penetration delayed development in the hinterland. Even the railway and road systems, such as they were, failed to stimulate economic growth beyond Manchuria and the treaty ports.

The situation now is that the Peking regime by the destruction of the old order and the elimination of imperialism has ridded the system of its in-built resistance to industrial growth and has substituted a system which demands it at a rate never before attempted in any country, and this despite the fact that China began its industrial advance facing even heavier handicaps than most underdeveloped countries face. Its estimated per capita income of $27 in 1949 was one of the lowest in the world. It was struggling, as it had always struggled, to grow enough food for its own needs. And it had resolutely set itself against accepting economic aid from the one country with the capacity at that time to provide it in meaningful quantities —the United States.

There were some favorable factors, however. Few countries in the world were so well endowed with mineral resources. Wu Ching-chao, Chief Secretary of Chiang Kai-shek's War Production Board (now in Communist China), discussing China's known resources in 1946, said that reserves of iron ore were sufficient for the next fifty, or even a hundred years. Its known reserves of coal were among the largest in the world. Among the metals needed in the manufacture of ferroalloys, there was sufficient manganese, plenty of tungsten and a little nickel and cobalt. Copper, lead and zinc were insufficient but there was more than enough antimony and tin. For a regime bent on rapid, heavy industrialization, such resources were sufficient to make a substantial beginning, always provided, of course, that the investment capital and the managerial and technical skills were available for future exploitation and development.

The resources picture today is even more favorable. Since 1949 teams of geologists have scoured China. Their findings are that China has 10,000 million tons of reserves of iron ore, that coal reserves are at least 100,000 million tons (though much of it is low-grade) and that there are ample copper, aluminium, tungsten, tin, molybdenum, manganese, lead, zinc and mercury. A significant weakness is oil. In 1956, the Chinese planned production of crude oil in 1962 to be between 5 and 6 million tons.

However, the minister in charge of the petroleum industry announced shortly afterward that proved reserves of petroleum in China were only 30 million tons, with an anticipated additional 100 million tons.

Industrialization does not depend on the indigenous production of oil, however. Of greater importance is the fact that in iron ore reserves China is almost as well off as the Soviet Union; in reserves of coal, it is even better off, even after making allowances for indifferent quality. Its hydroelectric potential is huge, and despite Professor Ma Yin-chu's doubts, the Three Gorges scheme on the Yangtze, which is being built with Soviet aid and technical assistance, will ultimately produce, though not for twenty years, as much power from this one scheme as is produced in all of Great Britain today.

Agriculture, despite its grave problems, is unlikely to stand in the way of continuing industrial growth, even though the rate of growth must be slowed. For China now has minerals and manufactured goods for export. In 1958, for instance, its exports included large quantities of cement, 1,200,000 tons of which went to the Soviet Union and 150,000 tons to Hong Kong out of a total production of 9,300,000 tons. China is also supplying Poland with mercury, iron, tungsten and molybdenum ore and manufactured goods. It is sending electronic tubes and radio parts and tungsten ores to Hungary. North Korea receives coal and structural steel. These items do not entirely replace China's agricultural exports, but they do mean that an important supplementary source of capital accumulation is available to meet the needs of industrialization, and this source will naturally increase in size and importance as industrialization continues.

Even more important in the Communist view are the reserves of manpower. China possesses the world's largest unskilled labor force. It is now well on its way toward the creation of a corps of highly skilled workers. By the beginning of the Second Five Year Plan it had 1,740,000 industrial and civil engineers and technicians with university or technical college training. Primary school students had increased in number from 23,680,000 in 1949 to 86 million, middle school students from 1,490,000 to 8,520,000, technical school students from 380,000 to 1,470,000 and college and university undergraduates from 150,000 to 660,000. By the end of 1958 there were more than 840 special research organizations in the natural sciences and technology and more than 32,000 research workers. As in so many other fields, China sacrificed quality for quantity; but a beginning, a tremendous beginning, had been made.

The Harbin University of Technology is fairly typical of the new technological universities. Staffed by more than 800 faculty members, almost all of whom received Russian training either in China or in the Soviet Union, and are members of either the Communist Party or the Young Communist League, it provides technological education for the basic industries and the advanced sciences. It also operates a branch school to serve heavy industry; advanced technological cadres are trained there. From this and other technological institutes throughout China and from Soviet universities, a steadily increasing flow of recruits is passing into industry each year. Manchuria remains a great industrial complex, but considerable industrial bases have appeared now in Inner Mongolia, Sinkiang, Chinghai, Kansu and other previously undeveloped areas in the Asian heartland beyond range of intermediate range missiles and Polaris submarines.

Transport remains a continuing headache. The Communists inherited a railroad system that was only 17,000 miles in length, mostly concentrated in Manchuria, complicated by different gauges and types of rolling stock and fallen into such disrepair that fewer than 12,000 miles were usable. The state of the road system was no better. Less than 50,000 miles of highway suitable for mechanized transport existed. Another 40,000 miles had fallen into disrepair; and the mountains and plateaux in the western part of the country with their deposits of minerals had no roads at all. Rail and road repairs proceeded swiftly, as did the construction of new highways and rail links. But strategic considerations—new railway links with the Soviet Union and new highways into Tibet and along the frontiers of India, Nepal, Bhutan and Sikkim—for a time appeared to loom too largely in the Communist plans. The pointless production of millions of tons of useless steel by backyard commune furnaces during 1958 caused a crippling bottleneck at the end of the year, when an estimated 40 million tons of freight were held up.

Shock brigades diverted to rail and road construction in 1959 added 3,500 miles to the rail system: in 1960 there was an even bigger leap with a further 5,500-mile expansion. These extensions included the development of the great trunk lines into Sinkiang and the linking up of Szechwan, Yunnan, Kweichow, Kwangsi, Hunan and Kwantung.

During the first part of 1960, other shock brigades built more than 80,000 miles of highways, or more than the total in existence before 1949 and built during the First Five Year Plan. That this effort has not yet succeeded in keeping pace with the flow of materials and manufactured goods is an outstanding example of the crisis of progress, and of the rate of progress. One of the major difficulties is the lack of adequate rail links between the mines and the iron and steel plants and other factories. In a typical effort to overcome the shortage at Anhwei in 1960 Communist officials improvised a "vigorous innovation of folk transport facilities" in which 900,000 wheelbarrows, flat-bottomed carts drawn by men, women and children, horse-drawn carts and other types of animal-drawn carts were pressed into use along with some 5,000 motorized sailboats.

Whether China's growth in gross national production has averaged the 9 per cent that Peking claims, or is 6 per cent, which some Western economists believe, is less important than the fact that growth has been considerable and promises to be considerable in future. That China can produce the goods has been demonstrated in its exports to Cuba and Guinea, in the displays at the Canton commodity exhibitions, where heavy industrial equipment, automobiles, tip-trucks, buses, motorcycles, motor-tricycles and a wide range of consumer goods, reflect its expanding industrial development.

Due to the demands of the Communist bloc, and the political need to expand its influence elsewhere, China has not yet fulfilled its threat to dominate Southeast Asian trade. But twice it has entered the market to cause something approaching panic on the part of its competitors. In 1953 Japan supplied Hong Kong with 32 per cent of the colony's imports of unbleached cotton, while imports from China were negligible. By 1957, China had captured 84 per cent of the trade and Japan's contribution had fallen to 2 per cent. On the Indian market, China, in 1958, outsold Japan in industrial machinery; in Indonesia, during the same year, China's sales of tool steel, cotton fabrics and caustic soda doubled those of Japan, which previously had monopolized the trade.

China's diversity of exports troubled its competitors more than its volume. Initially it competed only in textiles and traditional Chinese exports such as rice, soya beans, oils, fats and mineral products. By 1958 it offered an impressive array of capital and manufactured goods that provided direct competition not only with Japan and India, the United States and Western Europe but with the Soviet Union and the Eastern European satellites, also. Japan sold metal manufactures on the great Southeast Asian entrepôt in Singapore at an average price of $111 a ton: China's price was $92. Bicycles, watches, clocks, sewing machines, textiles, canned foods and a vast array of other goods undercut every other "lowest price" on the market. The view of New Delhi's *Eastern Economist* was that "China has made such great strides in building up her economy that she is in a position not only to penetrate every Asian market, but also to oust from these markets the long-established and traditional suppliers, Western as well as Eastern, including even powerful countries like Japan, let alone this country." Japan shared this view, and a Japanese trade delegation to Southeast Asia went home to report that not only the pattern of trade but the very structure of Japan's industry would have to be changed to meet the competition from China.

The following table sets out Chinese production claims. All these figures include varying degrees of inflation produced by the political pressures of the "great leap forward," inexperienced officials and the inclusion of low-quality production in the national totals. These exaggerations are particularly important in the agricultural sector and also significant in the production figures for local small-scale plants. On the other hand, production figures for large-scale modern plants are probably only slightly exaggerated; and in spite of these difficulties the official Chinese figures remain, in most cases, the best indicators of production currently available.

China's claim to have increased coal production from 31 million tons in 1949 to 520 million in 1960—leaving both Britain and the U.S. far behind—is probably reasonably accurate since the open-cut fields are easily exploited by unskilled labor. Yet throughout 1960 there was a shortage of coal. The *People's Daily* called for vigorous effort to develop mining operations. Coal was the raw material for iron smelting and more iron would be produced if more coal were produced. The article called for self-sacrifice for the sake of meeting

PRODUCTION FIGURES AND TARGETS

	1959 Target	1959 Production	1959% Increase over 1958 Production	1960 Target	1960 Target % Increase over 1959 Production
HEAVY INDUSTRY					
Steel	12,000,000 tons	13,350,000 tons	66.87%	18,400,000 tons	38%
Pig Iron	13,690,000 tons	20,522,000 tons (deduced)	49.9% (approx.)	27,500,000 tons	34%
Electricity	40,000 mill. kwh	41,500 million kwh	50.9%	55,500–58,000 mill. kwh	34%–40%
Coal	335,000,000 tons	347,800,000 tons	17.7%	425,000,000 tons	22%
Oil	Not known	3,700,000 tons	63.7%	5,200,000 tons	40%
Chemical Fertilizer	1,300,000 tons	1,333,000 tons	64.3%	2,800,000 tons [a]	110%
Power Generating Equipment	2,800,000 kw	2,150,000 kw	168.7%	3,300,000 kw	53.9%
Machine Tools	70,000 units	70,000 units	40%	90,000 units	28.5%
Locomotives	555 units	533 (deduced)		800	50%
Railway Wagons	27,000 units	20,100 (deduced)		33,000	50%
Tractors	3,000 units [b]	5,597 (deduced)		No absolute figure	150% [c]
Timber	Not given	41,200,000 cu. meters	17.7%	47,000,000 cu. meters	14%
Cement	12,500,000 tons	12,270,000 tons	32%	16,000,000 tons	30%
Sulfuric Acid	Not given	1,050,000 tons		1,500,000 tons	42%
Spinning Equipment	2,500,000 spindles	1,304,000 spdls (deduced)	30.4% (approx.)	2,400,000 spindles	84%
LIGHT INDUSTRY					
Cotton Yarn	8,500,000 bales	8,250,000 bales	35.2%	9,000,000 bales	9%
Cotton Cloth	7,200 mill. meters	7,500 million meters	31.6%	7,600 million meters	1.3%
Salt	13,000,000 tons	11,040,000 tons	6.15%	14,000,000 tons	27%
Edible Vegetable Oil	1,800,000 tons	1,460,000 tons	12%	1,700,000 tons	16%
Sugar	1,500,000 tons	1,130,000 tons	25.5%	1,300,000 tons	15.4%
Paper	2,200,000 tons	1,700,000 tons	4.3%	2,830,000 tons	66.4%
AGRICULTURE					
Food Grains	275,000,000 tons	270,050,000 tons	8.02%	No absolute figure	About 10%
Cotton	2,300,000 tons	2,410,000 tons	14.7%	No absolute figure	About 10%
Pigs		180,000,000		No absolute figure	About 35%

[a] This figure is described as the amount to be allotted from heavy industry. [b] 1 unit = 15 h.p.
[c] The figure of 22,000 tractors to be allotted to agriculture was also given.

the over-all needs. Commune dining halls were ordered to cut consumption of coal, and again the Chinese man-in-the-field and factory found himself obliged to make sacrifices. Cadres, it appeared, had failed to take into consideration the fuel consumption of the newly established commune dining halls and the consequent drain on coal supplies. They had also failed to plan the ratio between increases in the number of iron and steel plants, together with increased output, and the supplies of coke and coal available. If this reflected haphazard planning and much inefficiency, the poor quality of China's coking coal and the low ratio of pig iron production to coal consumption, it also indicated that the blast furnaces were extremely active and that steel production must have risen sharply, perhaps to the figure of 18,450,000 tons claimed by Vice-Premier Po I-po.

Road transport strains caused by the constantly increasing demands of industry also produced an acute shortage of oil. Economies included the changing of routes and motive power of public transport in the cities and the use of battery-charged tricycles for light transport. Technicians were set to work to produce the petroleum equivalent of the backyard furnace. A Cantonese institute extracted a motor spirit from "horse-tail pine needles," and in Hupeh a gas derived from burned rice husks was claimed to be 190 times cheaper than gasoline.

The picture that emerges from this sort of industrial development is certainly one of contradictions, some of them quite deliberate contradictions—"walking on two legs," as the Chinese call it—of large modern plants and primitive cottage industries, of the over-laden donkey laboring along a modern highway, of the carrying pole lingering in the atomic age, of spectacular production figures but widespread inefficiency, of high output but heavy fatigue in men and machinery, of quantity, as usual, at the expense of quality.

There is need for greater, ever greater, quotas; and since more steel demands more iron and more coal, and more iron and coal demands more railway lines, more locomotives and freight cars, more roads and more trucks, there is also a demand for more workers and more work. But too much work produces too much fatigue, and too much fatigue means that there must be less work and more rest if production is to be maintained.

Of all this the Chinese Communist leaders are aware. But having started the "great leap forward" in 1958, they are determined not to abandon their attempt to achieve in a few years what other nations have done in a hundred years or more. Where other industrial countries, including the Soviet Union, have grown industrially through three clearly distinct phases, China is not only leaping from the pre-Christian era plow to atomic reactors but tackling all the intermediate stages at the same time. It is a program that holds the promise of blood, sweat and tears for generations to come. But it also promises a continuing high rate of growth.

China, with few exceptions, has the industrial raw materials. By the total regimentation of the country's wealth, labor and time it is finding the means of capital accumulation. By U.S. standards its investment in capital construction of $13 billion in 1960 is not high; in China it is revolutionary. In ever increasing quantities it is getting the technicians. And thanks to aid from the Soviet Union and, to a lesser extent, the other satellite countries, it has the nucleus of heavy industry needed for an economic take-off. Already it has revealed surprising economic resilience and strength. The official admission at the end of 1960 that crops had failed disastrously during the year, that natural disasters had not been worse for a century, that Party officials in agriculture had proved slack, inefficient and sometimes even treacherous, and that several tens of millions of Chinese people had still not given up hope of throwing out the regime, led to some hasty foreign conclusions that the Communist regime itself was on the brink of disaster. The communes had failed, it was said, and would be abandoned. Tens of millions of Chinese would starve to death, since China could neither fed itself nor pay for food imports.

Peking's immediate task was to find sufficient food to tide the country over the winter and spring. Crop failures in the Soviet Union precluded assistance from that quarter. China therefore turned to Australia and Canada in search of wheat and barley and to Burma for rice. Australia hesitated—not because of any doubts about the propriety of helping the Communists out of their difficulties but because it wanted to be assured it would see the color of its money. China replied to its query with cash down for approximately a million tons of wheat costing $60 million. In all, China within a few weeks found sufficient ready money to buy for emergency delivery $200 million worth of grain and to begin negotiations for much larger deliveries. It also honored its contract with Cuba to pay four cents a pound, a cent above the world market price, for a million tons of sugar to be delivered in 1961; and in addition it embarked on a new economic aid program in which, during three extremely critical famine months, Cuba, Cambodia, North Vietnam, Burma and Albania were promised more than $500 million in gifts and long-term, low-interest loans. These were designed to expand bilateral trade to China's own advantage: and, as usual, they were made with political objectives in mind. They were, nevertheless, an effective rebuttal to those who had predicted disaster.

Despite China's agricultural difficulties and the effect they are having on industrialization, there still seems little reason to doubt Peking's boast that it will overtake Britain's output in basic industries by about 1967. The London *Times* said on December 27, 1957: "We had better watch out. There may be a dragon close behind us." There is. But a more dangerous and frustrated dragon the world has never known. Peking believes that Britain's output of steel will be about 31 million to 32 million tons by 1967, and that China's then will be about 40 million tons. Based on current and planned production, this ambition seems modest. In terms of steel production, the badge of industrial power as the Communists, and many others in the underdeveloped world, believe, the "lever to set everything in motion," China will rank third to the United States and the Soviet Union among the major industrial Powers. By 1967, however, China's population will have increased to approximately 755 million. Britain will produce substantially more than half a ton of steel per head of population: China about a hundred pounds.

If steel is truly the lever by which all other progress is set in motion and its production may legitimately be used as a gauge for measuring development, China with 755 million people would need to produce nearly 500 million tons a year to match Britain's per capita production. Similar ratios apply to power, cement and all other basic industrial products. Thus the world will soon be faced in China with a nation that will rank with the industrial giants in terms of gross output while its people remain desperately poor.

In 1959, in his attack on the Party policy of encouraging a large population, Professor Ma Yin-chu said: "You want more population and the population increased to 900 million or 1,000 million. Are you not dragging our feet that enter the gate to Communist society?" Ma made the point that the area of the national territory of the Soviet Union was two or three times that of China and that the Chinese population was more than three times that of the Soviet Union. If the Soviet population was to be brought to par with the Chinese population it ought to number more than 1,500 million instead of 208 million. Yet the Soviet experts had already begun to discuss how to make arrangements for the population after the introduction of automation.

This is a problem that Peking declines to face within Professor Ma's terms of reference. The great wheel of industrial revolution turns but the man on the treadmill never advances. Higher, ever higher will the industrial ouput rise: but for the 800 million, 900 million, 1,000 million Chinese men, women and children of the next generation even bare sufficiency in food, clothing and consumer goods, the rewards for these years of work, is not in sight.

For China there is only one possible escape from this dilemma and the tensions that the contradictions in industrial output and continuing poverty and population pressures will inevitably produce within its society: it must push on as rapidly as possible with the creation of its own internal power while channeling the emotions of its people against the external antagonisms, thereby forcing a breakthrough at the weakest point. The harder the internal struggle, the more bitter will the campaign to isolate and destroy the United States become.

There are extremely cogent reasons, therefore, why the apparent desire of Khrushchev for a *détente* in 1959 and the "Camp David spirit" resulted in the vigorous Chinese reaction discussed earlier. It was all very well for Khrushchev to talk in terms of disarmament and of Socialism burying the capitalist system by means of peaceful competition: after all, the Soviet revolution had long achieved its economic and technological take-off. The Russian revolution had reached maturity and the stage where some relaxation was permissible, even desirable. But to suggest that President Eisenhower was a man of peace, or that the imperialists had changed their ways—or could change their ways—was not only bad ideology but contained the seeds of disaster for China.

That Khrushchev could be unwise enough to suggest that it was possible for the Communist world to live without struggle with the predatory monster of imperialism was contrary to the fundamental teachings of Lenin. Here was China's essential external enemy about to be whitewashed and declared a champion of peace, when every Chinese child old enough to listen to the radio, or to sit in a schoolroom, had heard for years that it was the archprotagonist of aggressive war.

Could Chinese Communism continue to spur the people to even greater endeavor without this enemy, or a substitute for it? Could China, at this stage, contemplate total disarmament? State power rested on the strength of the army. Without the army there would be no power and without power there would be no State. With every Russian step forward, China therefore began to take a step back. Cautiously at first and with constant reference to the apostles of its creed, Peking opposed the Russian policy of *détente*. The ninetieth anniversary of Lenin's birth in April, 1960, was made the occasion for numerous statements and articles by leading Party ideologists. The basic theme was that while imperialism continued to exist war was inevitable, whether in the form of local wars, or an international or world war. Imperialism was doomed, as seen from the decline of the colonial system; but in its last, fanatical hours it would continue to be dangerous.

Mao Tse-tung had correctly assessed the world situation as early as 1947 when he pointed out that "the strength of the anti-imperialist camp has surpassed that of the imperialist camp." Though the United States had enlisted the support of the "political scum" of various countries, it had placed itself in a state of opposition to the whole world and focused on itself the hatred which all the world's people have for the reactionaries and made itself the public enemy of the world's people. This, in its turn, was causing the American reactionaries to sink steadily into the plight of isolation. The Western world was beset with a deepening economic crisis, and again, as Mao put it, "the economic power of U.S. imperialism, which grew during the Second World War, is confronted with unstable and daily shrinking domestic and foreign markets. The strength of the United States is only superficial and transient. Irreconcilable domestic and international contradictions, like a volcano, menace U.S. imperialism every day."

This situation was being aggravated—and could be further aggravated—by "just and patriotic wars of liberation" in the colonial and semi-colonial countries, by the struggle for "people's democracy" in the capitalist countries, and by the struggle for peace. All these movements for peace, democracy, national independence and Socialism had converged to form a colossal force, fundamentally changing the postwar balance of class forces and enabling the strength of the anti-imperialist democratic camp to surpass that of the imperialist camp.

That the West possessed nuclear weapons was no cause for concern. People were always superior to weapons, as the Chinese Communists had demonstrated in the civil war. The people ought to be told about the "objectively existing danger of war," but only to "enhance their vigilance and make them mentally prepared for it at an early date." People's mental preparation for war was an important condition for preventing a world war and defending peace. The higher the people's vigilance, the broader the section of the people mobilized and the greater their determination to defend the cause of peace, the better would world peace be obeyed.

American military bases on foreign territories were all like nooses tied around the neck of U.S. imperialism. "The Americans themselves, and nobody else, made these nooses, and they themselves put them round their necks and handed the other ends of the nooses to the Chinese people, the people of the Arab countries and all the people throughout the world who love peace and oppose aggression," Mao said. The Americans declared that the reason for the bases was to defend the United States against the Soviet Union. This was merely a smokescreen. They were designed to enslave the people of the world, to seize the vast intermediate area lying between the United States and the Soviet Union, an area including many capitalist, colonial and semicolonial countries in Europe, Asia and Africa, and almost the greater part of the world's raw-material-producing areas and markets. Obviously this had to be prevented. It was futile, Mao argued, to persuade the imperialists to turn over a new leaf. The only course open was to organize the Communist forces to fight them. "The people of the United States and the peoples of all countries menaced by U.S. aggression should unite to beat back the attacks of the U.S. reactionaries and their lackeys in these countries," he said. "Only victory in this struggle can prevent a third world war; it cannot be prevented in any other way."

It was permissible to conduct peace negotiations, to make some concessions, to arrive at agreements of one sort or another and to obtain compromises on the principle that the basic interests of the people were not impaired. Even when trying to reach agreements with imperialism and to achieve compromises with it there should be no letting up in the struggles of the masses against imperialism, however.

The diplomatic activities of the Socialist countries dealt with relations between countries. While Socialist countries made necessary and possible compromises with capitalist countries diplomatically, such compromises did not require the people in the countries of the capitalist world to follow suit and make compromises at home. "Peaceful coexistence between Socialist and capitalist countries does not require the exploited classes in the countries of the capitalist world to follow suit and cooperate peacefully with the exploiting classes," *Red Flag* said. "Hence, one should not confuse the peaceful foreign policy of the Socialist countries with the domestic policy of the proletariat in the capitalist countries. Still less should one think that the revolutionary struggles of the people in the various countries will obstruct compromises between Socialist and capitalist countries. The contrary is the case. The more developed the revolutionary struggles of the people in the various countries are, the more favorable is the situation to force the imperialist countries to compromise with the Socialist countries and reach agreement on certain questions, including agreement on certain important issues, and the more favorable is it for peaceful coexistence between countries with different systems, and hence for the defense of world peace."

From this it followed that "the greater the number of countries winning victory in the revolution, the more difficult it is for imperialism to launch a world war and the more secure world peace is." It was therefore necessary to unite the revolutionary forces of all countries, and to wage arduous struggles.

"Until U.S. imperialism is dealt crushing blows by the people of the whole world, until it suffers a crushing defeat, it will never give up its ambition to dominate the globe and enslave the world's people," said the *People's Daily*. "U.S. imperialism will not escape just trial and punishment at the hands of the Chinese people and the peoples of the world."

Although the target of the criticism continued to be the "revisionists" of Yugoslavia, who believed that coexistence with imperialism was possible, there were covert references to Khrushchev in Peking's I-told-you-so-ism. He was the "some" people who had been misled into thinking that the imperialist wolf was really a sheep.

That serious differences in ideology, and even in practice, now existed between the Soviet Union and Communist China was demonstrable. There was, nevertheless, a tendency on the part of the West to misunderstand the nature of the breach. A week or two before his death in June, 1960, after a visit to Australia, British Communist leader Harry Pollitt described the differences as a matter of emphasis. The Chinese were in a hurry, he said; the Russians felt they could afford to take their time. The solidarity of the bloc was not in question, nor was there any doubt as to the identity of purpose. All that remained to be decided was how far and how fast to go in speeding up the revolutionary processes designed to bring about world Socialism. Subsequent events confirmed the Pollitt thesis.

Most Western interpretations of the Moscow conference were that Khrushchev in his bitter, and even obscene, attack on the Maoist theories, had had a notable victory, that the forces of peace had triumphed over those in favor of "peace." This is a highly dangerous interpretation. Despite Khrushchev's anger, the conference decisions did not seriously inhibit the Chinese, but they did commit the Russians to Mao's "countryside" concept of the global guerrilla war, with the United States as the principal enemy. "More than any other capitalist country, the United States drains Asia, and especially Latin America, of their riches, holding up their progress," said the conference statement. "U.S. capitalist penetration into Africa is increasing. U.S. imperialism has become the biggest international exploiter." A great struggle was getting under way between the forces of labor and capital, of democracy and reaction, of freedom and colonialism. The victory of the popular revolution in Cuba had become a "splendid example" for the people of Latin America.

High praise for its part in the world revolution was given to China which had "dealt a crushing blow at the positions of imperialism in Asia and contributed in great measure to the balance of the world forces changing in favor of Socialism. By giving a further powerful impetus to the national liberation movement, it exerted tremendous influence on the peoples, especially those of Asia, Africa and Latin America."

Peaceful coexistence, it was agreed, did not imply renunciation of the class struggle. As long as imperialism existed there would be soil for wars of aggression. The war menace had, in fact, grown because of the wrecking of the Paris summit meeting by the ruling circles of the United States. The aggressive nature of imperialism had not changed. "But"—and here the Chinese conceded their major ideological point—"real forces have appeared that are capable of foiling its [imperialism's] plans of aggression. War is not fatally inevitable."

The "fight" for peace was the primary task of the Communist parties. But should the "imperialist maniacs start war the peoples will sweep capitalism out of existence and bury it." The broadest possible united front of peace supporters, fighters against the imperialist policy of aggression and war inspired by U.S. imperialism was essential to preserve world peace. In the furtherance of this cause, the peoples of colonial countries could win independence both through armed struggle and by nonmilitary methods, depending on the specific conditions in the country concerned. In the struggle for the "liberation" of the people from capitalist oppression, the working class and its revolutionary vanguard (that is, the Communist Party) would press its offensive with increasing energy. In the event of the exploiting classes resorting to violence against people, the possibility of nonpeaceful transition to Socialism should be borne in mind, for Leninism taught, and experience confirmed, that the ruling classes never relinquished power voluntarily.

In both Russia and China the propaganda machines swung into action to publicize the new accord and undying friendship of the two Communist giants. The *People's Daily* declared that China and Russia were "united by a common cause, common interests and ideals and no power on earth can disunite them." *Pravda* described their friendship as being "as firm and indestructible as the Himalayas, as deep as the Pacific and as vast as the Yangtse and the Volga." "Ours is a common destiny," said Liu Shao-chi; and Anastas Mikoyan toasted the "eternal inviolability of the Sino-Soviet alliance."

What the Communist leaders agreed to was nothing more than a translation of the Chinese expression, "walking on two legs," into the world revolution. Khrushchev had Mao's blessing for summit meetings at which concessions appeared to be made and important agreements were apparently reached; at the same time, the more China and the rest of the bloc succeeded in stirring up trouble in the Philippines, Japan, South Korea, Laos, South Vietnam, Sikkim, Bhutan, Nepal, Algeria, Cuba and anywhere else in the world, the greater its contribution to the true cause of peaceful coexistence and peace.

Khrushchev confirmed this in an address to the Higher Party School of the Academy of Social Sciences and the Institute of Marxism-Leninism in Moscow on January 6, 1961. "It stands to reason," he said, "that we cannot completely exclude war [between the West and the Communist bloc] since imperialist countries continue to exist. There will be liberation wars as long as imperialism exists, as long as colonialism exists. Wars of this kind are revolutionary wars. Such wars are not only justified, they are inevitable. The Communists support just wars of this kind wholeheartedly and without reservation and they march in the van of the peoples fighting for liberation."

Only a little while ago, he said, Latin America was bound hand and foot to Yankee imperialism. Today it was no longer an American manorial estate but an active volcano. The eruption of the liberation struggle had wiped out dictatorial regimes in a number of countries. The "thunder of the glorious Cuban revolution" had "reverberated throughout the world." The Cuban revolution was not only repulsing the onslaught of the imperialists—it was spreading, signifying a new and higher stage of the national-liberation struggle. He predicted that the "Fascist dungeons" of the Union of South Africa would crumble to dust and that the national-liberation movement would spread everywhere.

That Sino-Soviet friendship is something less indestructible than the Himalayas is evident; that further rifts in the grand alliance will occur is almost certain. In the immediate future, however, there is little reason to doubt that the expedient Russian and Chinese decision to place unity first will be beneficial to both. By Peking's standards, Khrushchev has shown unnecessary restraint in international crises of recent years. But China has never been adventuristic to the point of folly. As it has indicated consistently in all its international dealings since the Korean War, it is prepared to go to the brink, but not, at this stage, beyond it.

Enlightened self-interest demands that the Sino-Soviet relationship should be maintained and strengthened in the present period of development. The future of world Communism depends on this unity. And whatever doubts Peking and Moscow may entertain about each other, both have clearly indicated by their joint development of the central Asian heartland that they are much less afraid of each other than they are of the Western Powers. The Korean War taught China the vulnerability of its Manchurian industrial complex and ever since it has been busy with the creation of new complexes far inland, not merely because these are areas both sparsely populated and rich in minerals but because they are safer from Western bombing or missile attack. That they are close, and, in some cases, contiguous to, the Soviet border, does not seem to have been a cause for concern: on the contrary, one of the earliest and most ambitious Chinese railroad building projects was to embark on a new line across Sinkiang to link up with the Russian central Asian system.

To Russia, China is a trading partner of constantly increasing importance. Between 1957 and 1959, for instance, its trade with China rose from 15 percent to 19.5 per cent and totaled more than $2.25 billion, which is roughly comparable with the United States' trade with Japan. Known Chinese exports to Russia include an annual average of approximately a million metric tons of food grains (and they may be very much more), a similar quantity of soya beans, and tin, antimony, tungsten, cement, mercury and precious metals.

This is the stiff price for Russian aid, perhaps, but, so far as China is concerned, worth every penny of it. The point is often made in the West—and sometimes even in China—that Soviet help has been less than generous, that the $3.75 billion which China has received is much less than its needs and given on such terms as to starve the Chinese people both of food and consumer goods by the repayment demands.

So far as the long-range Chinese plans for industrial development are concerned, this is not the most important point. China faced the problem of dragging itself up by its bootstraps. What it needed on a massive scale was Soviet capital and technical aid, including the services of teachers, scientists, agronomists and specialists of every other kind. These it received. There was no hint of ingratitude in Marshal Chu Teh's speech at the Soviet Embassy in Peking on February 14, 1960, to celebrate the tenth anniversary of the signing of the Sino-Soviet alliance. "The over 290 large-scale construction projects already completed or now undergoing construction with assistance from the Soviet Union constitute the nucleus and backbone of the industrial construction of our country and are of significant influence in the rapid completion of an integral industrial system in our country," he said. "The Soviet Union has dispatched many experts to help our country in construction, and has also assisted our country in training a large number of scientists and technicians. The Soviet Union helped our country in formulating the twelve-year plan for scientific development, and also provided us with great assistance in the research of peaceful utilization of atomic energy, thus considerably promoting the progress of research in science and technology in our country. On behalf of our Party, government and people may I now once again express heartfelt gratitude to the Party, government and people of the Soviet Union."

There would have been no "leap" in China without Soviet aid. Russia provided the hard core of China's new industries during the First Five Year Plan by building 156 separate projects, ranging from steel mills to hydroelectric stations. A second installment during the Second Five Year Plan carried the total to 291; a third will add another 78 major enterprises in the fields of power, metallurgical industries, chemicals, coal, petroleum, machine-building, electrical machinery, radio and building materials by 1967. In terms of money, the Russian loan does not sound much in comparison with some of the American Mutual Security Agency grants. But the difference between this aid and American aid to such countries as South Vietnam and South Korea, the two principal U.S. Far Eastern beneficiaries, is that it has been devoted largely to projects designed to help the recipient country to become self-generating industrially. It produced results. The Russians started with blueprints and worked through till the factories were in production. By the end of 1957, on the eve of the "great leap forward," 67 of the Russian projects were operating. This not only resulted in stepped up production but in the achievement of industrial skills which had been far beyond China's means, or know-how, in the past. For the first time, China was manufacturing heavy-duty trucks, locomotive engines and multiple types of automatic lathes. It was building ships of up to 10,000 tons' displacement and assembling both military and commercial aircraft.

The first three major iron and steel bases at Anshan, Wuhan and Paotow were all built under the Soviet aid program. Seven thousand

Chinese teachers and 6,000 students and postgraduate students had been trained in the Soviet Union by 1957 and returned technically competent for the tasks ahead; many thousands of others have since followed them to Soviet universities, where they are remarkable among the Russian students for their diligence and dedication.

The Russians set China's iron and steel industry in motion. They brought nuclear know-how. They started electricity flowing. They began by rehabilitating the Fushin power plant in 1951. In 1952 they built thermal power plants at Fushun, Sian, Chengchow, Chungking and Urumchi. They had vision and capacity. They saw water in terms of power irrigation and transport. They looked at the Yangtze at the Three Gorges and found that it carried four times as much water as the Volga but that the latter carried many times as much traffic. They said that with dams here they could not only generate as much power annually as all Britain generates but also make the Yangtze navigable by 10,000-ton vessels as far as Chungking.

In November, 1959, Madame Sun Yat-sen, first vice-chairman of the People's Republic of China, disclosed that the Soviet Union had sent 10,800 industrial advisers and other economic experts to China. This figure has since been repeated by other sources, including the *Sinkiang Daily* on February 14, 1960. How many left during the 1960 ideological dispute we do not know: but we do know that many have since returned.

All this is tangible evidence of Russian assistance. The intangibles are also important. If China had not been backed by the power of the Soviet Union would General Van Fleet's forces have halted at the 38th Parallel in the late spring of 1950? Would the U.N. planes have treated the Yalu River as the forbidden line beyond which they could not pursue the Communist planes? Would the United States have hesitated on the brink at Dien Bien Phu in 1954? Even if the answers to these questions are all in the affirmative, the fact remains that Soviet military strength has been an enormously effective military rear for Communist China. It has always been big brother back home with a mighty nuclear fist. Of this China has been fully, and, in its way, graciously, aware. It is also conscious of the fact that it is so deeply committed to an anti-Western, particularly anti-American, policy that, unlike Yugoslavia, it has no one else to turn to when it needs help—as it does now and will continue to do for many years to come. The primacy of the Soviet Union has not been questioned (even if the same cannot be said for personal leadership in ideological matters). On the contrary, even during the sharpest periods of the ideological dispute, the role of the Soviet Union was constantly acclaimed. Its scientific achievements were hailed as achievements with which China, as a loyal member of the Communist family of nations, was intimately associated, and a pilot commune was even named Sputnik, an honor that Moscow, with its heavy reservations about the communes and the challenge they imply in ideological leadership, may have regarded dubiously.

To sum up, there are main points on which the two nations differ even now and will differ in the future; but the reasons why these differences should be put aside, at least temporarily, in the interest of unity, are compelling. As the leader of a Russian delegation to Peking expressed it in February, 1961, the Sino-Soviet Treaty of Friendship is "a big shield protecting the peoples of the world but at the same time a sword that strikes fear at the enemy." In their disputes over the interpretation of peaceful coexistence and the inevitability of war the Soviet Union and Communist China are like two runners going in opposite directions around the same circular track. Though they go in opposite directions, they expect to reach the same goal. The difference is that Russia's path is reasonably clear and its pace more leisurely. It lacks the compulsions for haste that force the speed of its younger partner. Its tensions are easing, while those of China gather strength. It questions whether dogma laid down in days of conventional armaments holds good in the nuclear age. Within the framework of the Maoist guerrilla concept of the world struggle, this means that the Soviet Union does not believe that the "human" wave to capture the cities is either essential or desirable. If the Russians are correct in their assessment that stage will never be necessary. The vigorous struggles foreshadowed in the 1960 Moscow communiqué will have brought the United States and its allies to the point where their collapse will be inevitable.

Chapter IX   回回回回回回回回回回

SEATO'S SETTING STAR

THE West has failed in its attempts to discipline China. We have neither brought it to its knees in repentance nor caused it to change its ways. The inconclusive Korean War helped rather than hindered the regime. Like the American embargo on trade, it served to justify Peking's agonizing domestic demands and authoritarian excesses. Military alliances with countries on China's periphery have proved like ribbons binding the limbs of a giant: even now they are beginning to stretch and snap under the strain. In every continent and in every field China is beginning to break through. It is beginning to generate vast internal power; it has created far-flung ideological bases; it is being driven on by urgent tensions that are internally created and externally directed; and the scent of a first major international victory is helping to maintain its revolutionary dynamic. For whatever the changes in American policy that may precede it, the vote in favor of Peking's admission to the United Nations will be a profound diplomatic and psychological victory for China and a defeat for the United States. Peking could have eased its way into the U.N. by adopting a less intransigent foreign policy. It has chosen the hard way, the revolutionary way, in which, when it succeeds, it will crow in triumph over the American "paper tiger."

For years Japan, Australia and New Zealand, to mention only three U.S. allies, considered establishing diplomatic relations with Peking. They were inhibited partly by their allegiance to—and dependence on—the United States and partly by the fact that China wanted diplomatic recognition only so long as its "right" to "liberate" Taiwan was also recognized. Great Britain, which recognized the People's Republic early in 1950 in the fruitless hope of saving its investments in Shanghai, found its reluctance to abandon the 10 million Taiwanese a constant barrier to the establishment of full relations. "China is willing to see its relations with Britain improved, but it will never acquiesce in or tolerate the British practice of following the United States in creating 'two Chinas,'" Chou En-lai told the National People's Congress in 1958. "If Britain does not change its double-faced attitude toward China, Sino-British relations will inevitably be adversely affected. . . . The Chinese Government and people are firmly opposed to the scheme to create 'two Chinas.' We absolutely will not allow this scheme to materialize in any form or on any occasion."

In its quest for temporary allies, however, Peking is able to rationalize its association with many non-Communists who, for a variety of reasons, including their desire for a relaxation of international tensions, anticolonial and anti-imperialist phobias, a belief that China may have the answer to their own problems of industrial development, and fear, are willing to accept its protestations of friendship and its offer of aid.

Ignoring its own requirement on the "liberation" of Taiwan as a prerequisite to the establishment of diplomatic relations, Peking busied itself congratulating and recognizing each African state as it gained independence in 1960. It recognized Mali (June 19), Malagasy and Somalia (June 25), the Congo (June 27), Dahomey (July 31), Niger (August 2), Upper Volta (August 4), Ivory Coast (August 6), Chad (August 10), the Central African Republic (August 12) and Gabon (August 16). The decision of the Mali Federation to recognize Taipeh and not Peking led to some early hopes that Communist Chinese influence here and elsewhere in newly independent Africa might be minimal: but the Mali Federation split, and the new Mali was pro-Peking. Even countries that had no dealings with Peking were not prepared to vote against it. And in view of the attitude of the British Commonwealth, which favored China's admission to the United Nations as soon as possible, it became quite clear early in 1961 that possibly by the end of the year, or by 1962, Peking would command a sufficient majority of African and other votes to gain a seat.

Although the United States may elect to fight a rear-guard action, claiming that a two-thirds majority is required and that Nationalist China is, in any case, assured of retaining its seat in the Security Council with the right of veto, the Soviet Union, with the support of a majority of the Afro-Asian countries, will carry the day with the argument that the question is not one of a new admission to the United Nations but of which delegation may properly claim to represent China. The Congo provides a precedent: having been admitted to the United Nations, its opposing factions fought for recognition as the true representatives of their country and the issue was decided, this time in favor of the Western-backed candidate, on a simple majority.

The United States will have only two alternatives: to leave the United Nations, as the late Mr. John Foster Dulles threatened, or to accept the verdict of the majority. Both are difficult decisions, but the first would be easily the worst. Since Communist policy is to isolate the United States, China could scarcely hope for better than that its victory over the Nationalists would precipitate an American withdrawal from the world forum, which, for better or worse, is highly regarded by most of its more recently admitted members.

Withdrawal would place the United States in direct opposition to the winds of change in the underdeveloped world and would gravely aggravate the already complex problems that limit its effective association with many countries that have recently won their independence. Acceptance of the verdict of the majority, even in advance, is not calculated to produce much comfort, either. Most members of the United Nations would support a "two Chinas" solution. They would be more than happy to seat Peking as representing all of mainland

China and Taipeh as the government of Taiwan. Nationalist China's rejection of this solution sabotages all such comfortable solutions and greatly helps Peking, since it will not now be voted for as one of "two Chinas" but as the only China. Taiwan will lose in the eyes of the world the prestige it managed to retain by its membership of the United Nations. Its case will have been considered—and rejected. For Chiang Kai-shek this will be a defeat second only to the loss of the mainland.

All those nations which for varying reasons have hesitated to recognize Peking will no longer be inhibited, since any logic in voting for its admission to the U.N. will surely be destroyed if the process is not carried to its logical conclusion—the establishment of diplomatic relations. And "two Chinas" being out, China will regard diplomatic recognition as recognition also of sovereignty over *all* of its domains, Tibet and Taiwan included. We are in grievous error, however, if we think that this is likely to produce an amenable Peking, or that, in return, recognizing countries are likely to be able to exact a *quid pro quo*. Having watched our agonizing reappraisals, China intends to behave like the Emperor Frederick Barbarossa. In revenge for the expulsion of his Empress from Milan on the rump of a mule, Frederick besieged and captured the city and compelled all his prisoners, on pain of death, to extract with his, or her, teeth a fig from the anus of a mule. Peking's fig, and the condition under which it will take its seat in the United Nations, is the withdrawal of the United States from Taiwan and the Taiwan Strait. This is what Marshal Chen Yi told the Budapest Party newspaper, *Szabad Nep*, in March, 1961. And since Party newspapers are not given to mis-reporting high Party officials of other countries when they make statements on matters of policy, we may assume that Chen Yi means what he is reported to have said.

The outlaw intends to outlaw the United States. And until the U.S. behaves in a manner that meets with its approval it will decline to take its seat in the U.N. The proposition will then be advanced that China, having been snubbed for so long, is now merely being stubborn and getting its own back. Unfortunately, this does not happen to be the case. China is not being pigheaded but hardheaded, realistic and essentially practical. It never was a wooer of the West, and suddenly to find itself almost universally wooed strengthens its international hand in a way that it could not have achieved by itself, least of all by a humble and deferential entry into the United Nations.

The line Peking has been pushing for some years now among the neutrals and selected Westerners is that if only the United States would be reasonable about Taiwan, all would be well. China has no territorial ambitions, it says; it demands only its due. It sold this view to that distinguished British political expert, Field Marshal Montgomery, who visited China in 1960 for five days and returned to urge in a confidential report to the British Government that Taiwan rightfully belonged to Peking.

The wooing has not ended but only just begun. Anxious nations around the globe will press their suit ever more urgently as China's industrial, conventional and nuclear strength grows. It will not be merely nice to have China sitting down at the conference table, but urgent.

As Peking sees the future, those who were doubtful about China in the past will become increasingly concerned with removing the stumbling block in its path. Chiang Kai-shek, who is held in high regard only in South Korea, South Vietnam, the Philippines and parts of the United States, will now become a greater villain than ever. One can almost see the cartoons in the popular sections of the British press and hear the outrage of its commentators. Is a world war the price we are to pay for the protection of this worn-out war lord, who is occupying Chinese territory, rules by terror and survives on American handouts? they will ask.

The United States will stand fast. It is committed by treaty to defend Taiwan. Its moral obligations are even firmer. This, in turn, must have the effect of weakening American influence with its allies in the underdeveloped world and in the West Pacific, for Washington, to some extent at least, through its moral and treaty commitments to Chiang's now hopeless cause, will share Taipeh's isolation and the brickbats hurled against it. Everything favors Peking. The world needs a reasonable China much more than China feels obliged to be reasonable. And every attempt in the next few years to reach any sort of understanding with Peking on such matters as disarmament will inevitably be scuttled by its emphasis on the need to "liberate" Taiwan. In countries such as Britain the government is a long way behind public opinion in its reluctance to see a Communist take-over in Taiwan. But governments wishing to stay in power in democratic countries eventually find ways and means of accommodating themselves to public opinion; if they don't, and if the issue is regarded as important, they may expect to be thrown out. This is called realism. It may also be called appeasement, but whatever its label the prevalence of the anti-Chiang bias, not only in Britain and other European countries but in many parts of the underdeveloped world, also, can only have the effect of bringing Peking a shade closer to the achievement of its stated objective: the destruction of all American power and influence in the West Pacific.

Already the balance of power has changed so much that the United States is no longer the dominant authority in the Far East. The U.S. nuclear deterrent, the 7th Fleet, military bases in Japan, Okinawa and the Philippines and the existence of SEATO have created an illusory façade of strength. With the notable exceptions of Japan and Malaya, the economies of all countries in the region are insecure, and even these shining stars in the non-Communist Far Eastern camp cannot be considered as entirely firm politically. The security of the region is, in large measure, dependent on the security of its component parts. Military action on the off-shore islands of Quemoy and Matsu, for instance, has political consequences in Japan and every alarm there is recorded in Okinawa. South Korea's security is dependent on the military bases in Japan and Okinawa. Japan and Okinawa are, to some extent, at least, dependent on Korea, where both the political and economic situations are cause for grave concern.

Despite some technical progress, the state of the South Korean economy is chronically dismal. A slight improvement occurred in the financial year ending June 30, 1960; but the trade gap was a huge $291 million, with exports totaling only $19 million. For everything but rice, which went down and added thereby to the impoverishment of the already desperately poor farmers, prices of consumer goods continued to rise alarmingly.

Industry suffers from four major deficiencies—electric power, able management, skilled technicians and indigenous raw materials. Steps have been taken to remedy the power situation, but the other three cannot easily be improved. Management is especially weak, and the universities send their graduates to industry only half trained. South Korea has never been established as a going concern and, so long as present United States policies are maintained, is unlikely to be so established, though American economic aid through 1960 had reached a cumulative total of almost $2.5 billion.

It would be a gross misstatement to say there is no evidence of this aid. One can see the reconstruction of cities, towns and railways especially. But by far the greater portion has not been going to development projects likely to make the economy self-generating but to the import of "salables," which include a wide range of machinery, equipment, fertilizers, petroleum and raw materials, which simply keep the country going. These are sold for hwan to Korean enterprises, the hwan thus received going into a counterpart fund. Because of the artificial exchange rate, which was maintained until late 1960, the "salables" part of the program was for years wide open to racketeering. For instance, some of the $30 million worth of cotton, the largest single import, was brought into Korea in 1960 at a rate of 800 hwan to the dollar and sold at prices based on a ratio of 1,400 hwan to the dollar in the open market.

South Korea has become a permanent mendicant, with all that that implies in moral decay. Every part of the community, including the army with its eighteen infantry divisions, has been affected by this. Resignation by senior officers after the students' revolt against Syngman Rhee in 1960 helped to soothe feelings against Rhee appointees: but they did not alleviate the deeper unrest among ill paid junior officers who see little hope of enjoying the plums of office that came to many senior officers in their early thirties. At the time of the 1960 crisis an R.O.K. army major received 56,000 hwan a month (about $46 at a realistic rate of exchange), a captain 46,000 and a master-sergeant 36,000. Yet American economists believed that a married Korean officer with three children needed a minimum of 65,000 hwan a month for bare subsistence. Faced with the choice of hunger or of supplementing their income by outside operations, is it any cause for wonder that the Korean army fell back on looting supplies intended for the two American divisions and on the black marketeering of their own supplies of gasoline, tires and other easily disposed of materials? Or that in 1961 a military junta overthrew the short-lived, democratic but ineffective regime of Dr. John Chang?

Few South Koreans see any hope in the forlorn efforts to attract tourists as a means of raising foreign exchange, or of persuading foreign capital that its economic and political climates are healthy enough to encourage private investment. The restoration of trade with Japan has helped—but not enough to change fundamental prospects.

Despite South Korea's vigorous anti-Communism, pressures for unification will grow as the security situation deteriorates, not necessarily in the confrontation of South Korea's eighteen divisions and two U.S. divisions by nineteen North Korean divisions (plus Chinese Communist forces behind the Yalu River), but in the inevitable weakening of the American conventional military position in the Far East. When the Korean War broke out in 1950 the United States had four divisions of troops in Japan. Today the ground forces have all gone and the only immediately available regional reserves, the understrength Third Marine Division, are in Okinawa.

While it is possible that nothing will occur to upset the Treaty of Mutual Cooperation and Security between the United States and Japan during its ten-year span, the assessments of the Japanese reaction to the treaty that flowed from the quiescent months after the cancellation of the Eisenhower visit in June, 1960, and the national elections which followed, were much too optimistic. Mr. Ikeda, the Japanese Prime Minister, went to the polls with a breath-taking 16 per cent increase in the gross national product as the foundation for his unprecedented opportunity to offer both tax cuts and greater social welfare benefits. The Japanese voted for prosperity and not against the security treaty.

The state of the Japanese economy and U.S. trade are principal factors in Japan's alignment with the United States and the West. Numerous other factors will have a bearing on its future relationships, however. These include the establishment of diplomatic relations with mainland China; the widespread Japanese fear of war, especially nuclear war; the equally widespread desire to do business with both the Soviet Union and China; the demonstrable ease with which a small Left-wing Japanese minority can arouse the fears of the non-Left majority; the appreciation in Peking—and also in Moscow—that as Japan grows in industrial strength and capacity its importance in the struggle for global power also increases; and the weaknesses in the Japanese political system.

Since May 15, 1958, when a Soviet note to Japan implied that the

Japanese Government had permitted United States forces to bring nuclear weapons into Japan, Russia and China have conducted a war of nerves against the Japanese Government and people. This campaign has, as usual, been a mixture of club and carrot, on the one hand the threat that Japan could easily be drawn into an atomic war contrary to its wishes, or even its knowledge, and on the other hand a pledge to abandon the anti-Japanese provisions of the Sino-Soviet Alliance in exchange for Japanese neutrality. China has adroitly mixed appeals for a nuclear free zone and a "zone of peace" in the Far East together with its own plans for nuclear development. Through "people's diplomacy" it has held out the tantalizing promise of trade, while pursuing a policy of deliberate intransigence toward the Japanese Liberal-Democratic Party government, even to the point of establishing a Japanese school for subversion and sabotage in Peking.

This school, which was known as the Marx-Lenin School Second Branch, was under the direction of a Japanese Communist, who had a number of Chinese assistants. Its object was to train political and military leaders to form the nucleus of a *coup d'état* group in Tokyo. Japanese Communists were smuggled out of Japan to attend the school, which functioned from 1953 to 1957.* About nine hundred Japanese passed through the school, including former soldiers and others awaiting repatriation, and its graduates were among the participants in the spectacular anti-Kishi, anti-Eisenhower, anti-treaty campaign in Tokyo in May and June, 1960.

To what extent Peking helped to finance the Tokyo demonstrations is unclear. It is known, however, that yen transactions running into millions of dollars were negotiated by Chinese Communists in Hong Kong just before the demonstrations began, the assumption being that Peking was buying specifically to remit the money to sympathetic organizations in Japan. Shortly afterward Liu Ning-yi, who visited Tokyo to attend the annual congress of SOHYO, the Left-wing Japanese trade union congress, admitted quite freely that

* The Japanese school was only one of many established under the aegis of the Liaison Bureau, an offshoot of the Australasian Trade Union conference in 1949. For instance, a first contingent of fourteen Australians arrived in Peking in 1952 and remained for three and a half years. Other smaller groups have gone periodically and have stayed for generally shorter periods.

China had contributed some $25,000 to help striking Japanese coal miners on the island of Kyushu.

In the short term, the Chinese have been working for a situation that will merely nullify the value of the U.S.–Japan treaty: in the middle term they hope for a "united front" government as a prelude to a Communist take-over. With each year the potency in their anti-treaty propaganda increases. Because China lacked an air force, Japan and Okinawa provided invulnerable bases during the Korean War. This invulnerability is no longer assured, and, on the contrary, has become highly unlikely in the event that hostilities should begin again on the Korean peninsula, or elsewhere in the immediate vicinity of Japan.

This is serious enough while China remains a conventional military Power. Its impact on Japan and Okinawa will be shattering when China becomes even a token member of the nuclear club, especially if Chiang Kai-shek is still on his exposed position on the offshore islands and threatens thereby to involve Japan (through the U.S. military bases) in a war with China.

The official American view in Tokyo of the U.S.–Japan Mutual Defense Treaty contretemps which led to the cancellation of the Eisenhower visit was that the American need for military bases in Japan was not in really serious conflict with local political realities. The by-elections that followed the antivisit demonstrations in Japan and which returned Liberal-Democrats with increased majorities and the Liberal-Democratic convincing win in the national election later in the year were used as illustrations to defend this view.

The arguments are hard to justify. If the Japanese cast their votes for the Liberal-Democratic Party and the prosperity they associated with its rule and not against the security treaty, opposition to which was about all the Socialists had to offer, it does not necessarily mean that the "United States lost the Kishi Cabinet and the Eisenhower visit, but won the battle of the bases," which is the way one American official in Tokyo described the situation. "We've got ten years plus one under the treaty and that's about as far as anyone can expect to look ahead in these times," said the official, reflecting the embassy optimism that everything would be relatively plain sailing for the rest of the way.

It was given particular stress that even the Left wing would have greeted President Eisenhower with warmth and friendliness if there had been a moderately successful summit meeting and he had then gone on, as planned, through the Soviet Union to Japan. The U2 incident and the Chinese exploitation of it for propaganda purposes, the unpopularity of Kishi with the Japanese people, the hangover of anti-Americanism due to some unfortunate earlier base incidents, and difficulties arising over Okinawa, where the continuing American administration was regarded by many Japanese as a violation of Japan's "residual sovereignty" in the Ryukyus, were listed as having combined to produce a set of unfavorable circumstances which were unlikely to recur. The virtual disappearance of American ground forces in Japan, it was claimed, had eliminated one possible source of friction. Mr. Ikeda, who succeeded Mr. Kishi as Prime Minister, and his Cabinet were untainted by past association with the militarists and therefore more acceptable to prevailing Japanese sentiment, and, above all, there was scarcely a man or woman in Japan who did not live better and eat better because of the country's close economic ties with the United States.

Confidence that American optimism in Tokyo about the treaty was well based was shared, in its public utterances at least, by the Japanese Government. Mr. Kosaka, the Foreign Minister, who is the product of a rich family background and an early interest in Marxism (which have combined in middle age to produce an attachment to what he calls "new capitalism," with the accent on social welfare, a firm belief in close relations with the West and a desire to do business with the Communists), blamed the 1960 demonstrations on the Russians and Chinese, on the Japanese tendency to become quickly tired of their governments, on the failure of the Kishi administration to recognize the need for proper public relations and on the activities of a small Leftist minority. He inferred that the majority now knew where its bread and butter came from, that all was well with Japan, with the security treaty, with the bases and with Japan's relations with the United States. It was a comforting impression, but it was not wholly true.

In the immediate future the Western world in general, and the United States in particular can and must remain on close and friendly terms with the dynamic, prospering and stimulating Japanese nation. But no amount of wishful thinking will restore the significance to the treaty that existed before the cancellation of the Eisenhower visit. Though the Communists certainly exploited the situation to their own ends, the feeling against the treaty is widespread. Japanese youth, for instance, is almost solidly antitreaty. Japanese fathers who disapproved of the behavior of their sons and daughters during the riots said that their wives were solidly for the demonstrators.

In a state of isolation from its neighbors and neighboring events, the temperate atmosphere that prevailed in Japan late in 1960 and early in 1961 might continue indefinitely. But the Japanese do not want to be isolated; and there are forces at work, both internal and external, which will make the treaty a matter of major controversy again. To begin with, the Ikeda Government, while honestly determined, as Mr. Kosaka puts it, to stay on a peak with the West and not to descend into the valley between the two blocs, is no less concerned with the need for establishing normal relations, especially trading relations, with Moscow and Peking. During his visit to Tokyo in August, 1960, Liu Ning-yi had a long talk with Mr. Kenzo Matsumura, leader of the antimain factions of the Liberal-Democratic Party, in which he suggested that Sino-Japanese relations would improve if the Japanese Government refrained from (a) pursuing a policy hostile to China; (b) taking part in the "two Chinas plot"; and (c) obstructing and sabotaging the normalization of Sino-Japanese relations. Liu added that after the abrogation of the security treaty China and Japan could coexist peacefully and conclude a pact of mutual nonaggression.

The appeal did not fall on altogether deaf ears, for not all Japanese share their officials' fears of losing the assured Taiwan trade for the prospect of unreliable trade with the mainland. The political desire to reach an understanding with Peking is powerfully supported by many rich industrialists who are so lacking in political orientation that they determine the weight of their contributions to the opposing Japanese political parties, including the Communists, according to the size and influence of the parties. They will not be prepared indefinitely to tolerate the treaty if it stands in the way of what many still optimistically, and unwisely, view as the cornucopia of China trade.

The situation in Japan cannot be taken for granted. The relationship between the United States and this traditional lone wolf in the Far East will have to be cultivated with the greatest possible care. However devoutly a strongly anti-Communist Japan, unafraid of cocking its snook at the Communist giants in Russia and China, may be desired, a friendly non-Communist Japan is probably the best that can be hoped for. Most of the Liberal-Democratic Party backers are delighted with the tremendous volumes of sales and purchases that cross the Pacific between Japan and the United States; they would be even happier if this could be duplicated across the Sea of Japan (to Vladivostok) and the East China Sea (to Shanghai). Politics, they feel, should never stand in the way of trade. This attitude is reflected all the way down the Japanese social scale. Except for minorities on the extreme Left and the extreme Right and among the students, the Japanese have become apolitical. Pay checks mean more than political pledges, or the fate of political parties and their leaders.

There are appealing elements in a situation in which a country so demonstrably proves itself greater than its politicians. But there are also dangers. It is only when they resort to violence and mass demonstration that the Socialists and the extreme Left have scored points. In their frustration, this may seem the only way—and perhaps an easy way, too. If government decisions can be upset by force and the show of force, why not extend the process slightly and overthrow the government? The possibility may be remote, but not too remote to be entertained in Peking and by some of its friends in Tokyo.

The situation of the billion-dollar base of Okinawa is even less reassuring, especially since the island appears, in so many respects, to fulfill the requirements of the ideal foreign military station. Its nuclear capability is not subject to local political veto; its air and ground forces, unfettered by restrictive treaty obligations, are well placed to fill the role of a regional "fire brigade" in the event of a brushfire war; there is no time limit on American occupancy, which, as Washington has made clear in statements in the past, is scheduled to continue "so long as conditions of threat and tension continue in the Far East"; and the touchy question of jurisdiction, which caused trouble in Japan and remains a constant irritant in the Philippines, is automatically taken care of in Article 3 of the peace treaty with Japan, which stipulates that the United States has the right "to exercise all and any powers of administration, legislation and jurisdiction" over the Ryukyus.

Within the range of the sleek fighter-bombers at Kaneda airbase are the densely populated coastal areas of central China, the Communists' air switch point at Shanghai, and the build-up areas opposite Formosa on the Fukien coast. Within range of the Mace intermediate ballistic missile, destined according to Washington reports for installation here, are Peking, Mukden, Pyongyang and Vladivostok, the concentration area of Sino-Soviet Far Eastern air, sea and land military strength and from which any attack from the Far East against the United States might be expected to come.

During the Korean War Okinawa's two airfields provided a secure base for B-29 operations in support of the United Nations forces. Impressed by this experience, the United States, which had wrested the island from Japan at a cost of forty-nine thousand casualties in the last great battle of World War II, spent a billion dollars turning it into its major base in the Western Pacific. Everywhere the island reflects American technical skill and investment. Naha, the capital, which was once knocked flat by American bombers, has been rebuilt into a prosperous city of 225,000 inhabitants. A four-lane concrete highway runs between Naha's two deep-water ports and Kaneda, the principal military airfield. Typhoon-resistant installations and homes for approximately fifty thousand American servicemen and their thirteen thousand dependents have sprung up among the vegetable fields.

Thanks to American medical aid, the life expectancy of Okinawans has increased by twenty years, while infant mortality has declined by 80 per cent. Classrooms have more than doubled and now have room for all but 7 per cent of the children of school age. The base gives direct and indirect employment to fifty thousand workers, and the per capita income of the Okinawans has climbed to $282 a year. In short, the Okinawans have never been better off and may never be as well off again if the Americans move out, since the current trade gap of $60 million a year is covered by expenditure on military services.

It does not follow, though, that Okinawa is secure, either militarily or politically. The Korean War marked the birth of the Chinese Communist air force which, while still in its infancy when hostilities ended, played a purely defensive role behind the Yalu River base. Against the total Communist Far Eastern air force of approximately five thousand jet aircraft the United States and its regional allies in the Far Eastern area now muster fewer than two thousand operational jets. Even on the not fully warranted assumption that any limited Communist adventures are likely to be primarily Chinese, with the Soviet Union standing technically aloof, the Communists have an air edge that might not prove decisive, but would certainly raise formidable problems in the operation of the Okinawa base. The installation of the Nike-Hercules and the Hawk ground-to-air missiles compensates somewhat for this new air inferiority; but since there are no islands to the westward on which to establish listening posts nearer to the Chinese mainland, and the island's two airfields are close together, Okinawa's vulnerability in a brushfire war must be considered fairly high.

On Okinawa itself pressures to hasten the end of the American base continue to build up. There is a sense of hurt among the Okinawans that the Americans are depriving them of their rightful place within the Japanese community, infringing Japanese sovereignty, and, by the introduction of nuclear weapons, risking the "annihilation of the entire Okinawan population," a phrase used by the Ryukyuan Assembly in 1957 when it unanimously passed a resolution calling for the discontinuance of base construction for atomic weapons. Even such purely defensive weapons as the Nike-Hercules and Hawk missiles, which are intended to deal respectively with high-level and low-level attacks from the air, are vehemently censured by the Okinawans. The test firing of the Nike brought immediate attacks in both Okinawa and Japan on the propriety of all military sea ranges in the Ryukyus, and the construction of Hawk launching pads resulted in another outcry. With a population of 700,000 compressed into 463 square miles, Okinawa is about the most densely settled land in the world, and frictions between the military and civil populations in such a situation are self-generating. In any case, the anti-American elements in the community would not hesitate to create "incidents," just as they may be expected now to create the sort of devices for exploiting public sentiment that proved so successful in Japan when the Communists, the Zengakuren students' organization and SOHYO united to sabotage the Eisenhower visit.

The Communists in the United Nations will hammer the "colonial" aspects of the Okinawa base, not merely to force an American withdrawal but to discredit the United States in the underdeveloped world. This is also true of other American trust territories in the Central Pacific, where highly important second-line base areas, such as Saipan and Guam, are involved. "Oceania" was a significant addition to the Asian, African and Latin American areas specifically designated to be carrying out a "heroic struggle against imperialism" by the Moscow conference in 1960.

Pressures against the bases will coincide with a period in which the growing family of intercontinental and other missiles and the expansion of the fleet of Polaris submarines will tend to make many conventional base areas obsolescent as contributors to the nuclear deterrent. "Fortress" America and bases in a handful of reliable allied areas will provide sufficient launching pads to bring the entire Communist empire under missile attack. Will many of the bases then be worth the calumny that the United States will have to endure by their retention? This, in turn, poses a second question: Is a Thailand, or a South Korea, worth a nuclear war and the probable loss of between 50 million and 75 million Americans in twenty-four hours? The Chinese believe that the Western answer to both questions is likely to be "no." In other words, in Mao's classic concept of the city-countryside theory of guerrilla war, the stronger the United States becomes in missile capability, the weaker it will become in the "countryside" and the more easily will the weaker peripheral countries be subverted and taken over. America's isolation naturally follows.

In view of Khrushchev's repeated support for Peking's claim to Taiwan, the Moscow conference's failure to designate it among the crisis areas is merely confirmation of the view that Peking is satisfied that time is on its side, that Taiwan is crumbling and will one day fall. The Kuomintang's resistance to the "two Chinas" concept excludes, in Peking's view, the possibility of a settlement of the Taiwan issue except as a province of China. American protection will be effective only so long as the United States is in a position to make its pledges effective. It has the conventional capability today; within ten years, however, it will certainly need to fall back on nuclear weapons.

Furthermore, after Nationalist China's rejection by the United Nations, Peking reasons, it will not be difficult to channel Taiwan's hate emotions away from the Communist regime and toward the mutual enemy—"U.S. imperialism." The one real unifying factor in the Nationalist regime is Chiang Kai-shek. Under him and ready to contest the leadership when he passes from the scene are factions whose rivalries will certainly be divisive and perhaps destructive, and whose leaders cannot all be regarded as fully proof against the constant appeals from Peking for peaceful unification and the promise of good jobs in New China.

There will be no letup in pressure in the Formosa Strait. The prospect of pushing the button on Quemoy to ring the alarm bells in Japan and Okinawa—and Taipeh—is much too tempting to be abandoned. But every shell that lands among the garrison in Quemoy is fired, so the Peking propagandists say, in sorrow rather than in anger. The Quemoy bombardments are not directed against China's compatriots but against the American imperialists whose intervention has led to this Chinese tragedy!

There is little likelihood of an early attempt to settle the Taiwan problem by direct military force, however. Even if China had the military capability, which it lacks, the consequences could be highly damaging, since it would almost certainly involve the mainland in air attacks and industrial destruction. Moreover, for the time being, the American presence on Taiwan underscores the internal propaganda theme that the United States has "invaded" and is "occupying" part of China.

Overt Chinese military action of a type which will be universally accepted as aggression is unlikely to occur anywhere, in fact, in the next decade. This does not preclude the further use of "volunteers" in "just" wars to which Peking is committed; but China does not believe in crossing borders to achieve its objectives—only in dissolving them, and, having had a fright in Korea, it would prefer to follow Mao's dictum and fight only when it is confident of winning. This is a policy involving minimum risks and promising maximum returns. It is the policy it pursued in the Indo-China War and followed thereafter in the long and patient campaign to achieve its objectives in Laos, where the process of wearing down the anti-Communist forces went on continuously, but not in such form that China was directly involved or the majority of the SEATO Powers were anxious to accept as sufficient to justify invoking their ill defined treaty obligations.

Overt aggression was not necessary. By internal military pressures, the Vietminh, with both ideological and material assistance from China, brought the French to the Geneva conference table in 1954 and won the bases from which Laos and South Vietnam could be subjected to similar military pressures and ultimate political surrenders. Contiguous borders with North Vietnam and China and military bases across these borders facilitated politico-military intervention of a type that was almost impossible to prove, or to prevent. The borders are ill defined. The people who live on either side are of the same ethnic stock and speak the same languages, and no outsider can tell with certainty where Laos or Burma ends, or where North Vietnam or China begins.

As a consequence, Australia, Britain and France accepted the Communist Pathet Lao movement in Laos as the only grass-roots organization in the country, a view that overlooked its establishment by force of arms when the Vietminh "volunteers" from Tongking entered the northern provinces in 1953—and again in 1954—and there established the Communist puppet government under the leadership of Prince Souphanouvong. At the same time, the Pathet Lao's subsequent success in the countryside stemmed directly from the U.S. failure to appreciate the pointlessness of building up an army while completely neglecting the Laotian villagers, the poorest and most backward of all Southeast Asian people, and its apparent lack of concern with the corruption that this sort of aid bred among the Laotians—and among some Americans charged with its distribution. Nowhere among the shoddy little Western legations and embassies here and elsewhere in the region was there any apparent appreciation that the problem was in essence social and economic, and military only in its final expression. And thus, against this background of scandal and the expediency of one Western policy and the artlessness of the other, the way opened for the exploitation of peasant unrest by ideological and later military pressures as a first step toward another political conference at which such gains could be consolidated. Here was history repeating itself all over again. In 1954 the Vietminh's guns were trained on Dien Bien Phu and later on Hanoi, but their most impressive victories were scored at the conference table in Geneva, where they shot down the Western leaders in flames. In Laos in 1961 the Russian military build-up of the Pathet Lao forces had the same intention; and their guns had a similar impact. SEATO leaders at the Council meeting in Bangkok in March, 1961, grabbed for papers reporting the apparent conciliation of a *Pravda* editorial and its suggestion that the fighting could be ended by conference as if they had personally brought about a victory. At this stage in the shameful story of Laos, there was not much else they could do; but the spectacle of SEATO becoming an applauding witness of its own sorry defeat is scarcely less nauseating than that never-to-be-forgotten picture of Neville Chamberlain waving his umbrella and talking of "peace in our time."

A notable non-Communist figure in the Communist plans for this "peaceful" conquest of Laos was Prince Norodom Sihanouk of Cambodia, who, in the closing weeks of 1960, picked up in Moscow the promise of a Russian technical school, Soviet geological surveyors to explore Cambodia's mineral wealth and help in developing his country's hydroelectric power. From Peking, where he went to sign a treaty of friendship and nonaggression, Sihanouk neatly side-stepped the Western call for reconvening the Indian, Polish and Canadian supervisory commission as a means of bringing about a cease-fire and demanded instead an enlarged Geneva conference. The intention, as at Dien Bien Phu, was to present the West with a military *fait accompli.* Between the time the cease-fire was first suggested and May 3, 1961, when it was loosely established, the Communist forces seized control of all but the northwestern province and a narrow strip along the "sensitive" Mekong valley.

At a state banquet in Peking on the eve of signing a treaty of friendship and nonaggression with China, Sihanouk launched one of his now more frequent attacks on the United States. "All schemes to isolate China in the world will only isolate those who start these schemes," he said. "Any country in the world that faces unjust straits can have China's firm and eternal support." In the visitors' book at the Peking National Agricultural Exhibition, he wrote: "All that we have seen at this agricultural exhibition of the Chinese People's Republic greatly amazes us. The Chinese People's Republic is taking giant steps toward the world pinnacle. Long live the friendship between the Chinese and Cambodian people."

For his cooperation Sihanouk received another $12 million to improve the equipment of the Chinese textile, plywood, cement, and paper factories, what he described as "gratuitous and unconditional" aid of an undisclosed but similar amount to build a metallurgic foundry with a yearly output of 40,000 tons of cast iron, 20,000 tons of steel and 15,000 tons of rolled iron; also a small mechanical engineering factory; more technical aid to improve the organization of State-owned cooperatives and rice-growing projects; and—as a gesture of contempt to the American highway—a detailed survey of the railway from the capital to the port of Sihanoukville. In addition, China agreed to establish a joint Sino-Khmer shipping company, which, according to Sihanouk, "will permit Cambodia to lay the foundation for its national merchant marine, to build ships and to train sailors." In return, he said, Cambodia had only to offer China its gratitude— "and, on the international stage, to support China's legitimate rights, starting with its admission to the United Nations. . . ."

Against these combined politico-military operations SEATO, and the entire anti-Communist position in Southeast Asia, have been casualties. In Bangkok, on December 12, 1960, Mr. Pote Sarasin, SEATO's secretary-general, expressed what may yet become the treaty organization's epitaph. "While Laos is protected by SEATO against aggression," he said, "this does not mean that the organization is designed to prevent States from going Communist."

It was designed, of course, for no other purpose.

Chapter X

THE POWER OF THE GUN

The Chinese Communists realized much earlier than SEATO's members that the treaty organization was ill equipped to handle Maoist tactics. While the annual Council meetings earnestly debated the desirability, or otherwise, of creating a command structure to combat a direct, overt and improbable Chinese invasion of the treaty area, Peking labeled SEATO another "paper tiger" and proceeded quietly to subvert and capture the countryside of Laos and much of South Vietnam. It was not until 1961 that SEATO began to understand that it had been tilting at windmills. By this time it was too late to save Laos. Faced with the prospect then of using military force to fight the Communists' evanescent pressures and of colliding thereby with the material force of Russian-backed China, four of the eight SEATO Powers—Britain, France, Australia and New Zealand—glumly concluded that they could not win. Though all but France were prepared to take military action in the improbable event that the Communists did not agree to a conference at which everything was in their favor, the acquiescence of Britain, in particular, was reluctant and obtained only by firm American pressure and Washington's quite obvious determination, if necessary, to go it alone, or with the aid only of the Philippines and Thailand.

SEATO got a new, but brief, lease of life. "We are no longer a paper tiger," said one of the Asian delegates as the Council meeting in Bangkok broke up at the end of March, 1961. "We've become a papier-mâché tiger." The brutal fact is that though China is not yet a great military Power, it has served notice—and without firing a shot—that in a conventional war in Southeast Asia it has the means and the manpower to win. Or, as Mao Tse-tung would put it, political power has begun to grow out of China's gun.

According to Marshal Lin Piao, the Defense Minister, the Liberation Army today has a strength of 2,500,000. Compared with the divisions that poured into Korea in the winter of 1950, it is well equipped. From seventy army corps its strength has been cut to thirty-five corps, each of three divisions. The divisions no longer consist of anything from five thousand to seven thousand guerrilla-oriented infantrymen, but twelve thousand to fifteen thousand regulars trained to use fairly modern equipment. Firepower has increased threefold. In Korea the Chinese repeatedly failed to make proper use of their 250 Soviet tanks. Often they spurned their tactical value and deployed them as field guns. Their artillery was inadequate and indifferently used. Supply was a fearful headache, since weapons were a mixture of Russian, Chinese, Japanese, American and British guns.

By the time the fighting ceased, however, a Chinese division had achieved approximately two-thirds of the firepower of a Western division. At the corps and army levels its firepower was still low by Western standards, and this deficiency may still exist, though the modernization of the force has embraced the formation of two, and possibly three, armored divisions, and one, possibly two, airborne divisions.

The air force, which did not exist when the Korean War began, now consists of about 3,500 planes, of which about three-quarters are jets, operating out of 147 airfields stretching from the borders of Indo-China to Siberia. The navy is small. It consists of two cruisers, five destroyers, twenty submarines and a couple of hundred other smaller craft, including landing craft.

These forces have some notable deficiencies. One is an acute shortage of oil, which affects all three services. Another is the inadequacy of the transport system. A third is the purely military weakness caused in recent years by the Party's insistence on a widespread participation in industrial and agricultural production and security work in the communes.

As defense forces, however, they are strong enough to defend China against any conventional attack, especially when backed by hundreds of millions of at least partially trained militia. For fighting limited wars in peripheral countries such as Laos, China is so well placed that no predictable concentration of available Western conventional forces could beat it: and, though it has obvious offensive weaknesses, which may take years to overcome, it is well on the way to becoming the most formidable military Power Asia has ever seen.

If that is an overstatement, it is the situation as some of America's allies have restated it for themselves; it is an appreciation shared by those in the target area. China is not yet a nuclear Power, but this is a deficiency that will certainly be remedied, if only in token form, within a few months. It has substantial deposits of uranium ore, which, under the 1950 agreement with the Soviet Union, have been jointly mined and refined. The Soviet Union, hesitant about giving China nuclear weapons, has been much less hesitant about helping with nuclear know-how. It has trained Chinese physicists at technological colleges in the Soviet Union and provided substantial technical and material assistance, including a heavy-water moderated reactor. This type of reactor is useful mainly for research, but it is capable of producing small quantities of fissile material which can be used to make atomic bombs, and Western Intelligence agencies believe there are others like it. Chinese nuclear physicists are also known to be working with advanced research equipment, including cyclotrons and electron accelerators at several institutes in China, and with even more advanced equipment at the joint nuclear research institute at Dubna, near Moscow. According to the Peking *People's Daily* of October 11, 1958, many provinces, municipalities and autonomous regions have set up organizations to conduct research in atomic energy, and many universities and institutions are devoting courses to nuclear study. Repeated reports from other countries such as Japan and India refer to Sinkiang as an advanced center for nuclear research, and, in July, 1959, President Ho Chi-minh was reported as having said that China would soon have atomic bombs.

The need for nuclear capability is now accepted both by the military hierarchy and by the Party theoreticians. Long before the "great leap forward," the necessity for industrialization was stated explicitly in terms of the creation of military power. In a report on the modernization of the army on July 31, 1952, for instance, Colonel-General Hsiao Hua, a veteran member of Mao's study group at Changsha, and then deputy-director of the General Political Department of the People's Revolutionary Military Council and a member of the Central Committee Control Commission, said: "It has to be particularly pointed out that to build a powerful and modern national defense army we must build a powerful industry, particularly a powerful national defense industry. The production increase and economy campaign unfolded by the whole nation and the large-scale economic construction which is going to start soon will lay the foundation for the building of a powerful industry and national defense industry. National defense construction is closely related to, and cannot be separated from, economic construction. . . . Our economic construction cannot but be undertaken with an eye to national defense and cannot but be directed to the needs of national defense. Hence, economic construction shall prepare material conditions for the building of national defense army units, while modernization of national defense serves as protection for the economic construction of the State and also the motive power for economic construction of the State."

It is arguable whether the emergence of Communist China as a nuclear Power will make a third world war inevitable. For years the Chinese people have been told that they have nothing to fear in a nuclear war, that people are more important than weapons, that even if three hundred million Chinese die they will be survived by more than three hundred million, and that nuclear war will only hasten the end of the imperialist Powers and spread Communism all over the world. There are also legitimate grounds for belief that Mao Tse-tung's failure to follow through with a crash birth-control program is linked with the Peking view that though nuclear war is not "fatally inevitable," as the Moscow conference stated, it is, nevertheless, highly probable, and even necessary.

To regard the Chinese as adventuristic and opportunistic and intent on plunging into a world war at the earliest possible moment, however, is to misunderstand the Maoist strategy. The use of the bomb, the nuclear equivalent of the "human wave," to destroy the "cities" (that is, the United States) is a final step to be taken only when the "countryside" (that is, the underdeveloped world) is secured and the United States has been isolated. If the point is ever reached where China strikes because it thinks that final victory is at hand—and not out of desperation—the chances are that the third world war will have already been lost by the West.

In the immediate future the importance to China of nuclear weapons, as in the possession of a strong army, is not what it will do with them, but what it is capable of doing. The lesson it imparts is obvious in Southeast Asia, where many who cordially detest the Chinese now see the future not as a choice between Communism and anti-Communism but between the peaceful and the painful acceptance of China as the dominant power of the region. To suffer, like the Laotians and the South Vietnamese, by associating with the effete and decadent West, or to get fine new hospitals and factories, like the Cambodians, by accepting China's pledges of peaceful coexistence for what they may prove to be worth? Provided one accepts treaties of friendship without too many backward glances at Tibet and the minority regions of China and ignores Mao's 1939 references to China's territories and the deliberate subversion and penetration that have gone on behind the protestations of "peaceful coexistence," the choice does not seem difficult.

It has been particularly agonizing in the case of Burma, however. Ever since the Chinese Communists appeared on its northern border in 1949, Burma has pursued a policy of hoping for the best while expecting the worst. The Communists refused to recognize either the validity of the perpetual lease of a stretch of territory called the Namwan Assigned Tract by the Nationalist Government, or the McMahon Line demarcating the border which was agreed to by Britain and China in 1913–1914. Communist forces often crossed into Burmese territory and clashes between Burmese and

Chinese troops frequently occurred. To make matters worse for Burma, which was plagued by Communist insurrections of its own, a hangover from the 1948 Southeast Asian revolts, the northeastern border area became a passageway for Burmese Communists into China. Some twenty to thirty thousand refugees from China also crossed the border into Burma, including a number of indoctrinated Communists, who succeeded, among other things, in indoctrinating the Chinese schools in the border district of Myitkyina.

As early as 1954, when U Nu, the Burmese Prime Minister, and Chou En-lai, agreed to accept the five principles of peaceful co-existence as a basis for the relationship between the two states, Burma tried earnestly to reach a boundary settlement with China. China appeared determined at first to drive a hard bargain. It demanded Burma's abrogation of the perpetual lease on the Namwan Assigned Tract, an area of special significance to all of northern Burma since it has the only auto road linking the Kachin State in the northwest with the Shan State in the east. Events in Tibet and the strained relations that developed between India and China during 1959 and 1960 led Peking into a more conciliatory mood. In the agreement, which was concluded with a rally at the Peking Workers' Stadium on October 2, 1960, China finally abrogated the perpetual lease of the Namwan Tract and let it become part of Burma. In exchange, it acquired a highly strategic position on the Burmese side of the Hpimaw Pass, which gives direct access into northern Burma, opening the way northward into eastern Tibet, westward into Assam and southward into central Burma.

Communist China gave every indication of delight. The Burmese were much more cautious. The *Nation* in Rangoon said: "In a vague sort of way the people of this country realise that they have come off second best in negotiating with the Reds, but the general feeling is one of relief that a solution that is not too humiliating has been found." A Chinese interest-free ten-year loan of $85 million sealed the new accord, however, on terms that were clearly meant to impress the Burmese that it pays to be friendly.

Under the rule of Field Marshal Sarit, the Kingdom of Thailand has given the impression of being firmly behind the United States in Southeast Asia. It was strongly in favor of armed support in Laos for General Phoumi Nosavan, the Right-wing army leader, who is also Marshal Sarit's cousin. It has enjoyed its prestige as SEATO headquarters. As the only country in Southeast Asia which did not come under colonial rule, it has no color or colonial bias, and it has not yet been plagued by wars of national liberation. Its people generally are better off than their neighbors, though most are subsistence farmers: the Thai Communist Party has always been small. It is well to remember, however, that the situation in Thailand has not always looked so secure. Before the rule of Marshal Pibul Songgram ended with a *coup d'état* by Marshal Sarit in 1958, Thailand professed its allegiance to the Western cause while flirting quite openly with Peking. It gave the impression of going up on the down escalator—and therefore possessed of the best of explanations whatever destination it chanced to reach. Newspapers owned by top government leaders, including Marshal Sarit, were overtly anti-American and pro-Communist.

When SEATO was created the West envisaged Thailand as the treaty center, with a semicircle of pro-Western and anti-Communist countries in Laos, Cambodia and South Vietnam protecting it from Communist contamination. The idea was that these countries should be persuaded, under promise of American aid, to have nothing to do with the Communists, and to this end they were firmly discouraged from entering into diplomatic relations with Peking. In exchange, they were covered by SEATO's mantle of protection, as Mr. John Foster Dulles used to call it, and provided with the means to raise and train large armies to counter the regional strength of the Pathet Lao and the much more formidable Vietminh in North Vietnam. The idea was to base political strength on military force. If this had been accompanied by the creation also of economic strength, it might have worked. Unfortunately, no one seemed to think this was necessary.

Thailand with its large export rice crop has not done too badly. But Laos and South Vietnam are, and have always been, in desperate shape. Cambodia, now laden with Communist, particularly Chinese, aid, the reward for cooperation, is doing better than any. It is getting factories to make its own clothing, its own cement and its own timber products. It feels it is beginning to move; and it attributes its success to the friendship it has established with China. It has therefore tossed its part of the SEATO mantle into the dustbin.

The result of this and events in Laos and South Vietnam is that Thailand has lost its anti-Communist outer shield. It is no longer the well protected hub of SEATO but its forward patrol. Its vulnerable and semidissident northeastern provinces are wide open to penetration and subversion, and Bangkok can scarcely be blamed for beginning to have some agonizing second thoughts. We have no reason—or right—to expect that it will prove more resolute than its Buddhist neighbors in Burma and Cambodia, who, at heart, do no more than hope for the best in pursuing their policies of "peaceful coexistence." It will be subjected to strong internal and external pressures. The Thai Communist Party, as we have noted, is small, but the Malayan Communist Party has its headquarters in southern Thailand; the Vietnamese Communist Party is extremely active in the northeast, adjoining Laos; and the Chinese Communist Party is at work in Bangkok. Marshal Sarit's relationship with a leading Laotian is far from unusual. Thousands of families in the two countries have relationships that cross the borders, and the northeastern Thailanders are much more Lao in custom, language and appearance than Thai. Finally, the Chinese Communists have for years been using Nai Pradit, the former Thai Prime Minister, as a symbol of the "Free Thai" movement, which, as a long-range goal, aims to unite the Thais of southern China, with the Thais of Laos and the Thais of Thailand in one "big family."

Thailand also has grievances, some of which are legitimate. During the period when the Laotian crisis was building up, many Thais felt—with justification—that some of their allies were vacillating, weak and unreliable. Thailand was also angry with the United States for dumping surplus agricultural products to the detriment of its interests in what it regards as traditional markets for Thai rice. And it contrasted Russia's 1956 offer to buy Burma's surplus rice crop for the next twenty years with its own marketing problems and the few benefits that appeared to flow from its alliance with the West. Already, like Pakistan, it has considered Soviet offers of aid. When SEATO fades away, Chinese aid may be expected to follow.

As for South Vietnam, it is now in the comparatively early stages of an intensified Communist effort that has brought bloodshed and terror to the whole countryside. The army, created at great expense, is, unlike the Laotian Army, well trained and equipped; its real weakness is that it has been created as a conventional force to meet purely conventional attack. It is not equipped to cope with the politico-military techniques of the Communists, which, like an iceberg, are mostly unseen. Field Marshal Sir Gerald Templer, when he reorganized Malaya's defenses against Communist insurgency between 1952 and 1954, used to call his problem a "struggle for the hearts and minds of the people." It was a realistic appreciation. And partly because he had this realism—and partly because of the Communists' earlier blunders—Templer won the support of the Malayan people. Diem has not shown this insight in Vietnam. The situation is deteriorating and deteriorating rapidly. Ahead of us in the not too distant future, therefore, is another international conference at which the Communists will secure legal approval for their illegal conquests and we shall congratulate ourselves once again on having won peace in our time.

Malaya's first years of independence were so orderly, prosperous, efficient, democratic and cheerful under the Prime Ministership of Tengku Abdul Rahman that it seems almost treacherous to doubt that it does not have an assured, comfortable and non-Communist future. It finished off the war against the armed Communist guerrillas, though the hard core led by the veteran Chin Peng (who won a decoration from the British for his services during the Second World War and participated in the Victory Parade in London) remained intact in its Yenan-like sanctuary across the Thai border. It maintained the highest living standards and the highest per capita income (Japan not excluded) in Asia. It successfully encouraged private industrial development and the replanting of high yielding strains of rubber. It resolutely turned its back on troublous Chinese Singapore which wanted to join the Federation of Malayan States; but, once again, it has begun to come under heavy fire from Peking, which lists it high among the "U.S. puppets" and therefore marked for liquidation. The Communists' opportunity here lies in the strains in the communal alliance between the indigenous Malays and the much harder-working—and much wealthier—Chinese and Indians and Pakistanis, who together outnumber the Malays. Through the police and the army the Malays have the guns. The Chinese have the money and the Malayan Communist Party as an always available militant line of defense. When all else around is crumbling in Southeast Asia the Communists will strike again.

Separated from Malaya by a causeway and the mile-wide Straits of Johore is the city-state of Singapore with a population now of nearly 2 million, more than three-quarters of whom are Chinese. Five out of every hundred over the age of fourteen are unemployed. Teen-agers flood the labor market at the rate of about thirty-three thousand a year; and the birth rate of 3.9 per cent a year shows no signs of leveling off, despite an officially encouraged birth-control program. To meet this challenge the Left-wing government has a two-pronged policy: to reinforce the island's entrepôt economy by industrialization and in the process to make Singapore so attractive that Malaya will welcome it as its twelfth state, and thereby serve as an outlet for the island's overflow population.

For an administration that promised to be "as far to the Left as it is possible to go and yet remain within the democratic framework," Prime Minister Lee Kuan-yew and his People's Action Party have governed with extraordinary restraint and efficiency. Though the British retain the island as their principal Far Eastern base and are responsible for its foreign affairs and defense (in addition to sharing with Malays a responsibility for ensuring that internal security does not run off the rails), the People's Action Party has full financial control and all the authority that flows from that. Its pre-election bellicosity drove much foreign capital out, but its exemplary behavior since has encouraged some capital to return.

In some of his window dressing acts, Lee Kuan-yew appears to derive his inspiration from Peking. Like Chou En-lai he occasionally shoulders a spade and leads gangs of "volunteer" laborers conscripted from the civil service on "people's" projects such as the creation of a "people's esplanade," a "people's park" and a "people's beach," all of which were created by an army of human ants in the twinkling of an eye. But he is also talented and courageous and certain that if his experiment fails there is no hope and the Communists will take over; and in this he is undoubtedly correct. His problem is to retain his dynamic within the bounds of responsible government, a feat that is becoming more difficult with every year. Since the end of the Second World War, Singapore's inclination to the Left has been progressive and predictable. Just as Lee Kuan-yew waited for blunders by his middle-of-the-road opposition to bring him to power, so the left wing of the People's Action Party, and, behind that, the Communists, wait their turn. They have forced Lee to demand independence by 1963: it is a demand that Lee himself deplores, a policy of desperation, which may prolong his political life but in the end must bow to the forces of Chinese chauvinism.

Within sight of Singapore is the great Indonesian archipelago which stretches for 2,800 miles in a crescent around the southeast corner of Asia. In known natural resources the country is the third richest in the world, ranking after the United States and the Soviet Union. In population, with approximately 90 million people (most of whom are Muslims) it ranks sixth. Before the Second World War, under Dutch colonial rule, it supplied a third of the world's rubber, palm oil and coconut products, two-fifths of the world's kapok, four-fifths of the world's pepper and a fifth of the world's tea in addition to large quantities of sugar and coffee. The climate is tropical but benign, the soil volcanic and rich. Yet Indonesia, now in its second decade of independence, is host to the largest Communist Party and the largest Communist following outside the Communist bloc.

Since the failure of the Communist uprising at Madiun in Java in 1949 it patiently built up its strength from fewer than five thousand to a million and a half members and candidate members and a voting following of some 8 million. For years the Communists were helped by President Sukarno's warm admiration for the progress he saw in China and by the general conviction among his subordinates that colonialism, even after independence, remained a more serious threat than Communism.

President Sukarno borrowed his idea of "guided democracy" from China in 1956. It bears little resemblance to its prototype. The president is a dilettante with a liking for power but with singularly little interest in, or capacity for, hard work or the mechanics of government. Dr. Hatta, for many years vice-president of the Republic, believes that the cumbrous governmental edifice that Sukarno has constructed will last only as long as the president. That may be overestimating the president's capabilities, the tolerance of the Indonesian people for an uninterrupted decline in their living standards, and the inclination of the Communist Party to accept a passive role in general support of the president.

Judged by the Maoist formula there are weaknesses in the Indonesian Communist Party. Though it is extremely well entrenched in populous east and central Java, it has tended to follow the traditional Marxist-Leninist approach, concentrating more heavily on organized labor in the trade unions and in the cities generally than in the countryside. It has the mass organization, but the army with 110 battalions has the guns. Between the two, President Sukarno, with demagogy and charm, has preserved a following that so far has enabled him to weather repeated threats to his authority.

Despite efforts by the Army Chief of Staff, General Abdul Haris Nasution, to purge his forces of Communists, penetration still exists. Against this, the Communists, in pursuit of a policy that for years gave firm support to Sukarno in most of his policies, have tended to grow flabby and to lose their impetus. The same, unfortunately, is also true of the army. In the civil aspects of its martial law administration it has failed to prove itself more capable, or even noticeably less corrupt, than the politicians. It gives the impression of having neither the inclination or the capacity to govern.

The Communists are aware of their shortcomings. In 1959 they began to move into opposition to President Sukarno over his treatment of the Chinese minority, who, by voluntary contributions, or by squeeze, had been one of the principal financial mainstays of the Communist Party. Another manifestation of this tougher approach became apparent during the Moscow conference when the Indonesian Communists, who generally have been closer to Moscow than to Peking, gave at least qualified support to the Chinese demand for action.

China did not hesitate to show its mailed fist during the extremely bitter controversy over Indonesia's treatment of Chinese nationalists in 1959 and 1960. For a time Dr. Subandrio, the Indonesian Foreign Minister, was frank in expressing his views about China's expansionism. But thanks to a determined effort by Peking early in 1961, a visit by Foreign Minister Chen Yi to Jakarta, the offer of Chinese economic aid, and some welcome advice on how to conduct a war of national liberation in Dutch New Guinea, most of Indonesia's fears seemed to have been set aside. In any event, the prospects of an eventual Communist take-over in Indonesia are extremely favorable, for here, as in the United Arab Republic, where the Russian-built Aswan High Dam promises to bring 1,300,000 acres of desert under irrigation, the Soviet Union was quick to pick up on the swings what China lost on the roundabouts. At a time when Sino-Indonesian relations were at their lowest ebb in February, 1960, Khrushchev arrived in Jakarta, the Indonesian capital, on one of his extraordinary tours. At the time, the visit seemed a curious mixture of success and failure. Khrushchev was often bored, rude and undiplomatic. He sometimes looked like an angry Berkshire boar that had blundered into a graciously decorated sitting room and wanted only to find the door.

More enduring than his boredom and bad temper, however, was the blank check in his brief case and his plans for such high prestige projects as steel mills for the Indonesians. "Take a billion dollars if you want it," Khrushchev told his hosts. But the Indonesians, not anxious to lose their neutral balance, accepted only $250 million.

Khrushchev did not lose heart, however, and late in 1960 the Russians were similarly openhanded in an offer of arms. General Nasution, many of whose officers had been trained in America and were sympathetically inclined toward the West, found himself presented with the whole array of Soviet conventional military hardware and invited to pick what he wanted. The latest in jet fighters came in this Christmas stocking, and a cruiser. This may easily absorb Indonesia's available naval officers. It is also well calculated to put some shudders down Dutch spines in West New Guinea, which, the Indonesians claim, should have been handed over with all other Dutch territorial possessions in the Netherlands East Indies in 1949.

Indonesian army, air force and naval officers now go to Moscow for training—and to listen to the powerful propaganda line that only from the Communists can Indonesians expect genuine support for their patriotic claim to West New Guinea, and that American aid is prestigious since it denies Indonesia what it needs and gives only what Washington believes is good for it. All this has not increased the number of Communists in Indonesia. But it has extended Communist influence at the expense of the West in general and the United States in particular; it has helped to make Communism much more respectable in Indonesian eyes than the ideology of the colonial Powers, or the United States, which has taken a "neutral" stand on the West New Guinea issue, can ever hope to be; and it has given the Communist bloc another large chunk of Southeast Asian trade, which, in turnover, ranks after North America and Western Europe.

China is conscious of the suspicion with which it is regarded in Southeast Asia and does not appear to have had any misgivings about surrendering the initiative to the Soviet Union in many cases. In Laos, for instance, Russian, not Chinese, planes operated the air lift to Captain Kong Lae and the Pathet Lao forces in the winter of 1960–1961. China's repeatedly expressed desire during this period was to see a "zone of peace" established throughout the Southeast Asian area. The policy is expedient. It requires the elimination of American and other Western influence—as a prelude to the extension of Chinese influence. Peking may be more than willing to coexist for a time with some of its Southeast Asian neighbors, just as it once declared its willingness to coexist with the minorities of China. In this even "bigger family" the problem is unchanged, however: China needs living space. Moreover, to leave pockets of potential counterrevolution within the region would be to run the risk of rotten apples in the barrel. Communist leadership must eventually be established, therefore, just as it was established in Tibet.

To the stock argument that Buddhist and Muslim Southeast Asians are not likely to "go Communist" because of their religions, the answer is that in order to resist they will have to prove more resolute in their faiths than the Buddhist Tibetans or the Muslim Huis of China. It is not so many years ago that some Westerners predicted with assurance that the Communists would never be able to control China because of the family system. We have seen what is happening to that.

A more valid suggestion is that the Communists will not find the Southeast Asians ready to accept the drive and hard work that has characterized the regime in China. Southeast Asia generally lacks the extreme poverty of China. Most Southeast Asians will not starve or lack for shelter even if they are disinclined to work. Southeast Asian Communism may well prove, then, to be a different sort of Communism; but it is unlikely to deny China access to its raw materials and the dumping ground it needs to dispose of its excess population. And beyond lies the virtually empty continent of Australia. Fewer than 11 million "white Australians" are scattered around its fringe. Its tropical north is almost totally undeveloped and unlikely ever to be adequately developed under the limited, and purely white, immigration policies that are common to all Australian political parties. Australia may survive longer, but should it also fall, historians will not pause to reflect too deeply on the fate of this handful of white men who thought they could live under the shadow of the Chinese phallus and, for perhaps two centuries, succeeded.

With a largely neutralized Far East covering its exposed Pacific flank, with great new centers of industry in Central Asia and strengthened by access to the wealth—especially the oil—of Southeast Asia, the hurricane from China will soon blow more heavily against India and countries far beyond.

The blissful era in which peaceful coexistence governed the relations between India and China lasted less than five years. By early 1959 Indian protests against Chinese conduct in Tibet had provoked Peking into the contemptuous attitude that had characterized its approach to India early in the fifties. "Interference in China's internal affairs by certain political figures in India is not fortuitous," declared the *People's Daily* on May 6, 1959. "It bears the signs of the times. India is a country that has gained independence after shaking off the colonial rule of British imperialism. It desires to develop its national economy in a peaceful international environment and has profound contradictions with the imperialist and colonialist forces. This is one aspect of the picture. Another aspect is that the Indian big bourgeoisie maintains innumerable links with imperialism and is, to a certain extent, dependent on foreign capital. Moreover, by its class nature, the big bourgeoisie has a certain urge for outward expansion. This is why, while it opposes the imperialist policy of intervention, it more or less reflects consciously or unconsciously certain influences of the imperialist policy of intervention."

In September, 1959, China suddenly reversed its official stand on the Indian border. Having led the Indian Government to believe that it accepted the traditional Sino-Indian alignment of the boundary, it occupied some twelve thousand miles of Indian border lands and disclosed claims to another 38,000 square miles of Indian territory, including 32,000 square miles (out of a total of 34,000) in the strategically important North-East Frontier Agency.

In a White Paper covering the period March–November, 1960, the Indian Government revealed that armed Chinese intrusions into Indian territory and air intrusions had continued through the summer, and that the two little States of Sikkim and Bhutan, on the southern slopes of the Himalayas, both of which are under Indian protection, were being softened up by a war of nerves in Tibet. In a note to Peking, the Indian Government said: "Persistent reports have reached us over a period of months that propaganda organs as well as officials in the Tibet region have been saying that China intends incorporating Sikkim and Bhutan, like Ladakh, into the Chinese People's Republic. On some occasions it was even stated that China might take military action to occupy these territories."

Peking's reply was to repudiate an assurance given by Chou En-lai to Mr. Nehru as late as April, 1960, that China accepted India's "protection" of Bhutan and Sikkim and to add another 2,000 miles to its border demands. As in Ladakh, which is part of Kashmir, the Chinese justified their claims on these tiny, backward states on the grounds that years ago they paid tribute to Tibet, which paid tribute to China, and that therefore Chinese suzerainty over Tibet meant Tibetan (that is, Chinese) suzerainty over Sikkim and Bhutan.

To pursue their objectives here the Chinese have a network of highways and airstrips in Sinkiang, which is now an expanding industrial area, a major center for the production of munitions, for nuclear research and a base for training large military forces. The Sinkiang-Tibet highway, which runs at an average height of 13,000 feet and was largely built with forced Tibetan labor, is of obvious strategic significance and purpose. Indian reports state that it has been used for the movement of troops and military supplies by "repeated convoys of ten-ton trucks." A second strategic highway, the Pamir Road, links Kashgar with Tashkurgan and the border zone in the Gilgit Agency of Pakistan, which China also claims. All along this great border area stretching from Afghanistan to Assam, the Chinese are concerned about external influences, especially religious influences, on their dissident minorities. In Sinkiang the worry is over the Muslim influence on the Huis, especially the influence of the Ismaeli sect, whose spiritual leader is the Aga Khan.

In Sikkim and Bhutan the concern is with Buddhism. Both these Himalayan peoples, in their own primitive way, have always tended to reflect Tibetan, rather than Indian, events. Even their rural superstitions, including the belief that devils always go uphill and never down, favor the Chinese. And today, along with the genuine Tibetan refugees, who continue to flee from the Chinese Communists, are numerous indoctrinated agents whose task it is to turn popular feeling against the Indian protectors. By the end of September, 1960, a total of 43,500 refugees from Tibet had been counted, but the flow is now decreasing. On January 10, 1961, Reuters reported that Chinese troops had killed more than 4,000 Tibetans trying to escape to India, with the result that only about a thousand of the original band which had set out from Lhasa survived.

China's object here is threefold. It wants to contain the Tibetan problem within Tibet; it wants to stamp out external religious influences on the Tibetan people; and it wants to secure a foothold on the southern slopes of the Himalayas overlooking the plains of India.

Its objectives are similar in Nepal, but its methods differ. As in the case of Burma, border demands have been softened with bribes of economic aid, a first installment of $12.6 million in 1956 and a further $22 million on March 21, 1960. This latest aid agreement included the dispatch to Nepal of Chinese experts and technicians to help in construction and the now customary psychological insert that though the living expenses of the Chinese experts and technicians will be paid from the grant, their standard of living will not exceed that of personnel of the same level in the Kingdom of Nepal, a shaft of telling potency in the propaganda field against the United States, whose aid programs are often criticized on the score that many loans and grants are heavily reduced in value by the demands of American technicians for Stateside accommodation and living standards.

The Indian Communist Party has split over the border issue, one group siding with the government in its firm stand against Peking, the other protesting that the Chinese leaders really do believe in genuine coexistence. It is significant, however, that the West Bengal Communist Party has ranged itself alongside the Chinese. In Septem-

ber, 1960, the Indian Communist Party passed a resolution supporting Moscow's views on the ideological debate on the inevitability of
war. A month later the West Bengal Communist Party dissented
violently. Believing that it is assured of victory at the next election, it has adopted a tough, pro-Chinese line against the Indian
Government. It feels that its chances of consolidating Communist
power here are sound and that advantages will flow from its proximity
to China that were denied the Communists in the isolation of the
south Indian State of Kerala, where the first democratically elected
Communist government in the world failed to convince the electors
that it merited a second chance after the central government, to prevent bloodshed, had dissolved the Communist administration and
introduced "President's rule."

Fewer than 13,000 Chinese are registered as living in India, but
most of these are in West Bengal. According to officials who fled
from Lhasa, they form part of a gigantic spy network for Communist
China. A former deputy chief of security in the Tibetan district of
Amdo, who reached India in May, 1960, said that the Chinese operated this ring from two bases in Tibet—the Lhoka district on the
border, and Gyantse, bordering Sikkim—and that the bases were controlled by high-ranking Communist intelligence officers, who worked
through Chinese nationals living in Bengal. Just before his report
was made public, the Indian Government deported thirty-four Chinese, including two high-ranking officials of the Bank of China, on
charges of espionage.

The subsequent failure of Indian and Chinese officials to reach
any sort of agreement on the border dispute, and repeated Chinese
ground and air violations of Indian territory have led India to match
China's strategic road-building program in the border areas and to be
prepared, if needs be, to meet force with force. Thus a new, if
inevitable, element has been added to the struggle for Asia. Again,
there is little prospect in the foreseeable future that it will be decided
by military force. China is confident that India's parliamentary democracy will fail, thereby leading to a political and economic collapse
and the emergence of a government in which a judicious change of
policy on the border issue, a substitution of the carrot for the club,
could have the desired effect. So far as India is concerned, Mr. Nehru
feels that any step to push the Chinese out of India territory would

only lead to war between India and China, "which is bad at any time but more so in the present world situation." Mr. Nehru does not dispute the possibility that India's economic efforts will fail. But he says that Indians lack the "inner self-discipline" demanded by Communism and that chaos and anarchy are the alternatives to success in the attempts to industrialize India and to raise the living standards of its people. At this stage, India's future is unpredictable. Everything depends on the quantity and quality of foreign aid that it receives, for this is the only alternative to the draconian forms of capital accumulation practiced by the Chinese Communists.

India's discovery of the true nature of the Chinese Communist regime is one of the more important developments of recent years, however, since it represents a marked narrowing of the gap between Western, especially American, and neutral, especially Indian, thought on China. The spirit of Bandung flickers only feebly now. And it has not been notably rekindled by China's friendly, and successful, overtures to Nepal, Burma, Cambodia and Pakistan, which reacted to the Sino-Indian crisis by seeking a border settlement with Peking as a means of further isolating India.

Inspired editorials in leading Pakistan newspapers early in 1961 suggested that Pakistan was too small to line up with one giant or the other. When it joined SEATO, Pakistan, like the Philippines and Thailand, hoped for greater quantities of economic aid—and for material backing in its struggle with India. With the passing of Mr. John Foster Dulles and the advent of the new American appreciation that a non-Communist India was at least as important—and perhaps even as deserving of economic aid—as a non-Communist Pakistan, frustrated Pakistani officials began to regret their haste and impetuosity in aligning themselves with Western Powers who, so it seemed, did not have Pakistan's real interests at heart but only their own. The acceptance of Soviet aid was a first step toward a policy change, tentative approaches to China to settle the border issue including areas which India claimed from both, a cynical second.

Peking could afford to chuckle. Here was demonstrable evidence that when it openly played the bully it could count on expanding its international influence, even if the relationship it enjoyed with most countries was likely to be of a different order from that which Mr. Nehru once envisaged.

The hope of bringing China into the family of Asian nations as a law-abiding, civilized member at this time and under these circumstances was always slight. Communist China could not be agreeable and trustworthy and at the same time achieve its goals. Mao did not think of the world revolution as "fancy needlework" when he set out its terms of reference. The Indian approach was important as a determinant, however. Mr. Nehru's carrot and the U.S. club were complementary. That both were likely to prove inadequate always seemed obvious. For the Indian premise to have been correct, Peking would have had to deny its charter. In the end, however, Nehru's try was no less, and no more, effective than the U.S. military deterrent, which could raise barriers, but, short of a major war, could neither bring down the Communist regime nor prevent Communist infiltrators from slipping around the mountaintops while it guarded the valleys.

The extremely deep doubts and suspicions now entertained about China by India must nevertheless be considered a major setback for Peking in its campaign to unite with all those available to be united with in the struggle against "imperialism."

China's quarrel with Yugoslavia has also had wide and unfavorable repercussions for Peking. Marshal Tito is a respected figure in much of the underdeveloped world, and repeated attacks on the Yugoslav "revisionists" have succeeded only in discrediting China in areas where it hoped to win friends. Its influence has also diminished in the United Arab Republic, where its encouragement of Communist groups opposed to Nasser weakened both Chinese-Egyptian relations and the impact of the Afro-Asian Peoples' Solidarity Council in Cairo, which Peking had once hoped to use as the spearhead of its penetration of Africa. Its prestige has declined among Iraqi leaders, also, despite a statement by General Kassem at the opening of the first Chinese Industrial Exhibition in Bagdad on November 5, 1960, to the effect that the Chinese people had brought their country to its present greatness by throwing out imperialism and Iraq would follow the same path.

China's breakthroughs have more than compensated for these setbacks, however. At this stage it is concerned primarily with subversion, the exploitation of distress and anticolonialism and the establishment of ideological base areas which are capable of expansion. In all these fields it has been successful. In an interview with the New China News Agency on October 31, 1960, Ferhat Abbas said: "The Chinese revolution was a great revolution which has had a vast influence on Asia and Africa, because Asia and Africa alike have been subjected to colonial rule. China's achievements of today in industrialization, technical progress and other fields set an example for Asia and Africa." A month later the spokesman for the Algerian Provisional Government in Cairo said: "The Chinese revolution offers a historic contribution to the general liberation of the peoples of the colonies."

Before the end of 1960 Algerian troops were busy applying the Chinese experience of civil war to their own war against the French. Wang Wei, a New China News Agency correspondent, who visited the front on the eastern border of Algeria, reported on November 8, 1960, that what struck him most was the frequent talk by the Algerians about the Chinese war and China's experience. On the bed of an officer at general staff headquarters he found a book on revolutionary war which devoted a chapter to the military thinking of Mao Tse-tung. The officer told him he had been studying Mao's works.

China sees in Algeria the opportunity to present Africa with a case study of Maoist revolutionary war, and the Algerian rebels are willing collaborators. In an editorial commemorating the sixth anniversary of the revolt on November 1, 1960, the rebel newspaper *Al Mujahid* said: "Today our revolution enters its seventh year. This is a major event in the history not only of Algeria, but of the entire African continent, and in the history of the struggle of the peoples against imperialist rule and exploitation. Our revolution has destroyed the foundation of the French colonial empire and accelerated the historical process of the liberation of the dominated peoples. It has illumined the path of the oppressed peoples and torn off the mask worn by the allies of colonialism." Another article pointed out that the myth about the invulnerability of the colonialist countries had vanished. Every African had seen that the fight of the Algerian people had accelerated the process of the decolonization of Africa.

On December 13, 1960, Ferhat Abbas appealed for further help from the Chinese, urging them to "take every measure in order to stop immediately this crime of genocide of the Algerian people."

Chou En-lai answered on the same day in a note expressing "infinite indignation" against the French colonialists' "atrocities and massive slaughter of the Algerian people." If the Algerian war is settled by negotiation with France, Peking will get the credit for having helped the Algerians, like Ho Chi-minh in Indo-China in 1954, to negotiate from a position of strength. If, on the other hand, the war drags on, China's assistance will increase and it will gain greater glory in Africa as a champion of anticolonialism.

In the hope and expectation of further "anti-imperialist" and anti-colonial revolutions, Peking plans to get fully behind the main stream of African nationalism. It knows it cannot fail to win African support when it lists Africa as a region for continuing revolution and perpetual struggle against Western aid and investment. South Africa promises a rich harvest in blood and Western ill will. Portuguese Angola proved overripe. The Congo was ready-made. Demonstrators in tens of millions jammed the city squares of China in February, 1961, to condemn the murder of Patrice Lumumba, who had been Peking's man long before his name hit world headlines and whose close associates had been early and honored visitors to China. Peking moved swiftly after Lumumba's death to establish diplomatic relations with the Gizenga group at Stanleyville, and, despite its own acute shortages, to exploit this beachhead with a consignment of food, medicines and gasoline and the promise of "support and assistance in all fields in the struggle against colonialism and imperialism."

It was farsighted in Kenya, tipping Jomo Kenyatta, the detained Mau Mau leader, as the man who would matter most when the country went to the polls and began its advance toward self-determination in March, 1961. A week or two before the election Chou En-lai cabled the Kenya African National Union in protest against the "British colonialists' brutal act," in keeping Kenyatta under detention and pledged China's "firm support."

Its reward came at the All-African People's Congress in Cairo at the end of the month where delegates openly quoted Mao Tse-tung and roared their approval when Ronald Ngala, of the Kenya African Democratic Party, said: "We are fed up with European supremacy and European exploitation," and added that the United States believed that "British, French and Belgians in Africa should be replaced by another white Power."

On another tack, it was hard at work selling itself as a model for economic development. An exhibition of its economic construction achievements, which opened in Conakry, the Guinea capital, on December 28, 1960, was seen by hundreds of thousands more Africans than there are in the city. Among these was President Keita, of Mali, who said he was "greatly impressed by China's industrial achievements and particularly by the concrete improvements in the people's life as a result of technical progress." President Keita especially admired "various practical machines produced in small Chinese plants, which could also be built in Mali at little cost." Even the communes impressed, and a statement by the frankly admiring Mali Foreign Ministry declared that they had played a "decisive role" in the development of China's economy, "have bigger economic possibilities," and offer a "greater scope for economic cooperation."

Where there was change, or trouble or discontent Peking had its agents. Sometimes it was clandestine and underground, as in the shipment of guns and ammunition through Somalia to insurgents in French Somaliland, Ethiopia and the Gizenga faction in Stanleyville. Sometimes it managed to combine covert subversion with overt friendship. It missed few opportunities. With a large part of the French Army tied down in Algeria, French Guinea, Martinique and Guadeloupe became immediate targets for wars of national liberation. With few Spanish scholars in its ranks, it recruited translators from British and other European parties and was soon attracting attention in Latin America with its Spanish-language editions of its glossy and spectacular magazines. By espousing Indonesia's claims to Dutch New Guinea, it began to mend its broken fences with Sukarno. In addition to Angola, it had the Portuguese territories of Guinea, Mozambique and Goa squarely in its sights.

As Peking assesses the international situation, however, the most pregnant breakthrough has been the success of the Castro revolution in Cuba. Southeast Asia is crumbling; but that was surely to be expected, since it is in China's own "tribute" area. Africa is in arms against colonialism and "imperialism"; but it is still tribal and its internecine quarrels are unpredictable, or perhaps too predictable for some of Peking's purposes. Cuba is, however, a textbook national liberation war in the heartland of U.S. "imperialism," opening up the widest revolutionary possibilities in a region where the peasant-landlord problem is in many areas similar to that which existed in China in the late twenties. Havana, as Mao sees it, is the Yenan of Latin America, the cradle of the revolution in the Western Hemisphere, "the trail-blazing vanguard of the Latin American peoples," as the *People's Daily* called it.

The Latin American equivalent of the All-African People's Congress is the Latin American Conference for National Sovereignty, Economic Emancipation and Peace. "The destruction of imperialism is the basic condition for the realization of any [development] plan of our countries," the conference declared at its meeting in Mexico City in March, 1961. "U.S. imperialism is the main force obstructing the development of Latin America. The close alliance of the United States with the Latin American oligarchic forces and the devastating consequences of its economic and cultural penetration show that these are the principal causes of the universal stagnation and backwardness in Latin America."

More than anywhere else the *People's Daily* saw signs of the Chinese hurricane at work here. "The Cuban people have pushed ahead with their revolution," it said. "The peoples of Nicaragua, Paraguay and the Dominican Republic persist in their armed struggles against dictatorial rule. In Guatemala, where U.S. control is tightest, armed resistance broke out against the puppet regime there. The struggle of the Venezuelan people in defense of democracy is surging forward. Anti-American demonstrations have developed on an unprecedented scale throughout Ecuador. In Argentina, Cuba, Brazil, and especially in various Central American countries, big strikes have broken out one after another, strikes which are, in fact, directed against the plundering activities of U.S. monopoly capital. All these facts demonstrate that the national and democratic revolution of the Latin American people is rising to a new height."

Here, as elsewhere, China's prospects cannot be adequately assessed without also considering the role being played by the Soviet Union, and, to a lesser extent, other members of the bloc. There are areas where Russian and Chinese policies obviously collide. One is India, where China's border pressures and attacks against Indian "interventionists" have not dissuaded the Russians from continuing large-scale economic aid. For every example of such contradictions, however, there are several which illustrate that Chinese and Russian

policies either run smoothly in tandem, or that bloc interests are
well served by this dualism. Russia moved neatly into the vacuum in
Indonesia caused by the 1959 rift in Sino-Indonesian relations, and
its dealings with the United Arab Republic, especially since the
Aswan Dam project began to take shape, for a time at least compensated for Cairo's coolness toward Peking (a coolness, incidentally,
which did not deter Nasser from acting as a forwarding agent for
Mao's military aid for the Algerian rebels). The campaigns in the
Congo and Cuba are bloc campaigns, as the Chinese have been at
pains to point out. In Cuba, for instance, China has promised $60
million in credits, Czechoslovakia $40 million, Hungary $15 million,
Romania $15 million, East Germany $10 million and Bulgaria $5
million. While China agreed to take a million tons of Cuban sugar
in 1961, the rest of the bloc shared another 3 million tons. For
obvious political reasons, all these deals were at prices higher than
the ruling world market rate.

Late in 1960 the Soviet Society for the Dissemination of Political
Knowledge set out the Party line on revolutionary prospects in Latin
America. In all aspects it faithfully reflected the Chinese policy, call-
ing for the exploitation of the Cuban revolutionary example, offers of
Soviet bloc aid, the encouragement of local Communist parties, and
the stirring up of revolution. The Cuban revolution it described
as having "priceless value"; hostility toward the United States was
Chinese in its intensity.

In Laos, where their planes shuttled supplies from Hanoi to the
Pathet Lao forces on the Plain of Jars in the early months of 1961,
the Russians not only showed their adherence to the principles decided by the Moscow conference but were ahead of the Chinese in
inflaming a war of national liberation.

In meeting this challenge in the underdeveloped world, therefore, it must be appreciated that China is not alone: in this, if in
nothing else, it has the unqualified support of the bloc. Where China
differs from its associates, however, is in the need for success. Its
pressures are violent and furious and will increase in intensity. Frustration and failure will cause it to redouble its efforts: success will
make its appetite insatiable.

CONCLUSION

IF THE Chinese plans proceed with the success they expect, and thereby provide the opportunity to postulate the argument that only the acquiescence and cooperation of the Soviet Union is needed to deliver the *coup de grâce* to the Western Powers, we may be sure that the 1960 Moscow debate, which ended in the inconclusive decision that a world war is not "fatally inevitable," will be vigorously renewed.

Assuming that the Chinese remain faithful to Mao's "countryside-city" concept, however, a conclusion that is likely to prove valid as long as nuclear equilibrium is more or less maintained between the two blocs and the Sino-Soviet alliance does not attain, or believe it has attained, such a stage of missile superiority that a single-punch war is a feasible proposition, the point of final action in the Maoist theory is unlikely to be reached in one decade, and perhaps not in two.

That is no cause for complacency. Even if events do not always favor Peking, by 1981 we must expect that China will rank third among the great military Powers of the world *and an easy first in militancy.* Its basic industrial output will be quantitatively inferior only to that of the United States and the Soviet Union. Steel production, which the Communists universally regard with ideological fervor, may well have reached 70 to 80 million tons a year, which is about the current combined production of Britain, France, West Germany and Japan. If we had any reason to expect that this might produce even a modest improvement in living standards, a mellowing in Spartan Chinese society, and a consequent lessening in revolutionary zeal, this would be a cause for satisfaction rather than concern. In per capita terms, however, even all this steel is likely to provide less than 200 pounds a year. Yet not even the food crisis in 1960–1961 persuaded Peking that it had too many people, or caused any official second thoughts about the creation of a predictable 1981 population total of a billion, which is more than the present population of North and South America, Europe and Africa combined.

Even if millions of people have been siphoned off into Southeast Asia, life in China will still be desperately hard. It is unlikely to be dull. With mass military demonstrations Nazi Germany created a militant nationalism in which guns before butter was a palatable slogan. In Communist China "people's culture" and mass rallies squander man-hours but make for a sense of national pageantry, which, like the campaign against the counterrevolutionaries, serves to identify the people with the regime and its ambitions. Lu Ting-yi, as propaganda chief, goes deeper than Goebbels ever went in Germany. Under his direction the entire educational system is designed to produce not only a new China but new Chinese. Even infants in kindergarten are introduced to manual work so that they will understand the importance of participation in "social labor." Confucianism bred a passive society; Communism demands that it should be active. Active it is, and active it is likely to remain. The commune, the creche and boarding school are not merely important economically, socially and ideologically to the regime; if Mao is to initiate something more than just another dynasty, the full communal life must be established and preserved. The "little family" will be absorbed into the "big family" of the communes, just as the "little families" of the minorities are being absorbed into the "big family" of China. In this maddened hive, filled not only with long-ings and needs and imperial visions and hatred of the United States, we shall no longer hear the cries of pain that once came from "class enemies" and the minorities of Tibet and Sinkiang. By reeducation and absorption they will have ceased to exist.

Even if it did not feel impelled to influence world politics and had no chauvinistic expansionist needs and desires, China, at this stage of development, would be a major world Power. In alliance with the Soviet Union and by the pursuit of a violent, revolutionary foreign policy directed to the destruction of American power and influence and the establishment of world Communism, it will pose the greatest challenge Western civilization has ever known. It may reasonably expect to have brought about the internal collapse of Taiwan, to have destroyed the military alliances that now girdle it, to have created by military pressures the political reactions needed to cause an almost total American military withdrawal in the Far East, to have "absorbed" all of Southeast Asia into the "great Com-munist family" and to have persuaded hundreds of millions in the rest of the underdeveloped world, whether by trade-and-aid, sub-version, persuasion or example, to turn away from the West.

If we are to have any hope of surviving this challenge it is im-perative that we understand its nature and intent. To this end I hope this brief book may serve as an introduction. We are, in effect, confronted by two complementary but separate threats. The first is purely military. Yet, if by a supreme effort we maintain nuclear and general military parity with the Soviet Union and China, we may still be left with our stockpiles intact and find ourselves so isolated from the world's materials, manpower and markets that we shall be an easy target for the knockout blow.

In this latter struggle, the balance of power is held by the 1,200 million still uncommitted people of the underdeveloped world. We have become increasingly aware of this in the past two years: but even today our approach to the problem is largely conditioned by the incorrect appreciation that it can be reviewed from year to year and that, in any event, if we contain the Communists militarily and prevent them from marching across the borders, we will be able to go quietly about the task of giving economic and technical aid and all will be well.

It is time this comfortable pipe dream was shattered. To begin with, much of the underdeveloped world is remote from both the Soviet Union and Communist China and therefore does not need to be isolated from them by military means. And in most countries under the Communist gun this emphasis on military deterrence as a counter to a threat which battens on economic and social grievances has failed to provide the stability, and the development, on which long-range optimism might be based.

In tiny, backward Laos even $300 million failed to create an army that could fight, or had any understanding of the tactics of the enemy. In South Vietnam something close to a quarter of a billion dollars a year produced a much larger and better-looking military result. But when the test came and the Communists raised the countryside, the army was quickly overextended. We built on sand and wondered why the castles fell. We also created and maintained governments which discredited both democracy and our claim to stand for "freedom."

We are perplexed and concerned when Asians and Africans fail to understand that Communism is not a greater danger than colonialism. "Colonialism is finished," we say. Asians and Africans do not think so. I once argued about this with Dr. Ali Sastraomidjojo, then Prime Minister of Indonesia, who claimed that the Dutch, who, albeit reluctantly, had given Indonesia its independence, were still a greater threat than the Communists, who threatened to take it over. "The Communists fought to throw the Dutch out," he said. "They are part of our revolution. Even now in Irian [West New Guinea], the Dutch are planning to come back and to steal our independence from us."

On another occasion I listened in a Singapore court while a tall, extraordinarily handsome young barrister with the confident culture of Harrow and Cambridge pleaded his client's case. His name was John Eber. He had won his Blue for cricket at Cambridge. He had a ready-made practice to step into in Singapore, an honored and much respected father. Yet six months later this same young man was detained without charge on St. John's Island, a green little knob in Singapore harbor and the residence at that time of men and women suspected of conspiring to promote the Communist revolution. The young man probably would have denied it and attributed his political outlook to other causes, but the fact that he was blackballed by a European club when he returned from the heady success of school and university days in England undoubtedly did not help. Of course, he should not have applied for membership in the club. His blood was not all European and he should have known better, even if he did want to play cricket. Just the suspicion of Asian blood was enough for the committees of Singapore's British clubs.

Leaving aside the behavior of the French colons in Algeria, the Belgians in the Congo, the Afrikaners in South Africa, the comparatively enlightened colonialists in India, Indo-China and the British territories in Southeast Asia consistently invited resentments that have never been forgotten. "You are my friend," a talented, sophisticated English-educated Indian journalist told me one day. "But to all white men in my country I say 'get out and go home.' " Collectively, we have been careless of custom and forgetful of the ethics of decent behavior. An acquaintance who owned a Jaguar blamed his Malay driver for the collapse of its gearbox and saw no evil in deducting eighty-five cents from his weekly wage of less than seven dollars to make good the damage. A prosperous British firm in Singapore, which employed skilled Chinese labor at fifteen dollars a week, found its illiterate, unskilled Tamil messengers could manage the skilled job reasonably well for less than six dollars a week and promptly threw all the Chinese into the street. Colonialism meant roads and schools and railways and fine buildings; but, fundamentally, it meant high profits and low wages.

Anticolonialism is a sort of Rotary badge of the underdeveloped areas. Nationalist Nehru can swap reminiscences with Communist Ho Chi-minh about when they were imprisoned by the colonial British. We are sometimes inclined to forget that Nehru, now an elder statesman of the Commonwealth, spent more than a fifth of his adult working life in British political prisons. Sutan Sjahrir, the most estimable and pro-Western of Indonesian political figures, shares his knowledge of Dutch colonial jails with President Sukarno and Vice-President Hatta. General Vo Nguyen Giap, the brilliant Vietminh military leader and conqueror of the French at Dien Bien

Phu, lost his wife in a French prison and his sister-in-law to a French firing squad.

We see Communism as evil and colonialism as defunct. To the Asians and Africans colonialism is evil and Communism more often than not an interesting "experiment." Asian anti-Communists are suspect by the majority as Western sycophants and satellites in a struggle which is not basically between freedom and tyranny but between two powerful blocs, both of which want to dominate the world. It is characteristic, for instance, that India fears Chinese chauvinism but not Chinese Communism. When the Communists equate colonialism with capitalism and both with the United States and its allies, they find ready listeners and friends, especially when they are so ready to respond to every anticolonial call. In this way, the Communist bloc profits from every Western error, and every Western act of intransigence in the underdeveloped world. Sukarno in Indonesia, Nasser in the United Arab Republic, Sékou Touré in Guinea and Ferhat Abbas in Algeria, to name only a few, are not Communists. They are nationalists, neutralists and anticolonialists, whose anger, frustration and ambition have made them bedfellows with the Communist Powers. Sukarno got support for his dearest ambition—the acquisition of Dutch New Guinea—heavy equipment for his armed forces and credits to make steel only from the Communists. Nasser got Aswan High Dam aid and heavy military equipment from the East after he had been turned down by the West. Sékou Touré turned naturally to the Communist bloc when the French tried to discipline him. Ferhat Abbas found the French willing to negotiate only when he took Chinese military assistance for his Algerian struggle. In agitating and uniting with leaders like Abbas who want to stamp out colonialism, the Communists identify themselves with revolutionary African nationalism, just as thirty-four years ago Mao saw the opportunity in China to indentify the Communists with the peasants and to lead them in revolution.

These colonial and "imperial" issues are powerful factors in the Communists' favor in their dealings with the underdeveloped world. There are others which seriously inhibit Western efforts to establish mutually satisfactory and beneficial relationships. Loss of confidence in Western capability is one. General Ne Win of Burma, a vigorous anti-Communist, thinks we have grown effete and soft. Neutralists like Prince Souvanna Phouma in Laos and Prince Norodom Sihanouk in Cambodia believe the Communists will eventually dominate the region. Non-Communist Lee Kuan-yew in Singapore says that the day he is regarded as anti-Communist he will fall.

Among Asian countries that gained their independence in the forties and inherited systems of government based on liberal democracy, India almost alone has persisted consistently with the democratic model. Pakistan is ruled by military dictatorship. The army took over to restore order out of parliamentary chaos in Burma, then handed it back to the politicians for one last try. Indonesia's democracy is "guided" by Sukarno, who has scrapped every truly democratic form.

Never-colonized Thailand sometimes has gone through democratic motions only to settle back under a military dictatorship. Of the Southeast Asian countries that have won independence more recently, North Vietnam is Communist; the South survives fretfully and temporarily under the authoritarian rule of Ngo Dinh Diem and his family; Cambodia is the feudal estate of Norodom Sihanouk; and Laos has been a political nightmare, in which the disciplined Communists alone have known where they are going and how to win. In this region only Malaya, with its economic feet planted firmly on the ground, pays more than lip service to the democratic forms.

Democracy has not failed in these and other countries; it never really existed. It is blamed, nevertheless, for economic failures, which in turn have led to a search for an economic-political system that may work more effectively in an underdeveloped environment. In 1958, eight years after the Colombo Plan was conceived "as a response to a condition of chronic poverty in an area inhabited by one quarter of mankind, within whose borders living standards were very low, challenging human conscience and constituting a threat to peace and prosperity throughout the world," even the prim and precise language of the Plan's official country-by-country survey reflected the heartbreaking lack of progress. The Indian economy continued to "show evidence of considerable strain." The year had been "generally unfavorable" for Burma. Indonesia was "confronted with a number of special problems and difficulties which hampered the government's development program." Malaya suffered from falling prices for rubber and tin. Singapore found trading difficult. Economic progress continued "though at a slower rate" in the Philippines. Everywhere the dream of economic progress and rising living standards remained a dream. If it does not follow that effective government necessarily accompanies economic progress, it is true that weak government has mostly led to chaos, or Communism, and that economic inertia has produced weak government.

In the search for a system capable of pulling up a country by its bootstraps, China seems to advance a model that, in many ways, is tailored for the needs of underdeveloped countries whose only resources, like China's, are raw materials and manpower. Parliamentary democracy is nice in theory but impracticable: Communism is not nice but it works; or so it seems to significant numbers of intelligent young Asians and Africans who want, and demand, progress.

Anyone can play the numbers game with economic aid to win debating points. Without making exaggerated claims for Communist aid, however, there seems to be a dangerous tendency in the United States to underrate Communist efforts. By comparing totals neither Russia nor China is in the race with the United States. By selective aid, sometimes in extremely large quantities, however, the Communists have frequently scored major successes, and we deceive only ourselves by failing to recognize this. At a time when American aid to India was principally directed toward famine and emergency relief, for instance, the Russians built the Bihlai steel plant. The first was humanitarian and quickly forgotten, the second created smokestacks on the Indian skyline, or what Mr. Nehru described as "a symbol and portent of India's future, a dream come true." The 500-bed Russian hospital and the Chinese factories in Cambodia are much more highly regarded than all American aid projects in that country put together. Afghanistan, at Russia's Middle Eastern and South Asian gateway, has been given a lavish ruble coat to impress Moscow-bound travelers with the advantages, even in such a highly conservative Muslim society, that flow from "disinterested" Communist aid, while the canals of the Helmand Valley project, the principal American aid contribution, are contemptuously dismissed by the Russians as "flowing not with water but with unadulterated whisky." This is cheap but effective propaganda, for the Helmand Valley project has been an expensive white elephant. The Afghans complain that American technicians demand Californian bungalows, air conditioning, imported American automobiles and imported food, thereby soaking up the dollar loans, while the Russians, to quote one official, "live six to a room and travel to and from work in the back of a truck." The Aswan High Dam is shrewdly calculated to irrigate both Egyptian deserts and the mind and emotions of Africa.

Since they entered the field the Chinese have also and pointedly found no difficulty in living at the same level as the people they help. They operate at the grass roots, a constant reminder to all with whom they come in touch that though they themselves are still poor they have found the key to economic progress.

If we fail to respond to the challenge in the underdeveloped world with positive and constructive policies we must expect the Communists to prevail and to make the sort of breakthrough that will inevitably lead to our isolation and eclipse. The response, if we make it, will be agonizing. It will make wartime demands during a time of apparent peace. It will involve heavy sacrifice and the scrapping of some long-standing policies. And it will also demand the active cooperation of the entire Western world, since for many reasons, including cost and the essential preservation of unity within the NATO alliance, it cannot be undertaken by the United States alone.

Thanks to the initiative of Mr. Diefenbaker, the Canadian Prime Minister, the Commonwealth Prime Ministers' conference in London in March, 1961, gave us one lead. South Africa's policy of apartheid is headed for clear and predictable racial disaster. It cannot possibly succeed. Largely because of it, South Africa's continued presence in the Commonwealth had the effect of dividing the Prime Ministers into two distinct groups, the white inner club and the brown and black newcomers. The expulsion of South Africa—for that is what it amounted to—removed this formidable barrier to the creation of a multiracial Commonwealth partnership whose influence in the underdeveloped world may now be counted on to increase.

An essential follow-up is to hasten the process by which the anti-colonial propaganda of the Communists may become a rapidly wasting asset. This does not mean the hasty exit of colonial Powers from territories that are not ready for self-determination. One Congo is more than enough. But it does mean that the colonial Powers must expand and accelerate their efforts to create the conditions under which self-government is feasible. A special U.N. agency consisting of both the colonial Powers and former colonial territories is needed to supervise and to coordinate these activities. Anguished cries that this would constitute interference in the internal affairs of sovereign states may be anticipated; they will be nothing to the cries we will hear in future if the Portuguese, the Dutch, the French and all other colonialists fail to recognize the winds of change.

A thousand men, two hundred rifles and a vision of how to win China was all Mao Tse-tung had when he arrived on Chingkanshan thirty-four years ago. Today he guides a nation of 670 million. He has conquered China. Now he looks for world victory. His base is strong and growing stronger; his disciples have inherited much of his dedication; and he works in fields that are frequently receptive to his missionary endeavors.

It is not enough to thwart him, or to contain Chinese Communism within the borders of the Middle Kingdom. It is a truism that no meaningful decisions can ever be made on the control of nuclear weapons and disarmament without China's participation. And China's isolation and containment, if this were possible, would eventually bring its external antagonisms into conflict with its internal tensions, precipitating either counterrevolution or war. In the nature of the Chinese leaders and the controls they exercise, war would inevitably result.

Strong regional armies are certainly necessary in some countries to deter overt aggression, but, as the experience in Laos, South Vietnam and South Korea has demonstrated, the attempted creation of military strength is futile if it is not also accompanied by complementary economic development. Conventional armies are not the answer to a rebellion and Communist-infiltrated peasantry, as Chiang Kai-shek discovered in China and the United States has learned in Laos and South Vietnam.

The primary need is to create economic viability, to deny the Communists the opportunity of exploiting unrest and the dissemination of the propaganda theme that they alone have the formula for progress. Nothing less than a global Marshall Aid Plan is required to raise the living standards of the underprivileged—and to raise them fast. Such a scheme would not only be costly—it would inevitably cause a heavy mortality rate among our sacred cows.

We could find ourselves helping economies that were unashamedly

Socialist. There would be no strings, no assurances of support for military alliances, no certainty, or promise even, that some countries would not still be tempted to hang on to the Communists' coattails, and possibly even no thanks. Our only practical concern would be to provide the means by which the underdeveloped world might make the rapid progress it aspires to, and which we have too often deluded ourselves into thinking we have provided. We are all victims of Madison Avenueism, of public relations, of government officials who gild the lily to protect their own jobs. All of us in the Western world—Americans, British, French, Germans, Canadians, Australians and the rest—are being merely meretricious when we claim that we are seriously in the business of improving living standards in the underdeveloped world. The gap between the haves and the have-nots is growing all the time. It is a Marxist situation that Maoism is peculiarly well fitted to exploit.

In a country such as India where the prospect of an economic breakthrough is in sight and the nucleus of skilled administrators and technicians already exists, the principal requirement now is finance—a billion dollars in round figures for the next decade. In many other countries, large sums of financial aid at this time are likely to lose both themselves and friends. It is pointless to give financial aid to people who do not know what to do with what they are given: and even the most modern factory with adequate raw materials to hand is unlikely to succeed if management and workers are unskilled.

A starting point is a guaranteed minimum price level for the rubber, tin, rice, copra, coffee, tea, meat and other commodities produced today in the underdeveloped countries. The characteristic boom or price fluctuations bust in these commodities has tended both to discredit the efficiency of the capitalist system and to destroy the basis for effective long-range development planning. Since the Korean War boom prices for raw materials—the only significant exports of the underdeveloped world—have gone down sharply while prices for consumer goods manufactured from these commodities and imported into the underdeveloped countries have risen consistently. This is not merely damaging to the economies concerned but grist to the propaganda mills in Peking and Moscow. "Do you need to look further for proof of imperialist exploitation?" the Communists ask. It is a question that can be answered only by the establishment of a proper ratio in the prices of raw material to finished products.

This is, of course, only the beginning. At the second level, there is a need for improved agricultural techniques. In Laos, which has received more American aid per capita than any underdeveloped country, much of the agriculture has not yet caught up to the pre-Christian era plow. Seeds are planted by boring holes in burned-off patches of jungle. The ashes act as fertilizer for a season or two, and when the soil becomes barren the people move on to another stretch of jungle.

This is an extreme case, but the argument that the need is for spades and plows and tractors, fertilizers and improved seed and basic-level agricultural colleges holds good in this and in most underdeveloped countries. Trite as it may sound to say so, Peking must be countered where it is seeking its recruits—at the grass roots of every underdeveloped country.

At the third level, the requirement is for a vast, but not necessarily costly, increase in technical aid. The shortage of skilled technicians, managers and civil servants in almost all underdeveloped countries is of such magnitude as to defeat any meaningful economic aid program. The answer to this problem does not lie in the extension of scholarships for foreign study in the U.S. or elsewhere, but rather in the creation and expansion of educational facilities in the countries concerned. Too often foreign-trained students fail to become reassimilated comfortably into their indigenous environment. Some are overqualified for the posts offered; many become frustrated; and others (this is especially true in the case of Taiwan) do not return at all. American aid to such institutions as the University of the Philippines, which, with an enrollment of about sixteen thousand and a large and efficient faculty provides the education-hungry Filipinos with tuition of high and accepted standards, is an example of effective technical aid. A small but inexpensive American school for training rural teachers outside Phnom Penh, in Cambodia, is another.

The need is not for Asian M.I.T.'s but for large numbers of basic technical and administrative schools in which the external obligation need go no further than assistance with construction, the training of the teachers and some sort of supervisory eye on standards. These requirements may sound elementary. They are. They are also essential.

The fourth stage, which in countries such as India is also a first stage, is an aid program on something like the scale envisaged by Dr. Barbara Ward who urges that all countries with a per capita income of more than $600 a year should contribute 1 per cent of national income a year for five decades toward the economic development of underdeveloped countries. In round figures this would cost the United States about $5 billion a year (compared with the annual national defense budget of about $45 billion). It would cost other developed countries, which have been singularly laggard with their contributions and quite free with their criticism, proportionate amounts.

To these must be added another requirement: the widest possible dissemination of the latest techniques in birth control. Communist China is not the only underdeveloped country likely to develop intolerable internal tensions because of the high birth rate. India's population, for instance, will rise above the 600 million mark by 1980 and be close to 800 million by the end of the century. Because of a draconian birth control program, the population of Japan, on the other hand, though likely to rise for another thirty years, will then begin to level off and probably even to decline. Through its rapidly rising living standards Japan has demonstrated to the rest of overpopulated, underdeveloped Asia, Africa and Latin America that family planning need not wait on an improved living standard but can actually make an important contribution toward its achievement.

All this amounts to little more than putting real competition into competitive coexistence. It is only a one-legged hop on the path to peace. To succeed we shall have to "walk on two legs," and also pursue a policy which seeks to draw China into the community of nations and to help it with its own vast and formidable problems. The approaches will be rebuffed at first as Mr. Nehru has been rebuffed. Their long-term chances of succeeding are directly related to our ability to deny China the recruiting grounds for world revolution and Mao Tse-tung the opportunity to wage his last and greatest guerrilla war.

INDEX

205